STYLE
BOOK

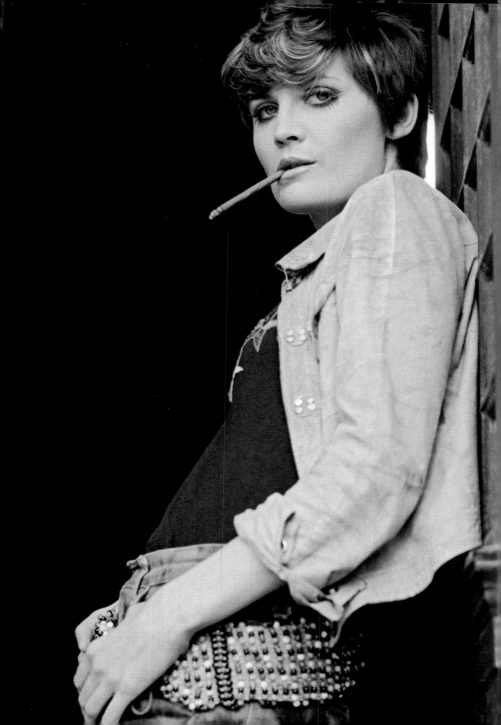

ELIZABETH WALKER

STYLE BOOK

FASHIONABLE INSPIRATIONS

Flammarion

Concept and Design: Tea Aganovic
Picture Research: Jennifer Jeffrey
Production: Mary Osborne
With special thanks to Liz Ihre and Ben Bonarius
Printed in China

Originally published in Great Britain:
Copyright © Endeavour London Ltd. 2010

This edition © Flammarion, S.A., 2011

87, quai Panhard et Levassor
75647 Paris Cedex 13

editions.flammarion.com

11 12 13   3 2 1

ISBN: 978-2-08-020082-2

Dépôt légal: 04/2011

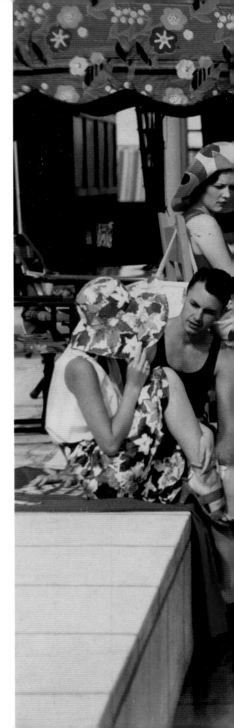

Right: Tableaux on a terrace, cartwheel hats
and wide trousers in florals or bright hues.
1930   Models around a swimming pool,
Ladies Home Journal magazine, USA.

Previous page: Relaxed cool in a jean jacket,
baggy trousers, and a very wide studded belt.
1972   English singer Sandy Shaw, the barefoot pop princess, smoking a cheroot.

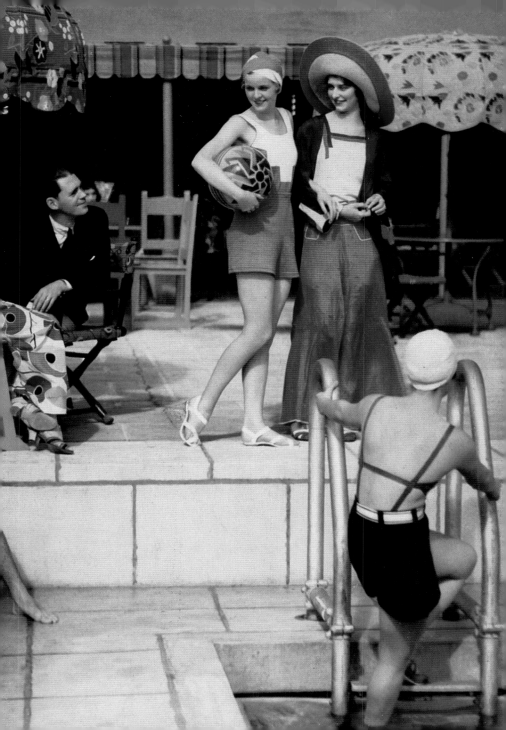

CONTENTS

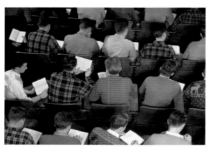

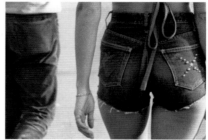

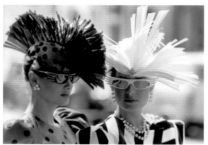

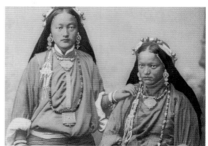

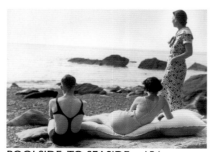

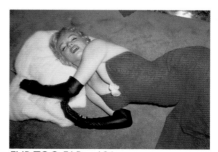

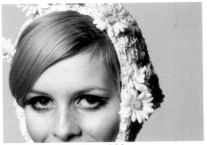

FLOWER POWER 222

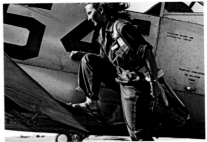

ALL IN ONE 256

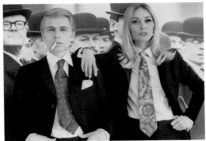

BUTTON UP 276

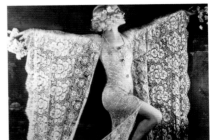

FRILLS AND FURBELOWS 322

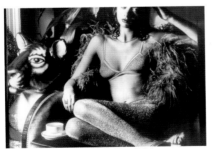

SHIMMER AND SHINE 356

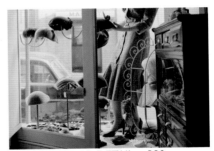

ATTENTION TO DETAIL 390

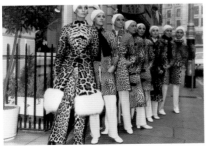

ANIMAL MAGIC 446

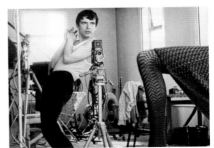

PICTURE CREDITS 476

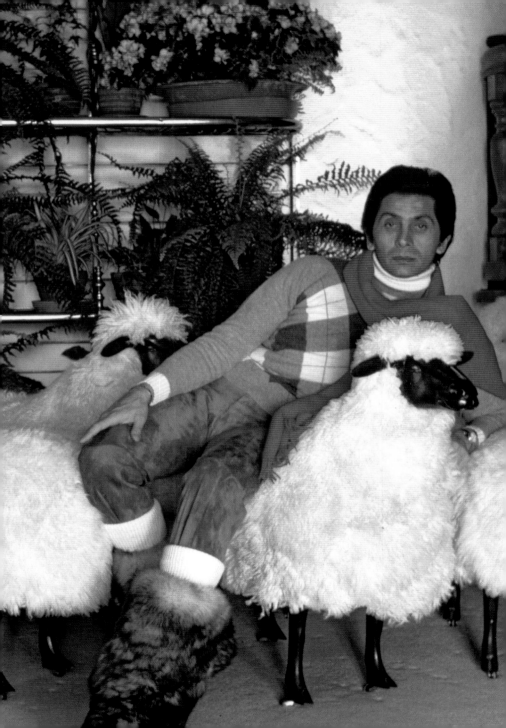

fashionable inspirations

"One picture is worth ten thousand words"* and these carefully selected images are set to inspire anybody fascinated by either fashion, foibles, or simply the photographs themselves. It is all about stylish contrasts, strange situations and rarely glimpsed pictures; all set to get the mind buzzing and the creative juices flowing.

The photographs have been gleaned from film sets, from fashion shoots and from unknown fields afar. Men and women, from differing decades, are intermingled with worldwide exoticisms. The juxtaposition of figures from different eras lends a remarkable insight into the progression of fashion.

The earliest example in this little book is a portrait of an Indian army commander clad in tartan and taken in 1865; facing him is a picture of a Japanese painter in the 1920s, also dressed in plaid. One can imagine either of these gentlemen gracing the catwalks of a Comme des Garçons show in Paris.

There are enormous bathing suits from neck to knee and itsy-bitsy bikinis, exotic hair-dos and oriental gems, knobbly knits and loads of lace. There is a smattering of celebrities; Twiggy is teamed with a swaggering fish-seller, Brigitte Bardot gazes at the Dutch painter van Dongen, and models, singers, sailors, and even royalty, all strut their stuff.

From flowers to furs, from pearls to pools, there are all things here for all folk.

ELIZABETH WALKER

*Frederick R. Barnard 1927 *Printer's Ink*

A wolf on sheep's clothing, laid back in suede jeans, bright scarf and furry boots. 1977 Italian dress designer, Valentino, in a ski chalet, Gstaad, Switzerland.

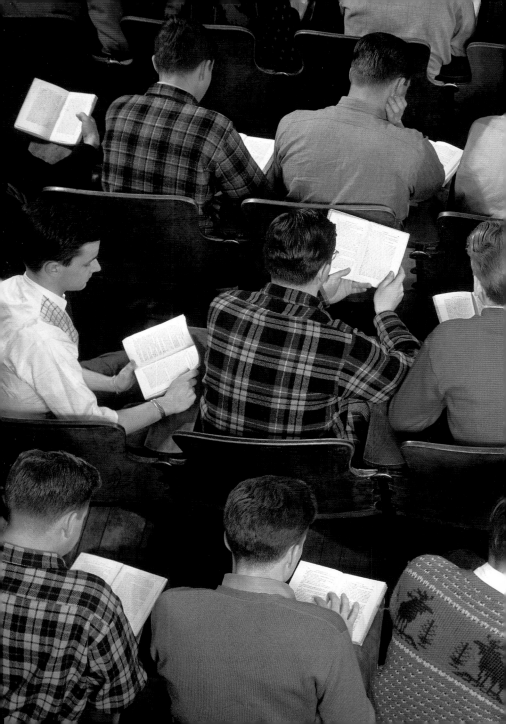

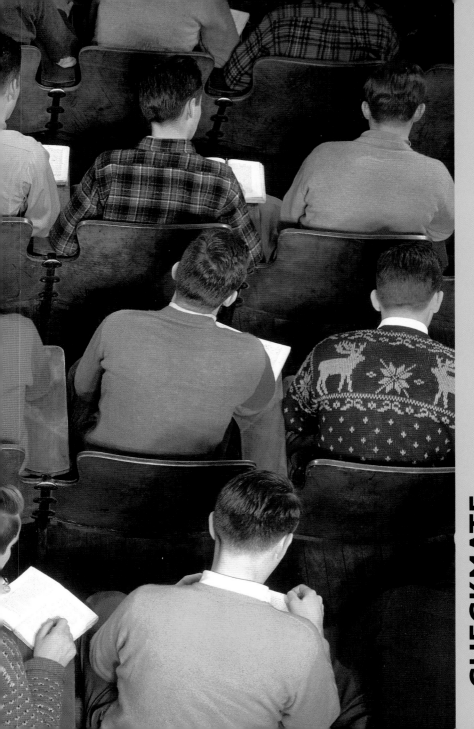

CHECKMATE

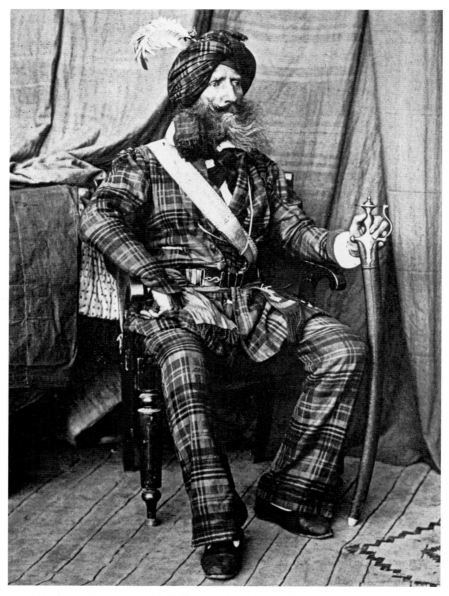

Head to toe, in tartan topped off with an exotic turban, egret feather and all.
1865   Colonel Gardiner, Commander of the Maharajah's troops, Kashmir, India.

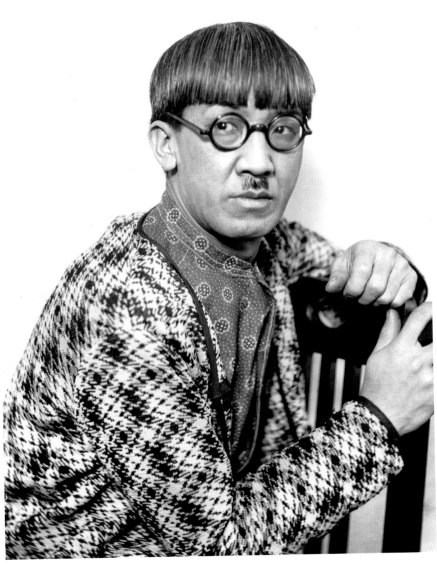

Painterly prints, a master of woodblock in a combination of checks and spots.
1924 Tsuguharu Foujita, a Japanese painter, who worked mainly in France.

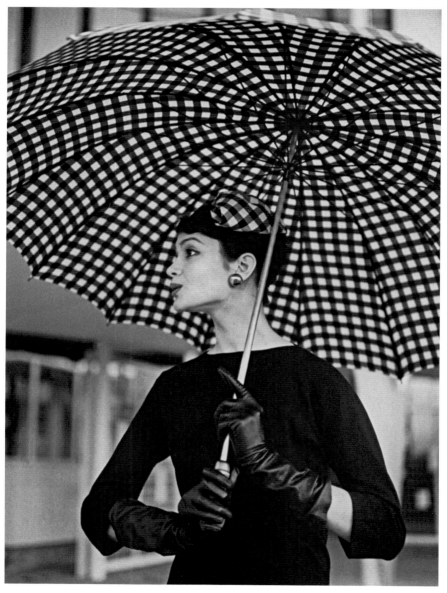

Rain check, an umbrella and matching cloche hat, perfect with a plain black shift. 1958   A new trend in women's accessories for the racetrack.

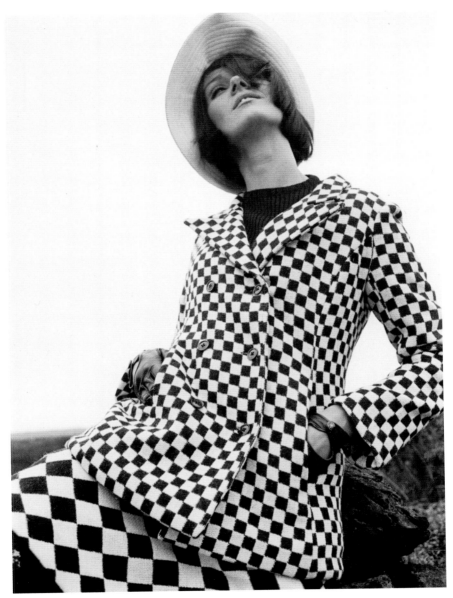

Chessboard checks, both little and large, teamed for a contemporary look.
1966   A model strutting her stuff.

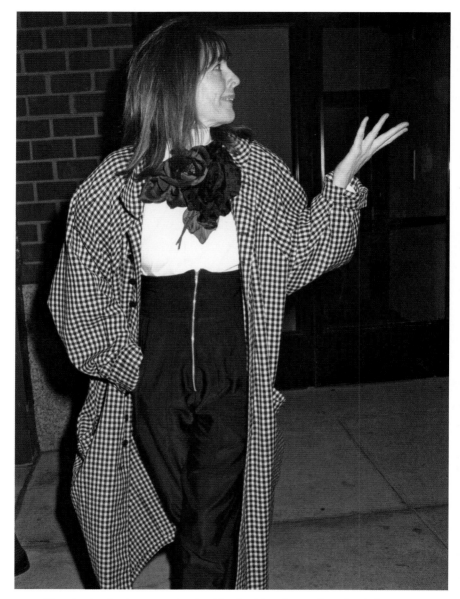

Man-sized, a classic coat contrasts with a feminine, flounced scarf and slim pants.
1988   Diane Keaton, actress, leaving trendy restaurant Primola, New York City.

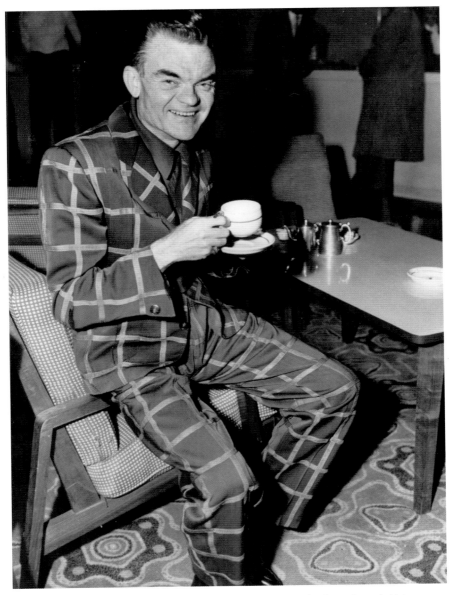

Shockingly bright, a suit of blue and orange windowpane checks, and a red shirt.
1955 Spike Jones, leader of the band *City Slickers*, Melbourne, Australia.

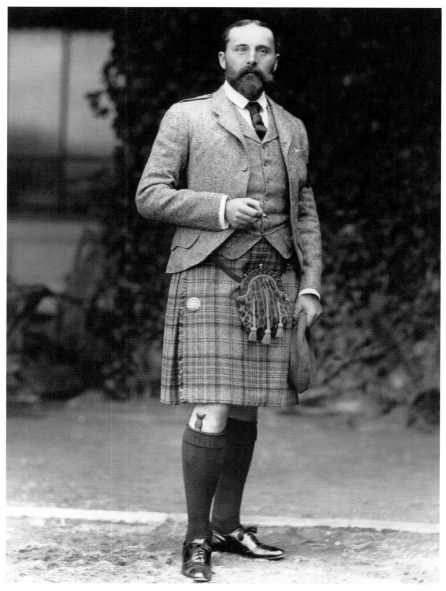

Tartan and tweed, a highland gentleman down to the last detail, dirk and all.
1895 Prince Henry of Battenberg, the husband of Princess Beatrice.

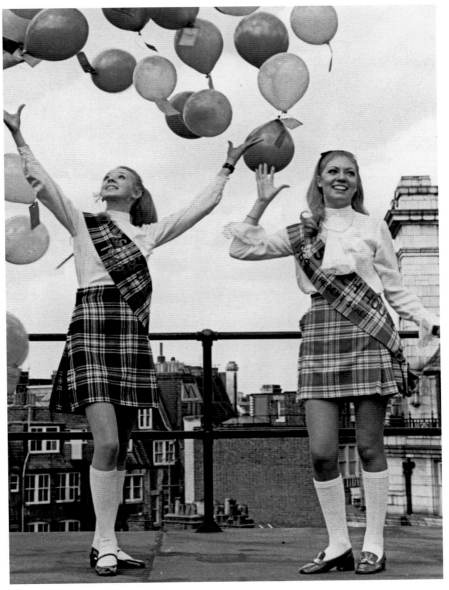

Cutty-sarks, very mini-kilts, worn with sixties socks in white and polo necks too.
1969 Teresa Banfield and Rosemary Reed on the roof of Scotch House shop, London.

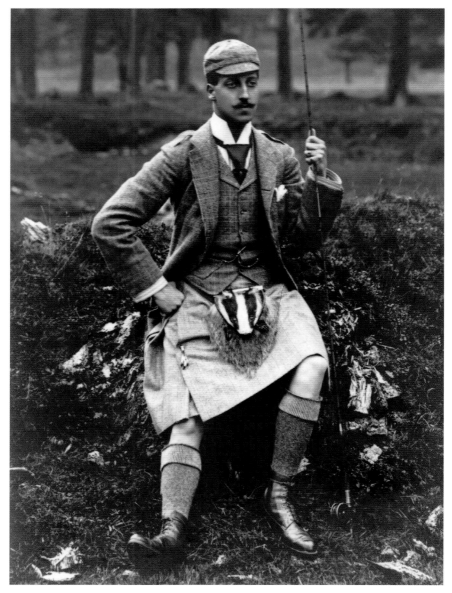

Scottish chic, a kilt and a badger-head sporran, a cap and a crop, and a black tie.
1888   Prince William Albert Victor, Duke of Clarence, son of Edward VII.

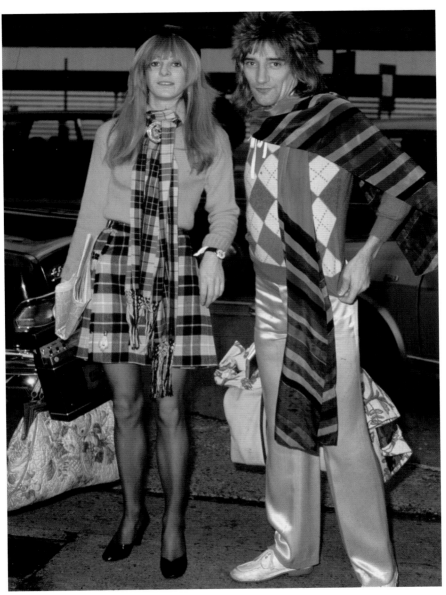

Travelling incognito, in egg-yolk yellow, in tartan, Argyll checks and satin strides.
1974 Rock star, Rod Stewart, with model Dee Harrington at London Airport.

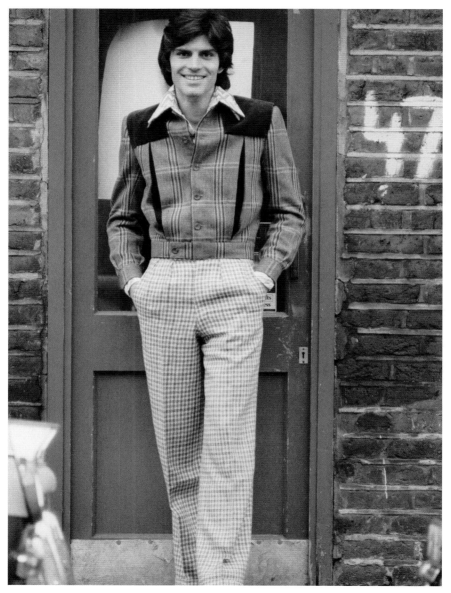

Small, smaller and smallest, differing-sized checks in trousers, jacket and shirt.
1972 A model posing nonchalantly against house number forty-seven.

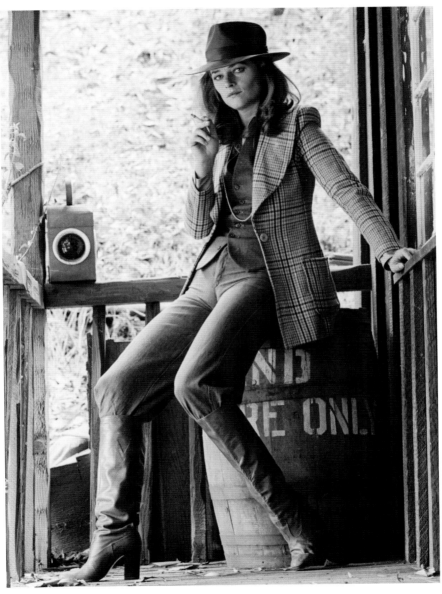

Mannish tailoring, waistcoat, fob watch, trilby, boots - and all, have a sexy slant.
1976 English actress, Charlotte Rampling, on a film set.

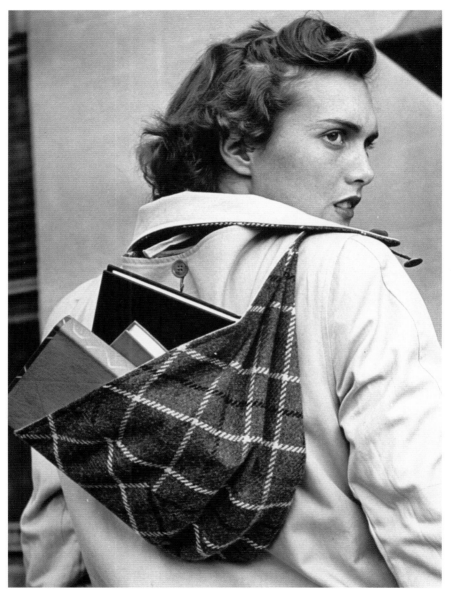

A reversible hood in tartan on this terrific trench makes a perfect carry-all.
1939 A young girl modelling the latest college fashions.

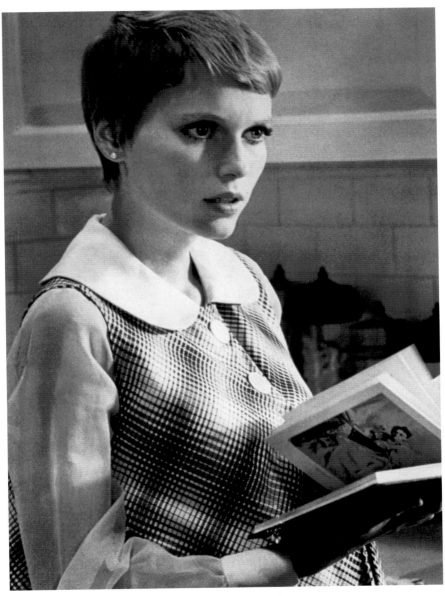

Prim in a plaid, a maternity dress worn with a Peter-Pan collared blouse.
1968 Actress Mia Farrow in *Rosemary's Baby*, directed by Roman Polanski.

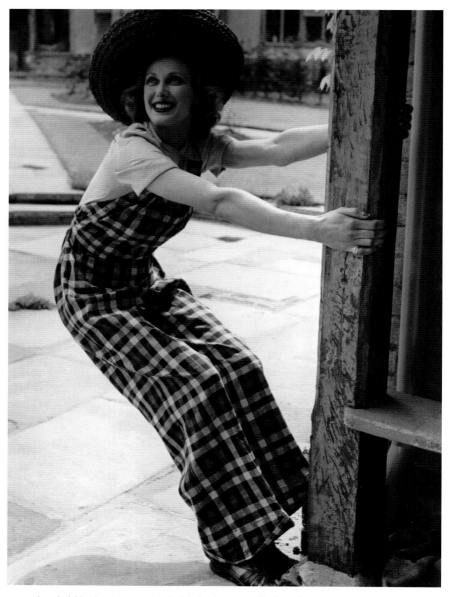

Land-girl looks, dungarees in bold checks, more Chelsea than cabbages.
1941   Clothes for *A Coupon Summer.*

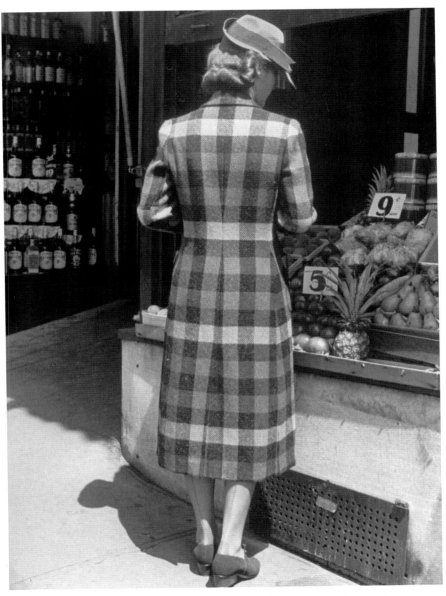

Cut cleverly, a block plaid coat, nipped in at the waist, worn with a jaunty hat.
1938 Autumn fashion in the USA, and pineapples for sale too .

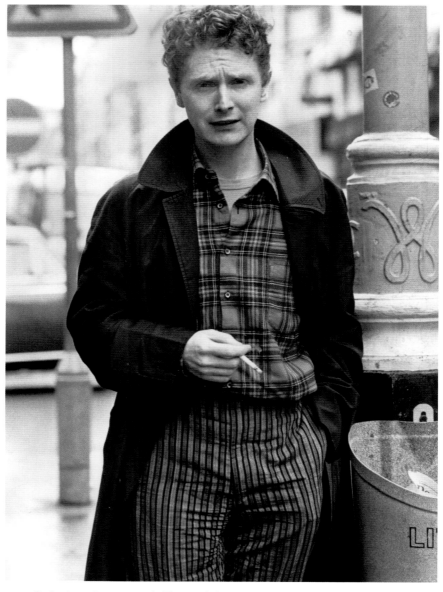

Perfectly punk, a young rebel in rumpled tartan shirt and striped trousers.
1980 Malcolm McLaren, manager of the British punk group *The Sex Pistols*.

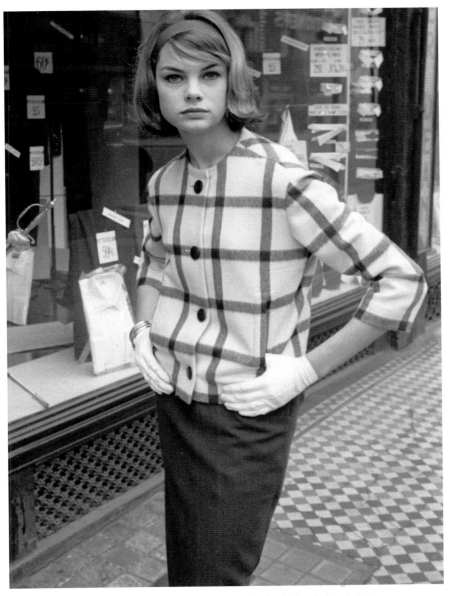

Legendary looks, pre the mini-skirt era, a classic, checked collarless jacket.
1960   English model, Jean Shrimpton, outside a shop, Jermyn Street, London.

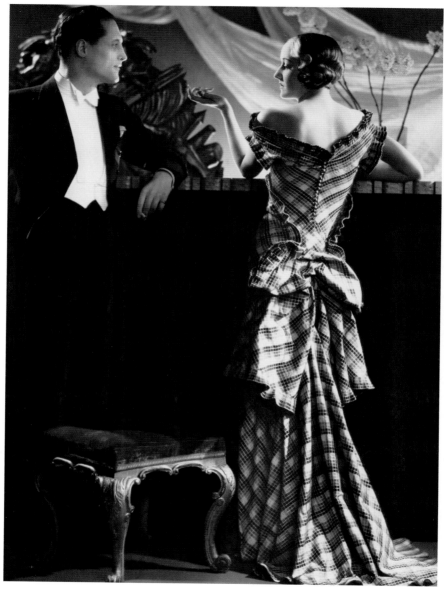

Instant impact, acres of plaid, and an enormous bow, make for a great exit.
1932   A fashion study for Liberty, London, famous for their printed fabrics.

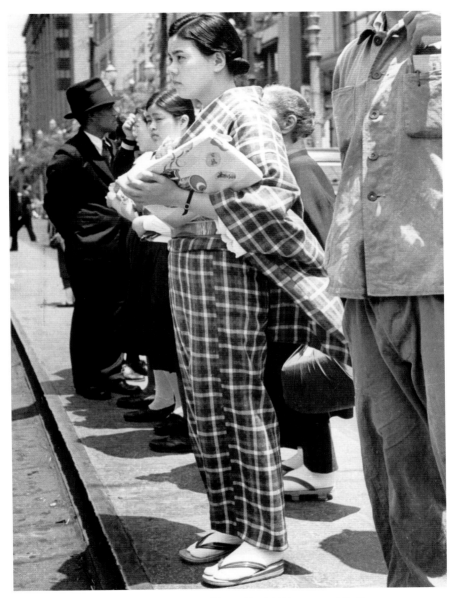

Garage-gear has never looked so stylish as this plaid kimono and flip-flops.
1955 A girl mechanic waiting with shoppers to cross a Tokyo street, Japan.

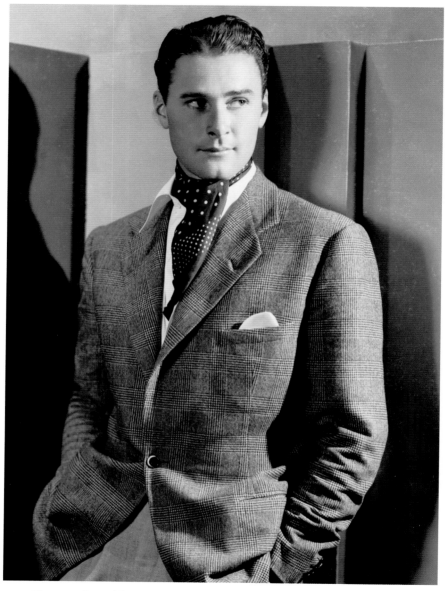

Elegant and superbly suave, in a checked tweed jacket and a spotted silk cravat.
1933   Hollywood film star, Errol Flynn, born in Tasmania, Australia.

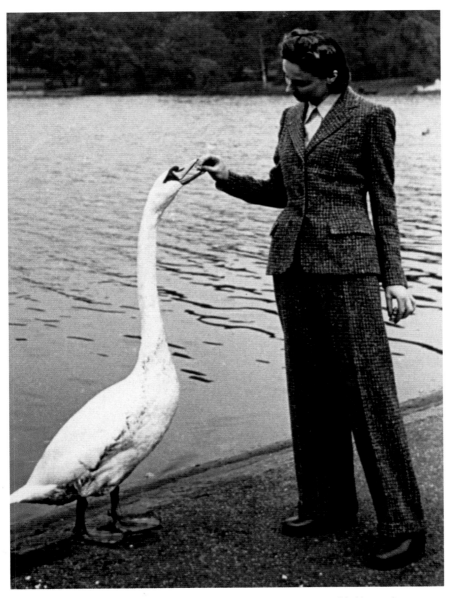

Tailored in trousers, a beautifully cut suit that would not be out of fashion today.
1941   Illustration for an article 'Should Women Wear Trousers?' in *Picture Post*.

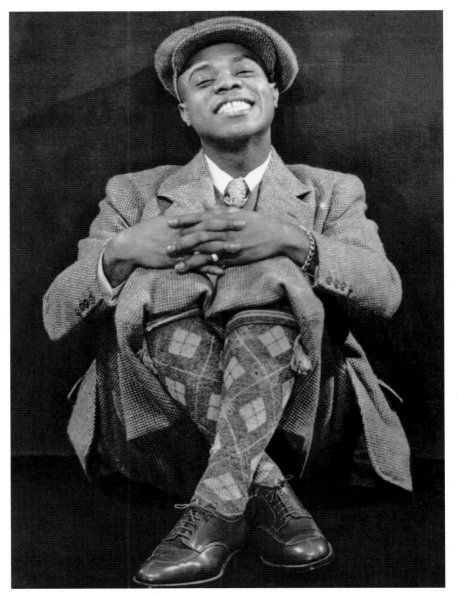

Knickerbocker glory, suit with Argyll socks and a flat cap, good enough for golf.
1933 American jazz musician, Louis Armstrong, on his first European tour.

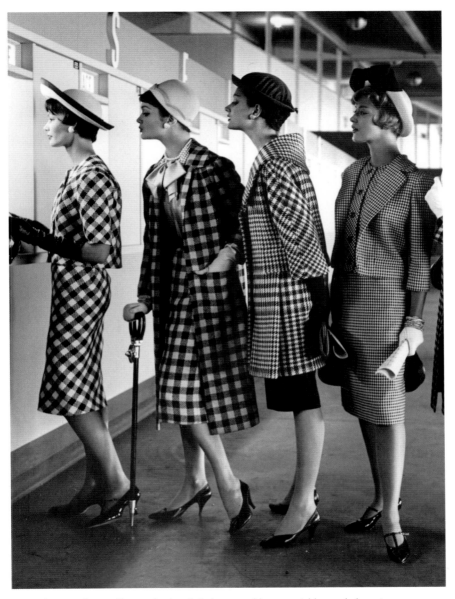

A marvellous mélange, checks of all sizes are chic, eye-catching and elegant.
1958 Four fashionable models betting at a racecourse, Roosevelt Raceway, USA.

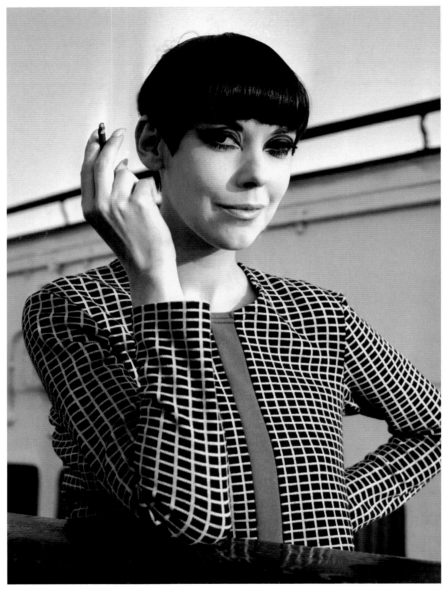

Graphic checks, in black and white worn with a severe fringe epitomize the sixties.
1965   American model, Peggy Moffitt, with her trademark bobbed haircut.

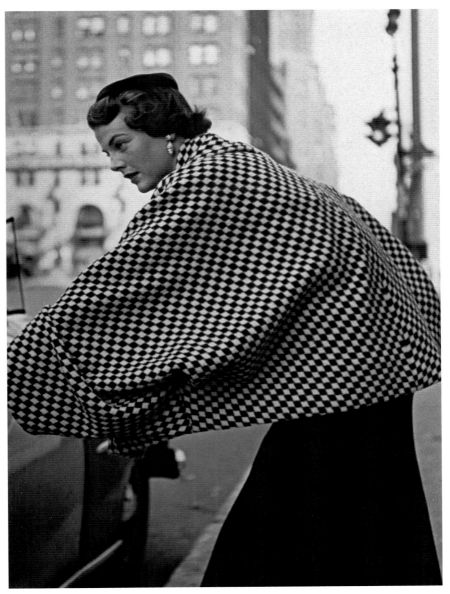

Cut in one, this creation was synonymous with Dior's New Look.
1949   Jacket by Pauline Trigère, Paris-born designer who gained fame in New York.

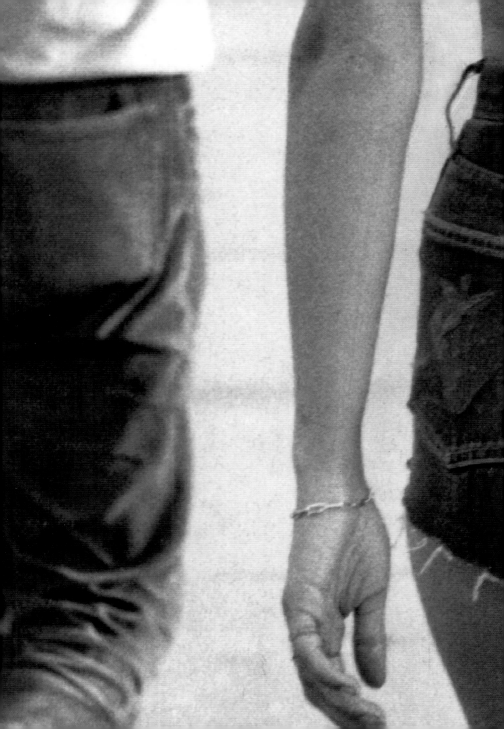

DIVINE IN DENIM

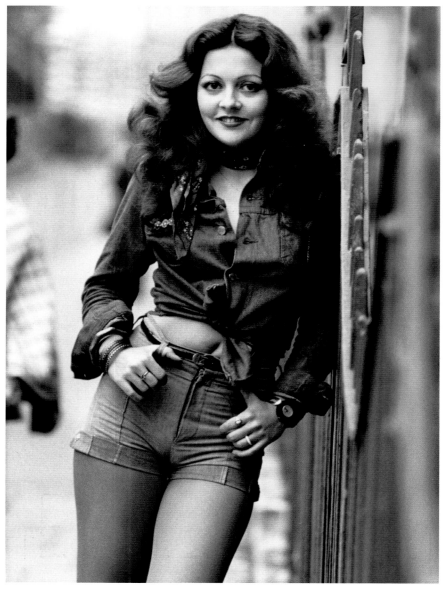

Clouds of curls, the tightest hot pants and a raunchy shirt was very Le Look.
1975 A young woman models denim shorts and shirt, worn with a spotty kerchief.

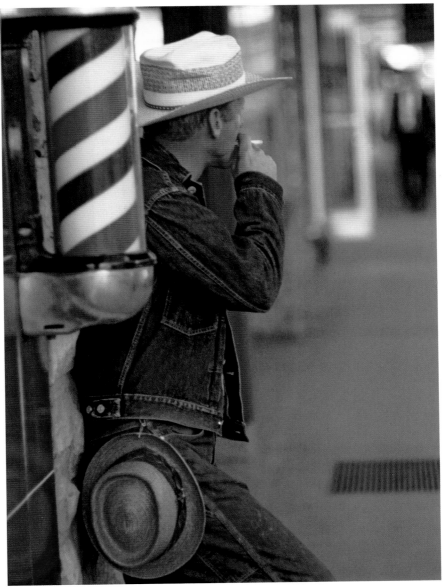

Work-wear, denim, a hardwearing cloth, was practical before it was fashionable.
1963 A cowboy takes a break, wearing a hat and carrying a spare, Wyoming, USA.

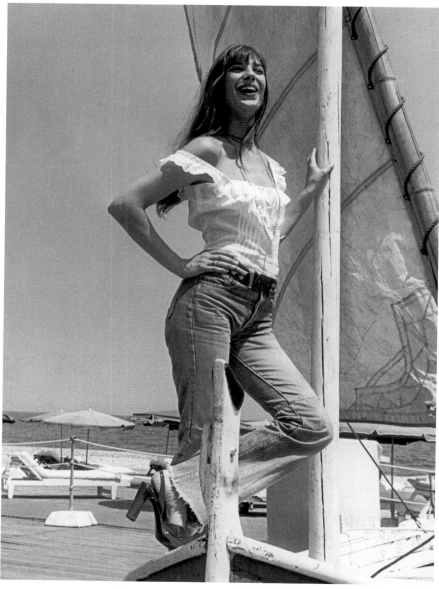

Distressed, jeans worn with a pretty broderie anglaise blouse and sling-backs.
1973   Actress, Jane Birkin, enjoys a sun-soaked holiday on the Côte d'Azur, France.

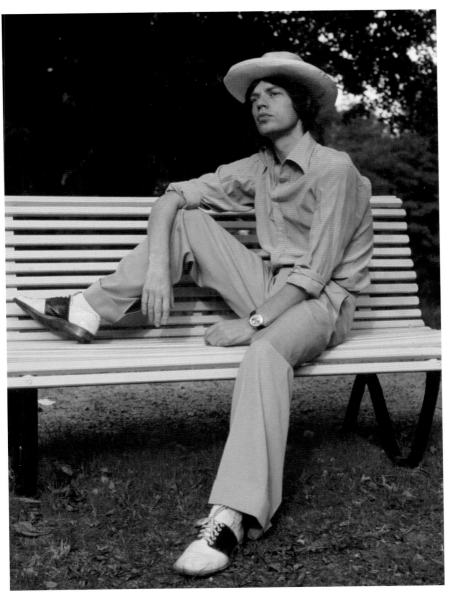

Smart but casual, a denim-blue shirt with co-respondent shoes and a panama.
1973 Mick Jagger of *The Rolling Stones* sitting on a bench in a London park.

44

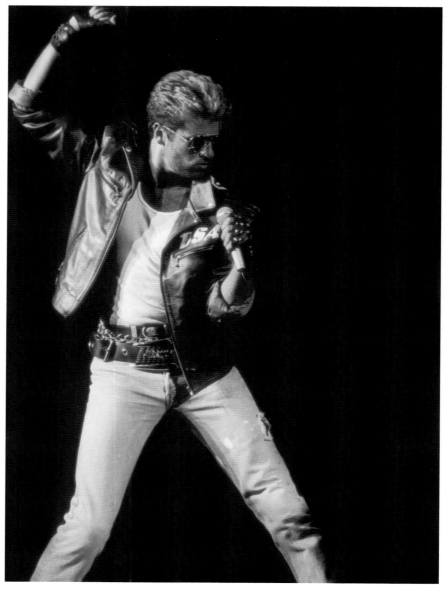

Very heavy metal, a leather biker jacket, studded gloves, chains and belts.
1988   British singer-songwriter, George Michael, strutting his stuff on stage.

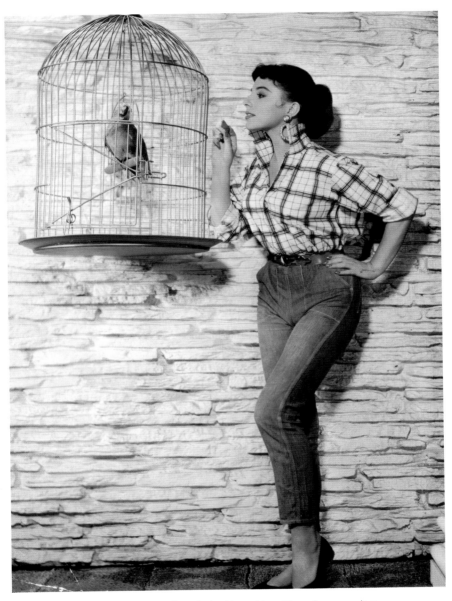

Sexy siren or beautiful beatnik, a cinched-in waist and huge hoop earrings.
1955 British actress, Joan Collins, feeding a parrot in a big birdcage.

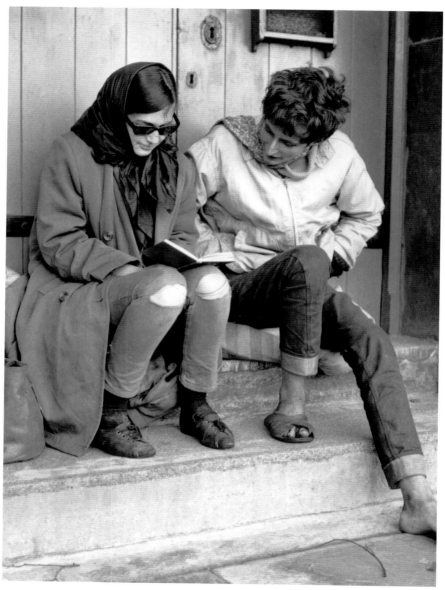

Demonstrating in denim, distressed or boyfriend jeans make a political point.
1965 Two girls at a 'Ban the Bomb' march, Trafalgar Square, London.

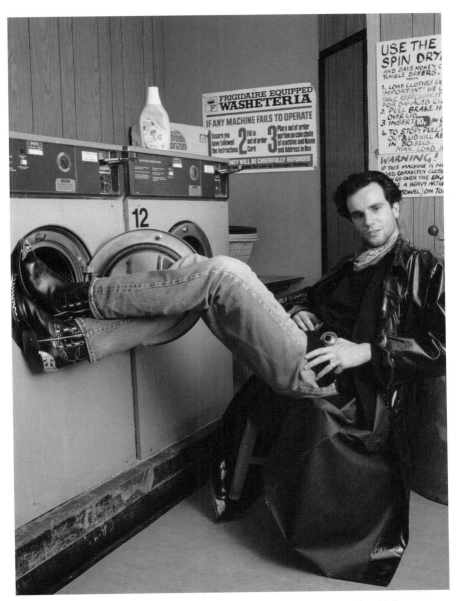

Cool and collected, cowboy boots, a long black coat and a gypsy neckerchief.
1985   Actor, Daniel Day-Lewis, in Stephen Frear's film *My Beautiful Launderette*.

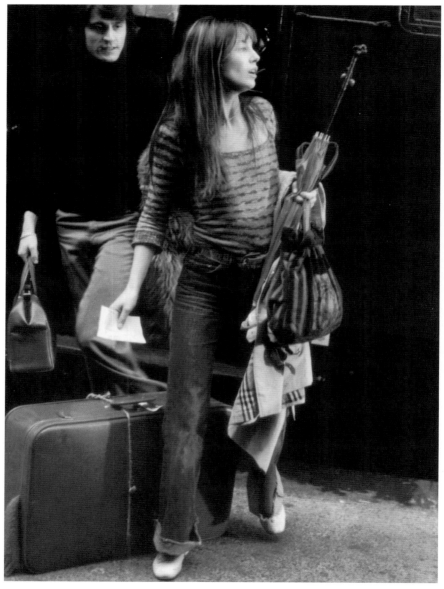

Bags of baggage, stripes and pumps, hippy vibes and with a boyfriend in tow, too.
1975 Jane Birkin as a prostitute in *Catherine & Co*, directed by Michel Boisrond.

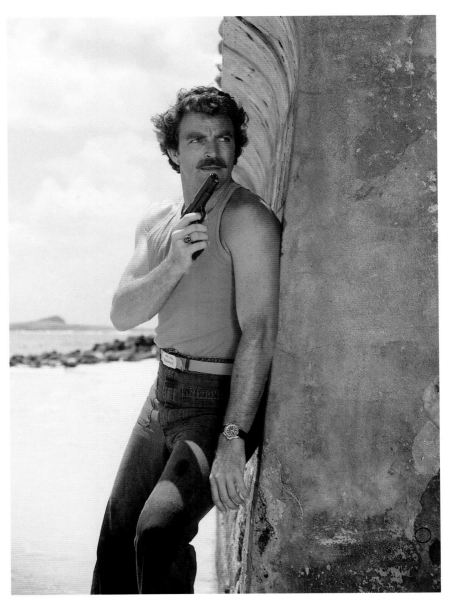

Mad, bad and dangerous to know, high-waisted jeans and a very small singlet.
1980   Actor, Tom Selleck, in the detective drama *Magnum, P.I.*, Hawaii, USA.

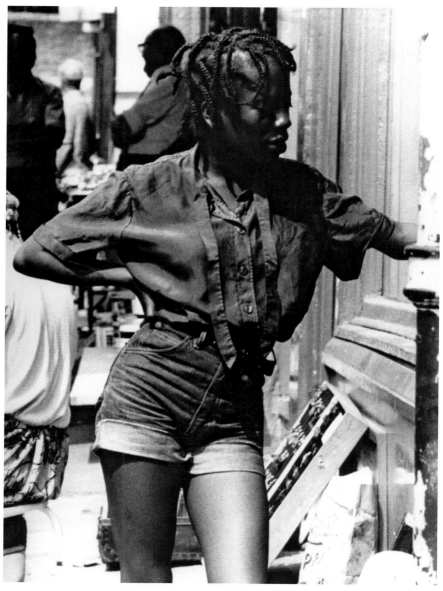

Dreadlocks and denim, an over-sized shirt and a tie, that man-woman mix.
1970 A girl wearing turned-up hot pants in Portobello Market, London.

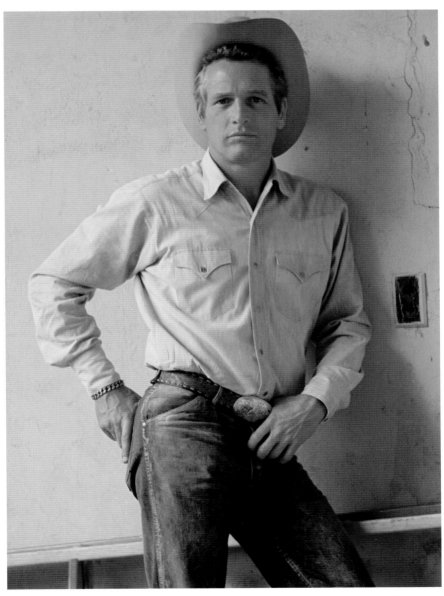

Tone on tone, blue eyes, blue shirt and blue jeans, how cool can a cowboy get?
1972 Actor, Paul Newman, in Western film *Pocket Money*, Tucson, Arizona, USA.

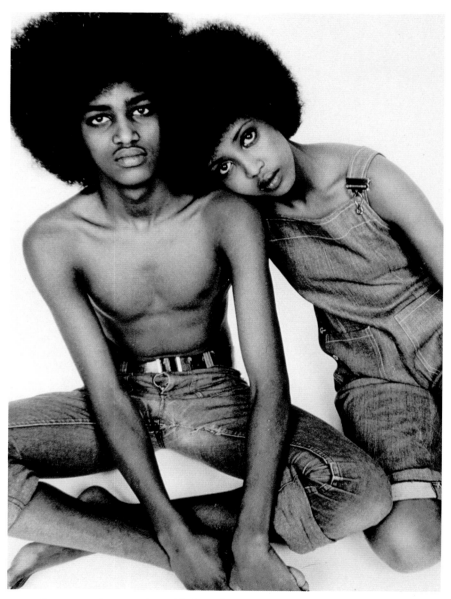

Gorgeous and groovy, oh-so-tight jeans for him and cropped dungarees for her.
1970   'Togetherness', a portrait of a man and a woman, both with Afro hairstyles.

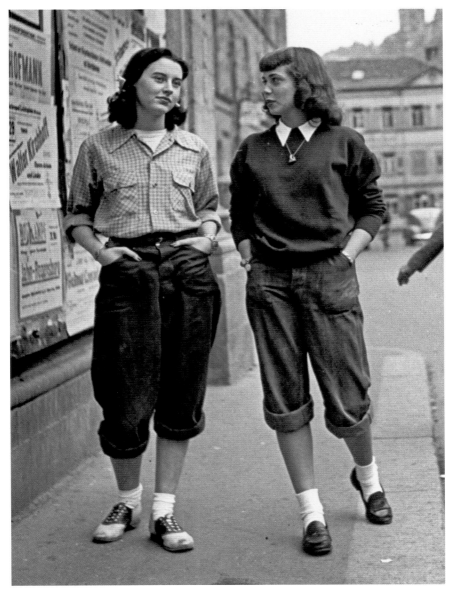

Shock horror, collegiates in trousers, men's shirts, bobby socks and even loafers.
1947   American students in Heidelberg, Germany, astound the local ladies.

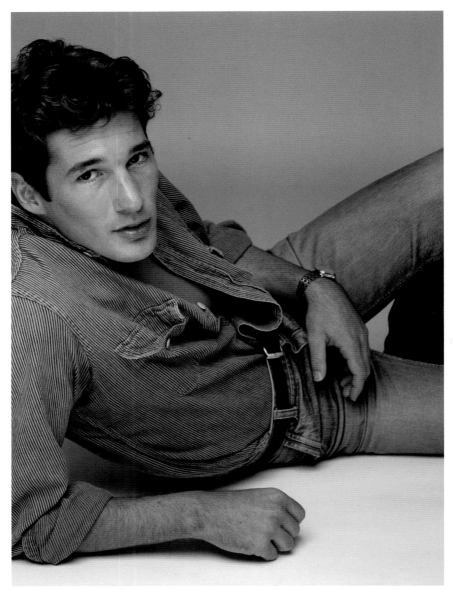

Laid back and casually cool, a simple striped shirt and jeans always fit the bill.
1980 In gorgeous gear, American actor, Richard Gere, as the perfect pin-up.

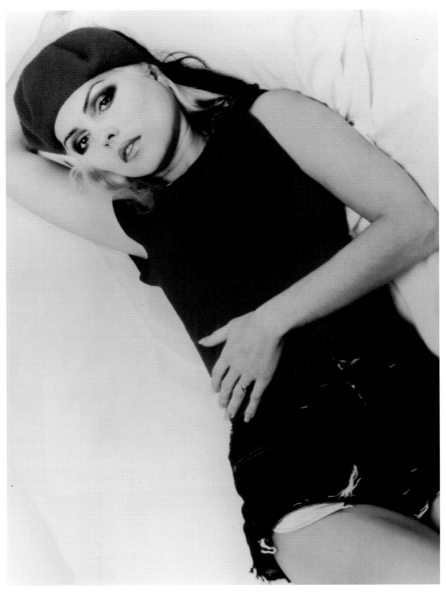

Simper and smoulder, in dark indigo denim cut-off shorts and a jaunty beret.
1977   Portrait of singer, Deborah Harry, of the band Blondie, reclining on a bed.

56

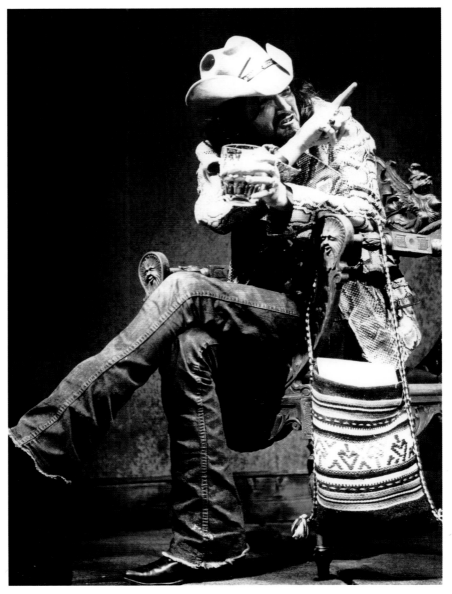

Wild and wonderful, rock-on-by in a Navaho jacket, jeans and a bashed-up hat.
1970   American pop star, P.J. Proby, points things out and pulls on a pint.

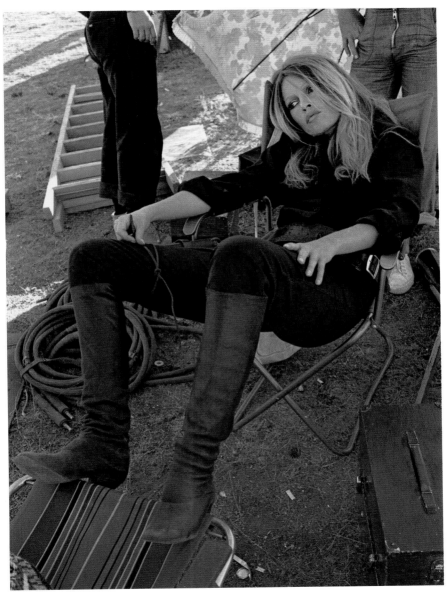

Blond and beautiful, hot stuff in knee-high boots, tight jeans and a polo neck.
1971 French actress, Brigitte Bardot, shelters from the sun while filming in Spain.

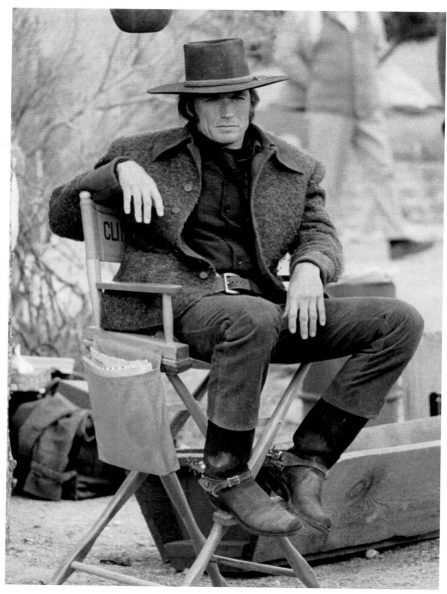

Buckles and boots, a huge hat and a tweed jacket, very like 'Cool Hand Luke'.
1965 American actor, Clint Eastwood, lounging on the set of a Western.

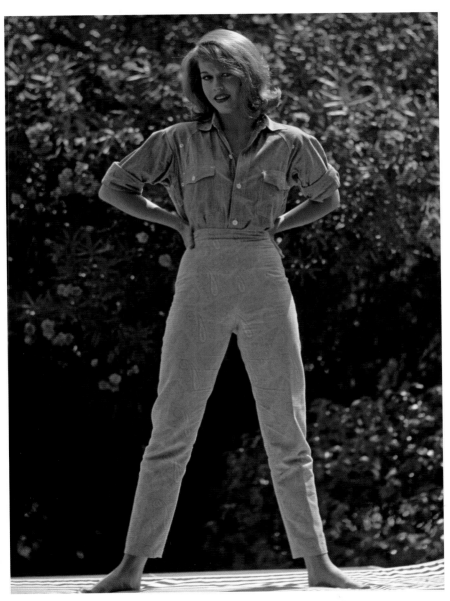

Feeling blue, looking lovely in a mannish denim shirt and slim Capri pants.
1956 American actress, Jane Fonda, in a gorgeous garden, California, USA.

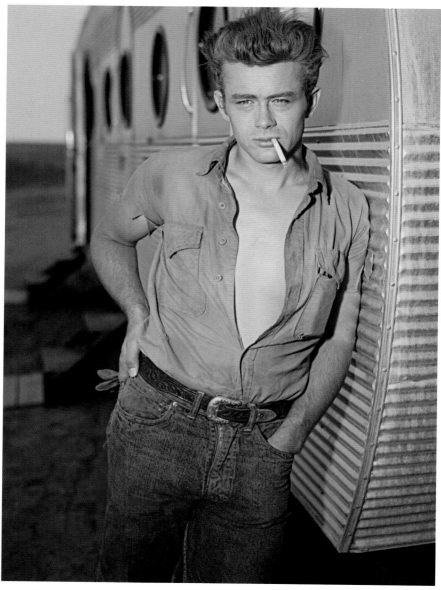

Casually iconic, clad in khaki with a quiff, this was the final film of the star.
1955 American actor, James Dean, in director George Stevens's *Giant*.

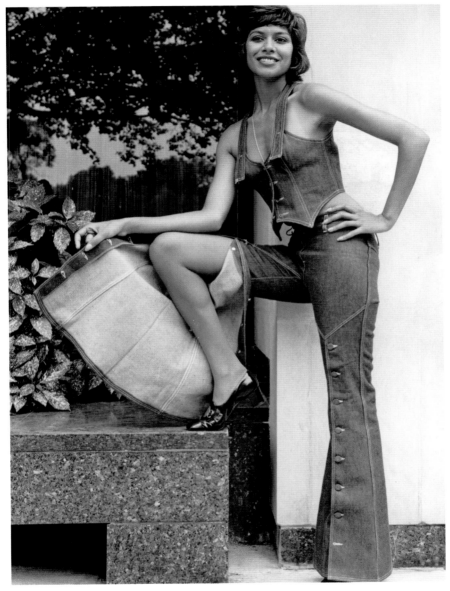

More buttons than bows, a tight waistcoat and jeans, all seriously Seventies.
1971   A model wearing the 'Miss Levi' Spring Collection' at a hotel in London.

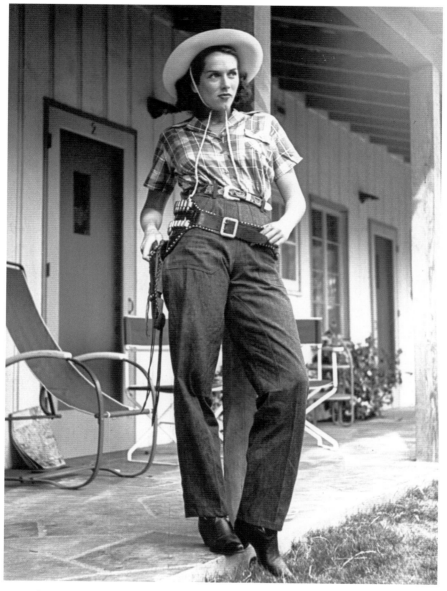

Cowboy queen, hat, plaid shirt, jeans and boots, gun-slinger belt and all.
1940   A model wearing an outfit by Marge Riley at a Palm Springs Dude Ranch.

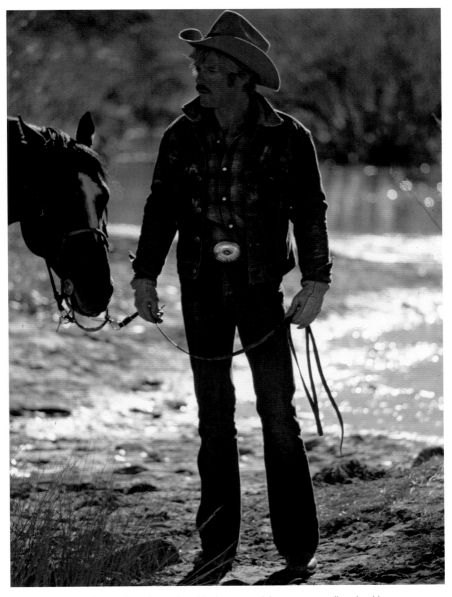

Rugged and magnificently rustic, with that essential accessory, a silver buckle.
1979 Robert Redford in *The Electric Horseman*, directed by Sydney Pollack.

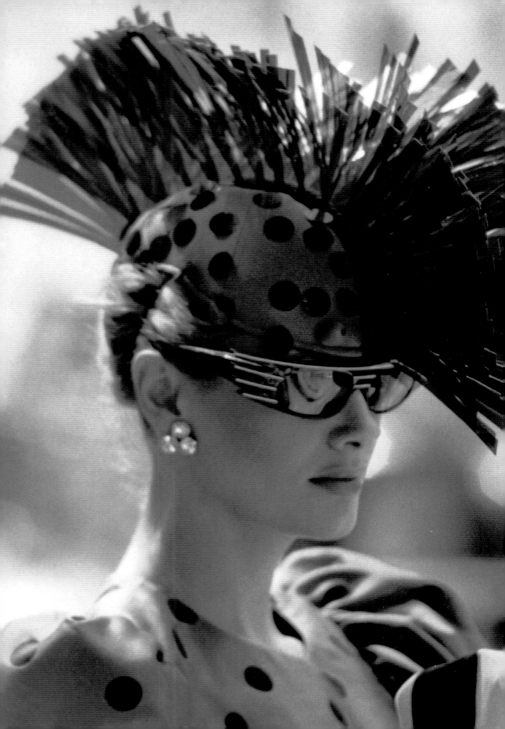

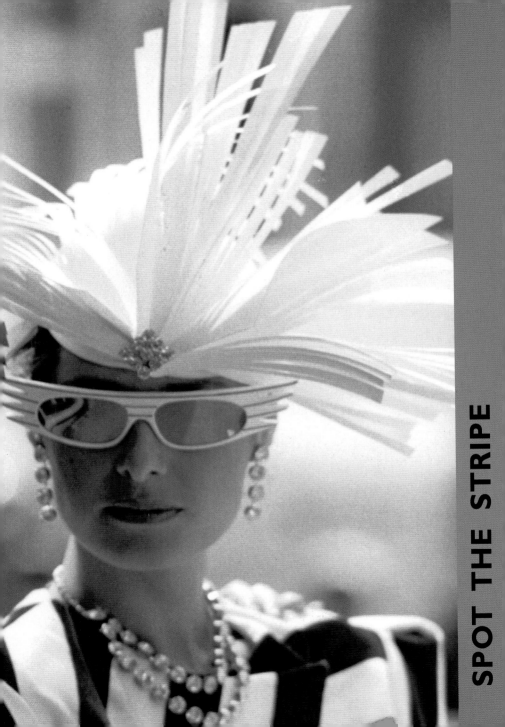

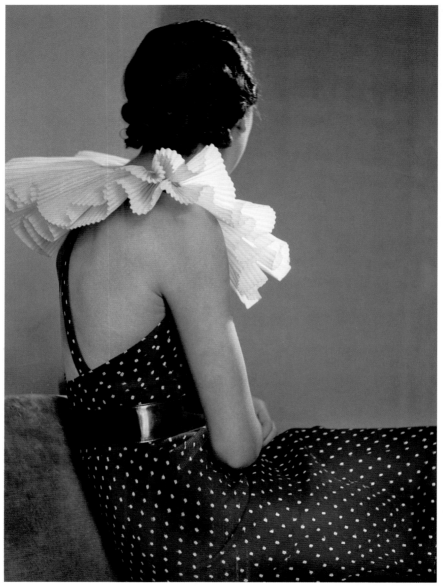

Perfect in polka-dots, a crisp Pierrot collar is a wonderful frame for a face.
1934 A model in an evening gown by French fashion designer, Jeanne Lanvin, Paris.

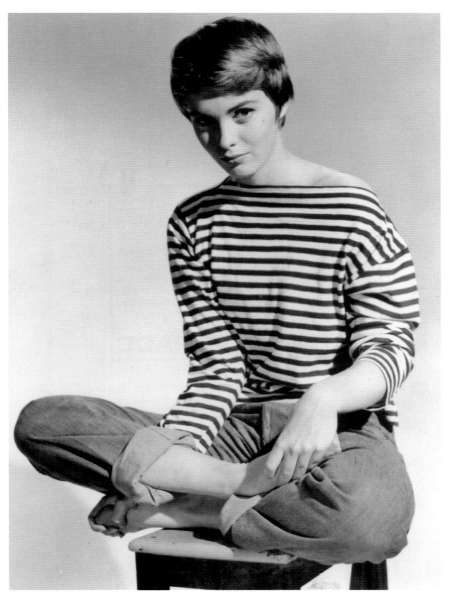

Boyish and yet beautiful, a sailor sweater with jeans, topped off with a pixie haircut.
1965   A portrait of American actress, Jean Seberg, sitting cross-legged on a stool.

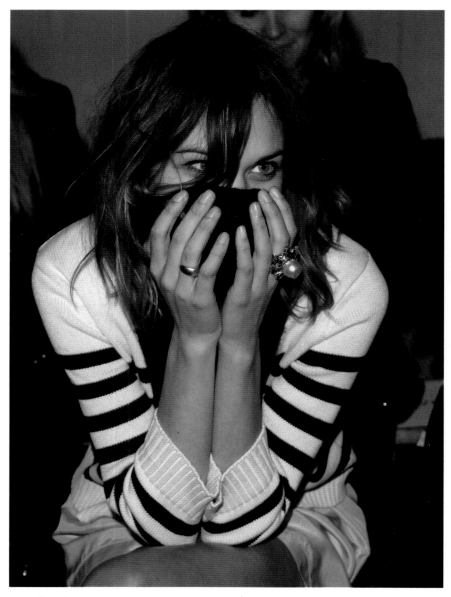

Sexy in stripes, pretty with a pink skirt, and worn with a very large pearl ring.
2009   Alexa Chung at the Autumn Twenty8Twelve show, London Fashion Week.

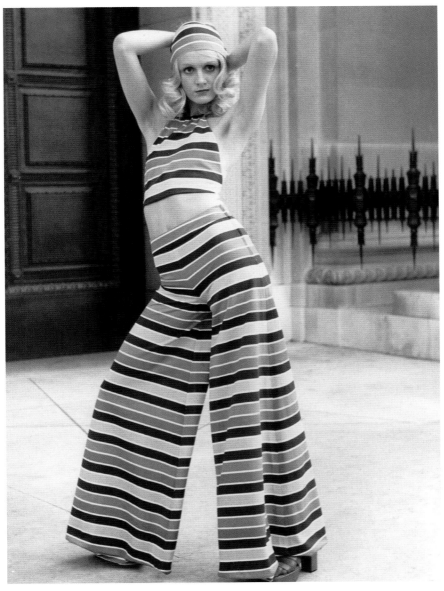

Matching moments, a cropped top, flared loons, topped off with a little beanie hat.
1971 A model wearing 'Lollipop', from the Mary Quant spring collection, London.

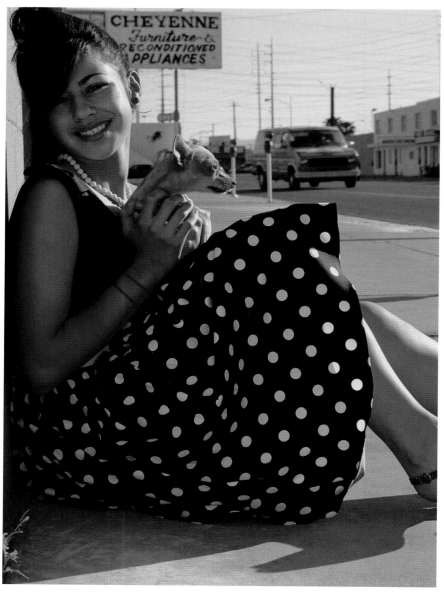

Very grown-up, a spotted prom skirt, a string of pearls and a chignon.
2000s A teenage girl sitting on the sidewalk with a Chihuahua dog, Las Vegas, USA.

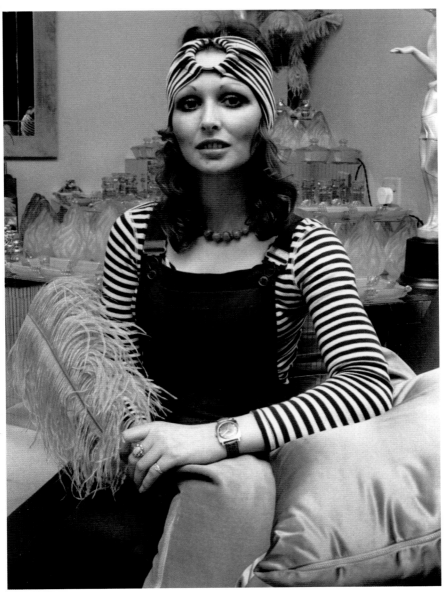

Sixties style, a headband and T-shirt in graphic stripes, and dungarees too.
1973 Jenny Cartwright, a shop assistant at the Biba boutique, Kensington, London.

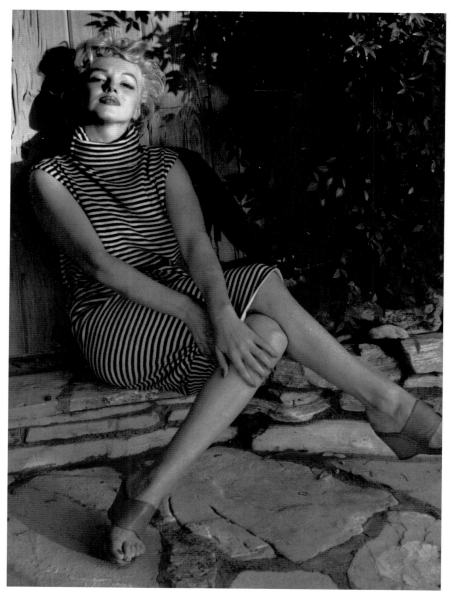

Shining siren, in the simplest striped dress, both beautiful and blonde.
1954 American actress, Marilyn Monroe, sits in shade against a garden fence.

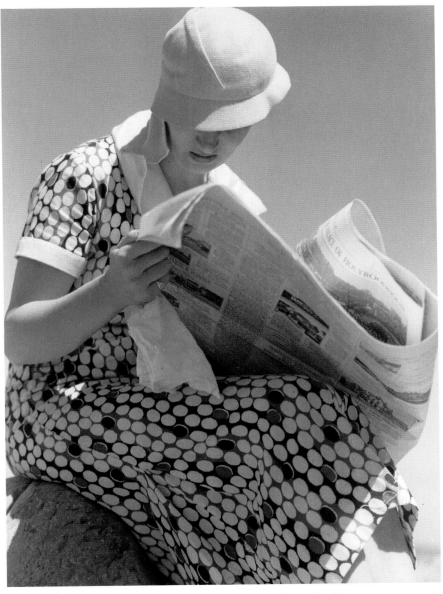

Smart and serious, a shirtwaister, with a crisp white collar and cuffs.
1930 A woman, in a spotted dress and a jaunty cap, catches up on the news.

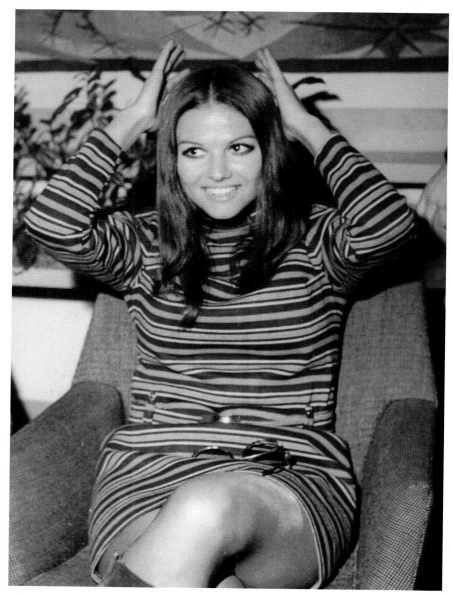

Horizontal stripes, both casual and kooky, worn with kinky boots and a polo neck.
1968   Italian film star, Claudia Cardinale, in a jersey suit with a mini-skirt.

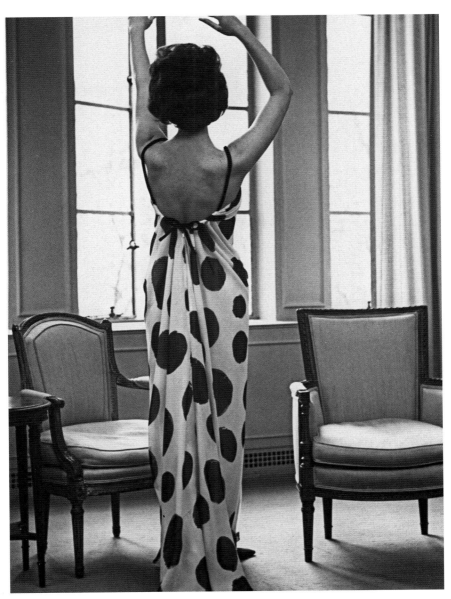

A very contemporary design, draped at the back, and cut in the boldest of dots.
1962 A fashionable French evening dress modelled at Ohrbach's, a New York store.

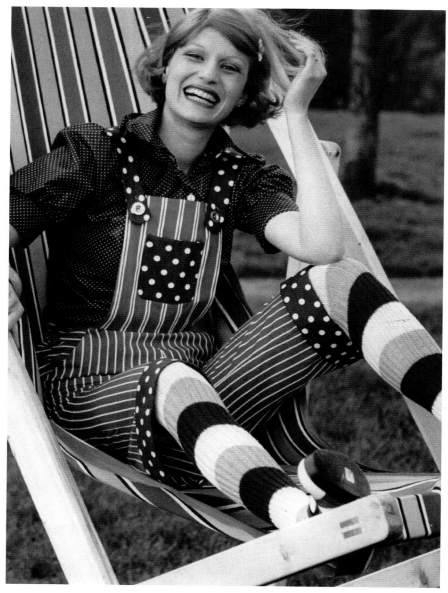

Andy Pandy comic-book chic, or Paddington Bear cool, a print too far perhaps.
1972 A model sports a spotted blouse, striped dungaree pedal pushers and socks.

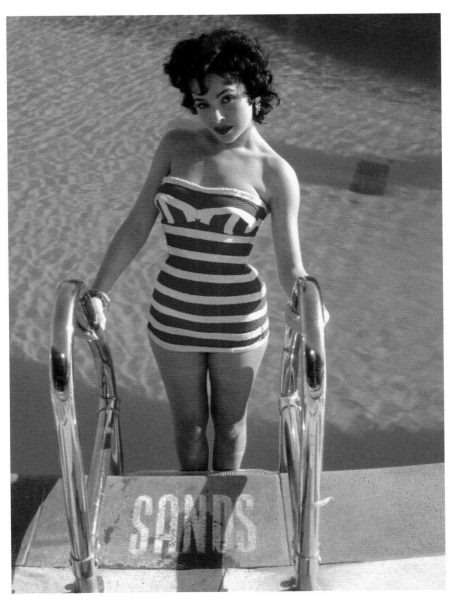

A pouting princess, all curvy and cute, in a bold, wide-striped swimming costume.
1954   Austrian actress, Mara Lane, posing by the pool at the Sands Hotel, Las Vegas.

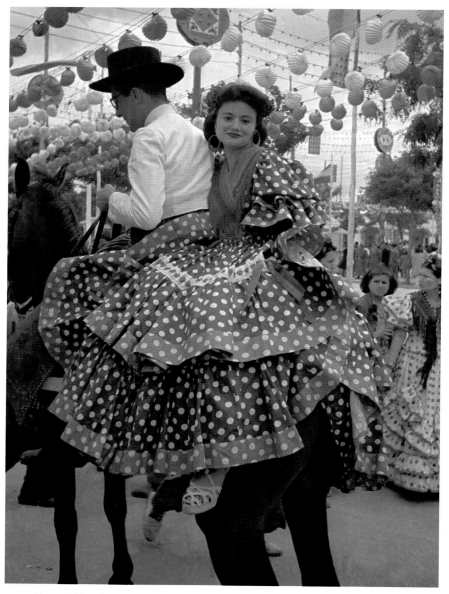

Fiesta fashion, flounced frills on the biggest dress ever, for all the fun at the fair.
1946   A Spanish couple riding in a procession and illustrated in *Picture Post*.

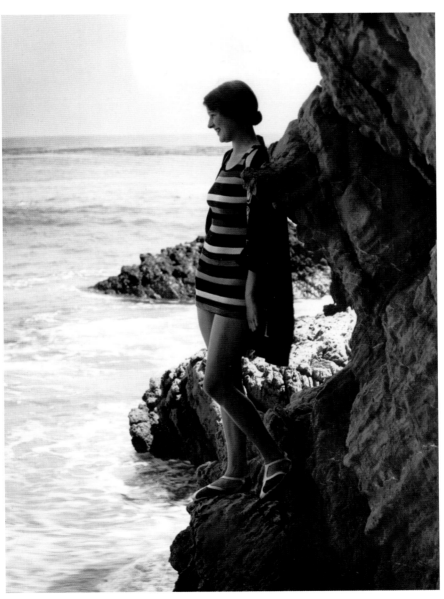

Sea style, a woollen costume and matching wrap, all covered up for a day in the sun.
1930 A woman wearing a then-fashionable bathing suit on cliffs by the sea.

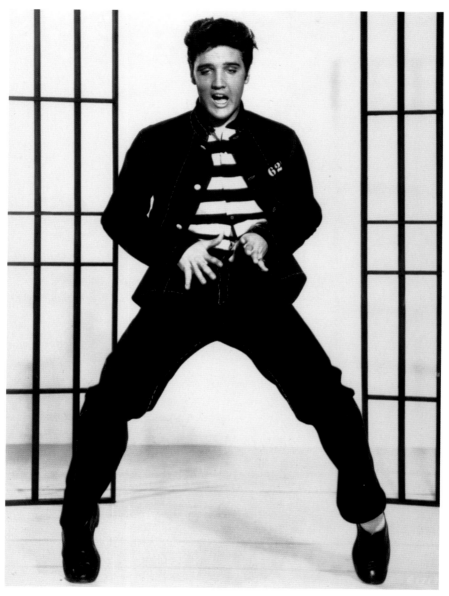

Rock and roll, all shook up, in dark denim, strong stripes, and that hip haircut.
1957   American actor/singer, Elvis Presley, appearing in the film *Jailhouse Rock*.

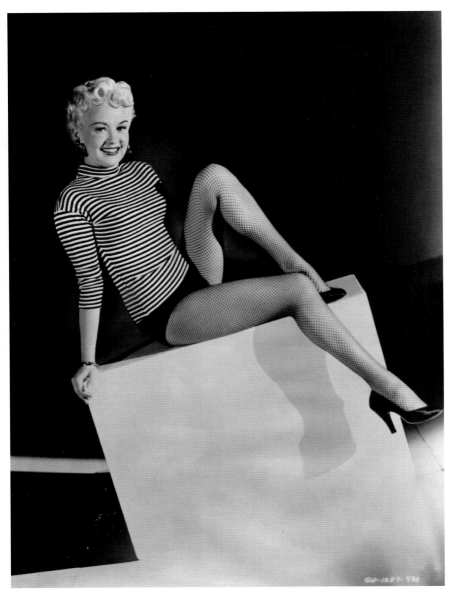

Pin-up perfect, in a simple striped sweater, tiny pants and sensible court shoes.
1955   Actress, Betty Grable, with her million-dollar legs, in *Three for the Show*.

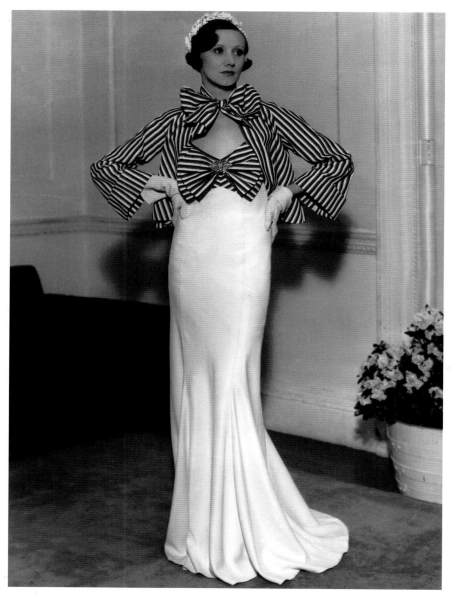

Elegance personified, with double bows, strong stripes over a satin sheath dress.
1934   An evening gown by Victor Stiebel, a South African-born, British couturier.

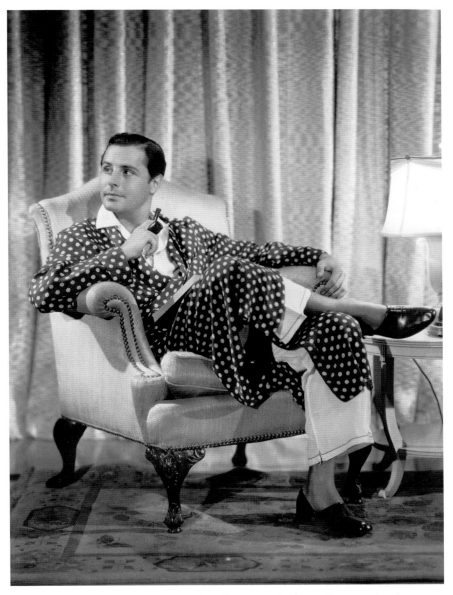

Dressed for bed, a gentleman clad in a silk gown and pyjamas, slippers and a pipe.
1935 Thomas Beck, the American actor, most notable in the role of *Charlie Chan*.

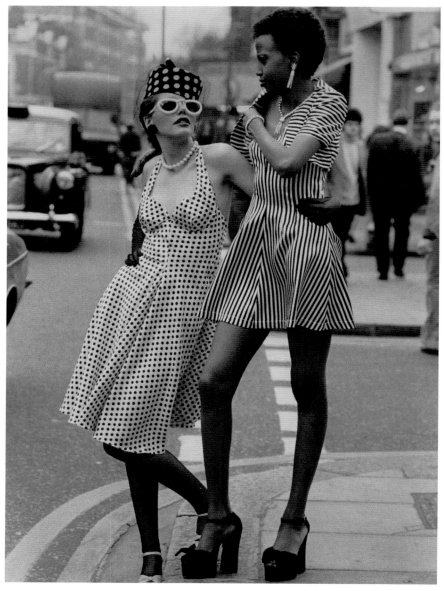

The long and the short of it, a sundress or a mini, both worn with towering platforms. 1973 Models at the opening of the Mr. Freedom boutique, King's Road, London.

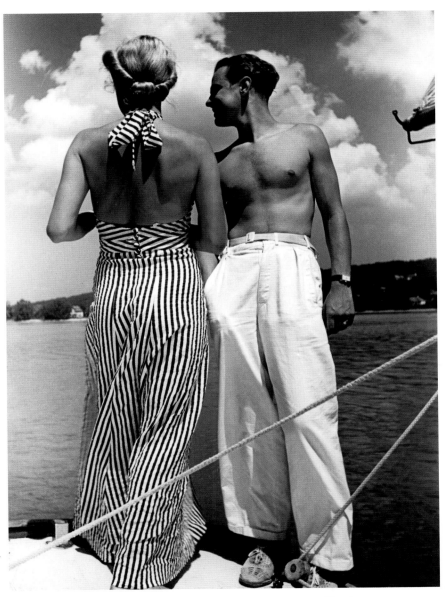

Hurrah for the white and blue, sailor style, carefully coordinated in crisp cottons.
1950 A couple, in white trousers and a striped trouser, suit gaze over the ocean.

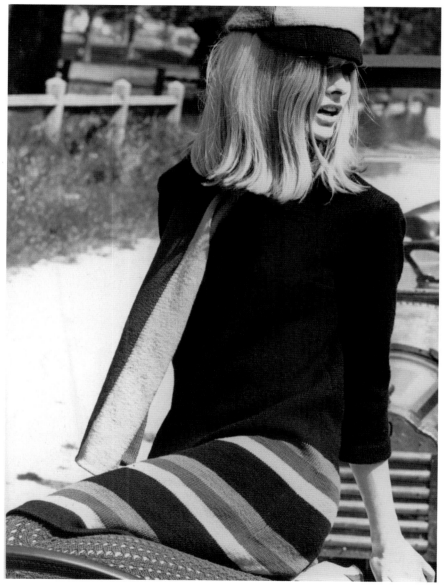

Student style, a polo neck, skinny skirt, jaunty cap and crochet tights, all in knit.
1970   A gorgeous girl, hanging out between classes, in a Parisian park, France.

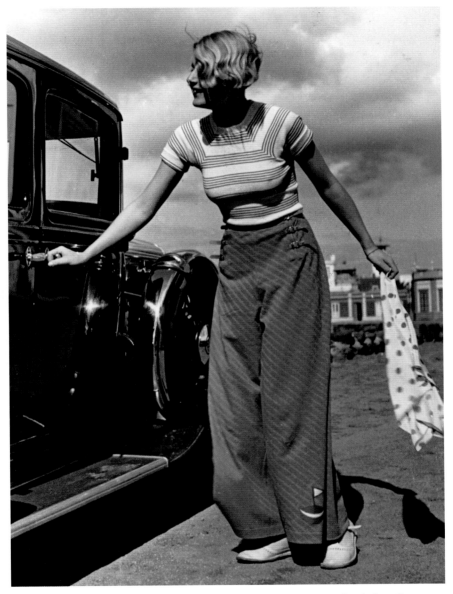

Beach babe, baggy bell-bottoms, a tight striped top, a spotted scarf and plimsolls.
1932 A girl, with a bobbed haircut, dressed for a day out on the boardwalk.

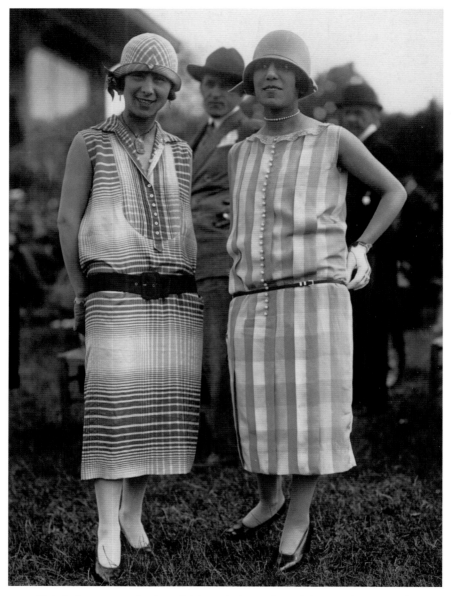

Style in the summer, checks and stripes, cloches and court shoes, and some pearls.
1924 Dropped-waist dresses, buttoned down the front, designed by Mlles Welly.

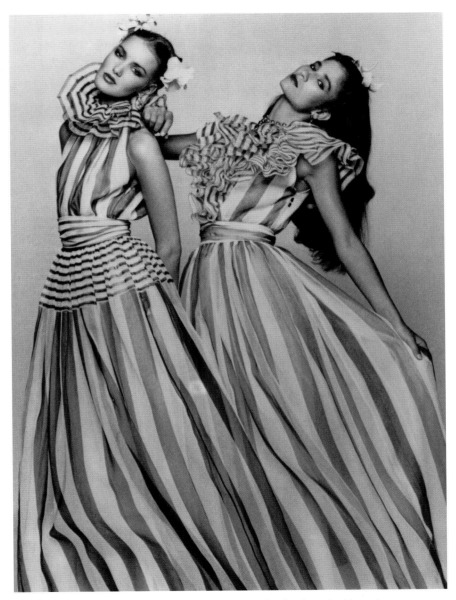

'In the Wind', organza evening dresses fluttering like flags in red, white and green.
1979 The Boutique Collection for spring and summer, Christian Dior, London.

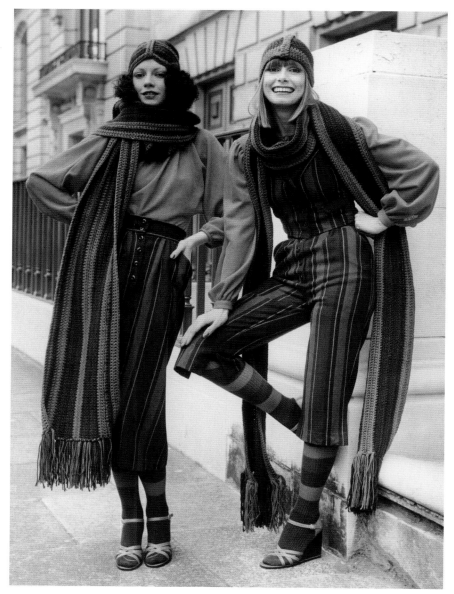

On trend, pedal pushers and wedges, batwing sleeves and *Doctor Who* scarves.
1975 'Skindles' and 'Hammersmith Palais', spring looks by designer, Mary Quant.

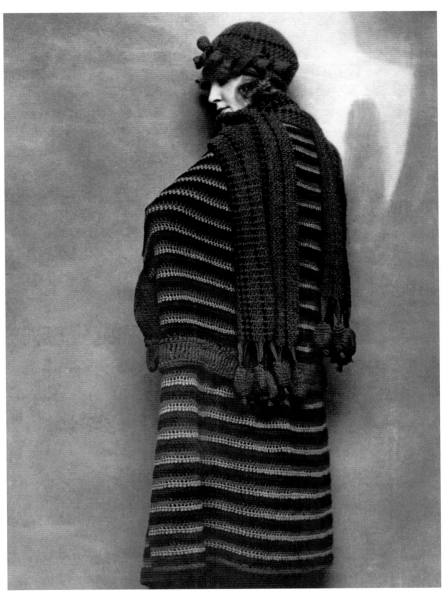

Knit one, pearl one, a coat, with a matching hat and scarf, complete with pom-poms.
1922 A model keeps cosy in an elongated, striped cardigan and all the accessories.

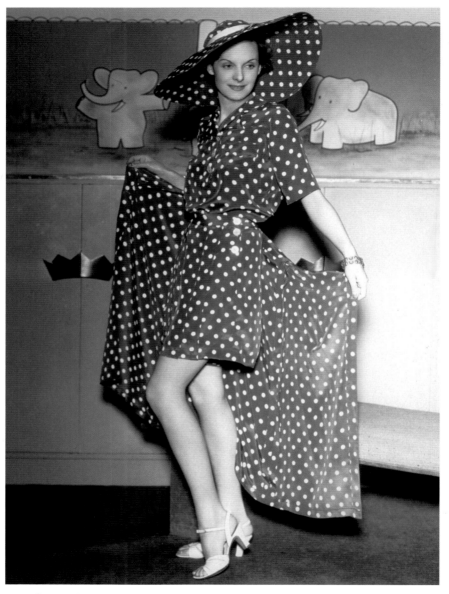

Summer in the city, spotted shorts, with a matching skirt, blouse and sunhat too.
1935   A model wearing Jaeger, at the opening of their Regent Street store, London.

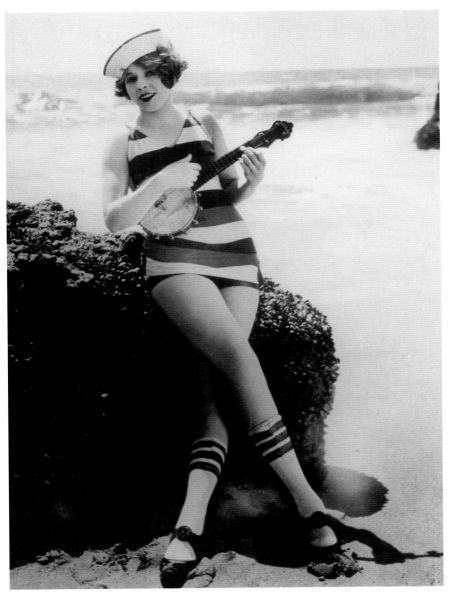

Hallo sailor, strumming a happy tune in a swimsuit, socks and shoes in the sand.
1923   A girl, in a striped bathing costume and sailor's hat, playing the banjo.

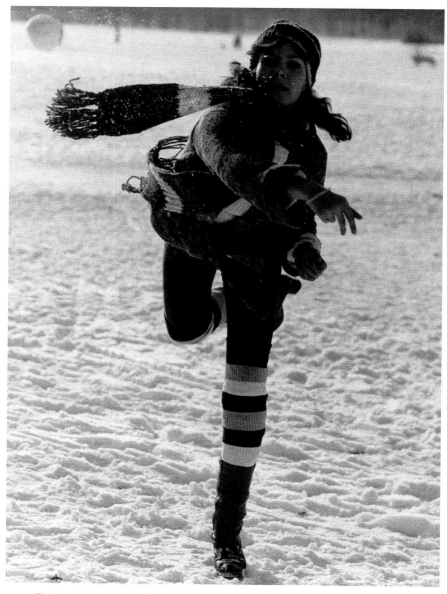

Fighting fashion, snowballing and stripes, and very *Flashdance* legwarmers.
1982   Knitting from head to toe protect a girl from the wintry weather.

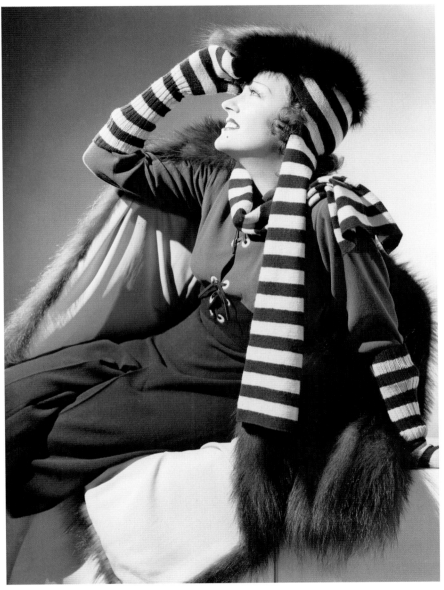

Star in stripes, skiwear in the studio, swathed in skins and smiles.
1931 American actress, Gloria Swanson, in a fur hat and coat, and loads of woollies.

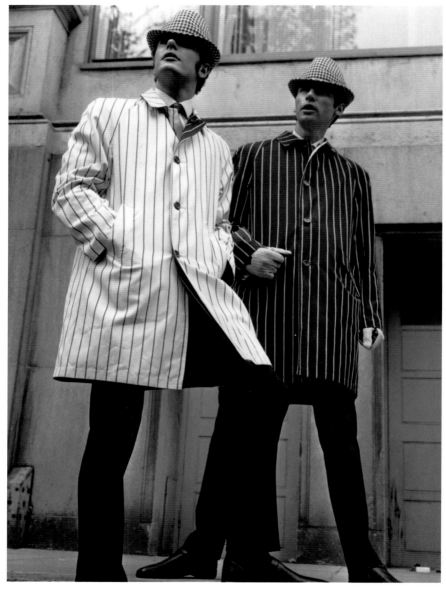

Lads in London strut their stuff, in stripes and suits, shirts and ties.
1967 Two male models wearing single-breasted raincoats and checked pork-pie hats.

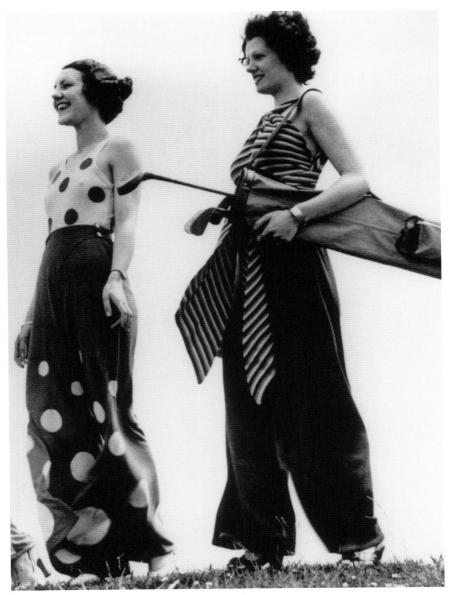

Gorgeous for golf, and not a handicap in sight, beach pyjamas in spots and stripes.
1935 Women playing golf at the Stanley Park course, Blackpool, Lancashire.

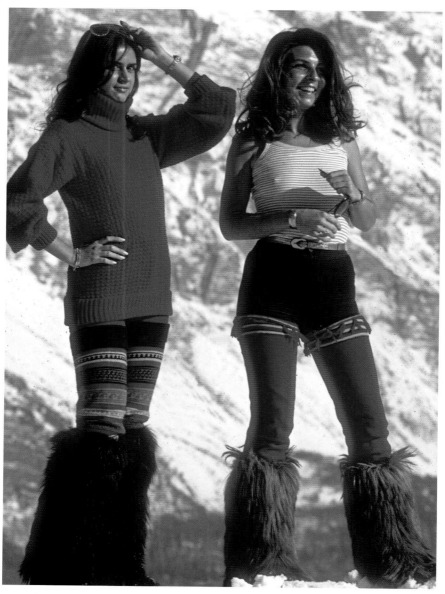

Sun and snow, furry yeti boots, knitted leggings worn with a polo neck or a singlet.
1976   Socialites on holiday in the ski resort Cortina d'Ampezzo, Italy.

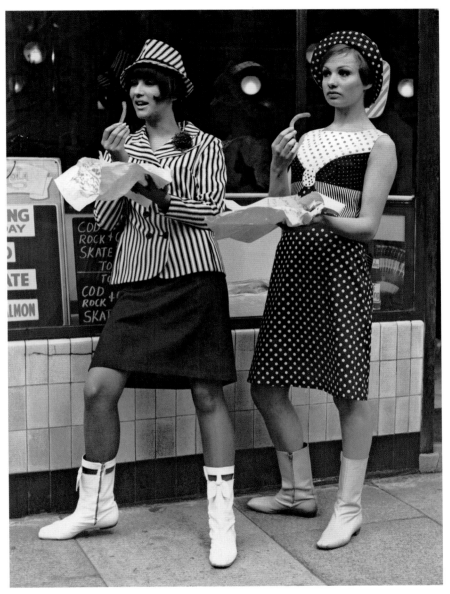

Fish and chips, curious clothes, polka dots and tram-track stripes with white boots.
1965   Jackie Bowyer and Judy Gomm in the Lee Cecil 'Jetsetters' collection.

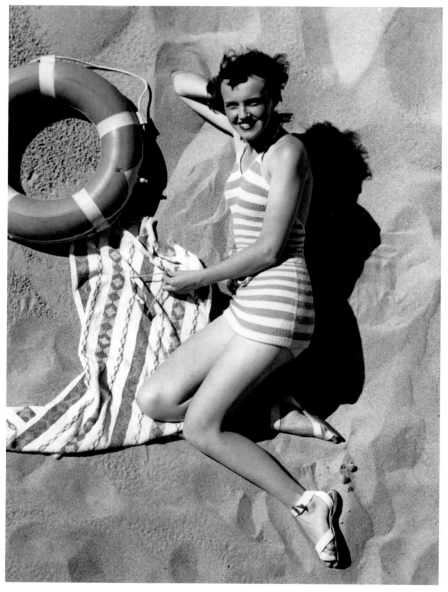

Surf city in the sand, sporting a tan, a halter-neck swimsuit and sensible sandals.
1935   A girl sunbathing on Palm Beach, Australia, life-ring and towel in tow.

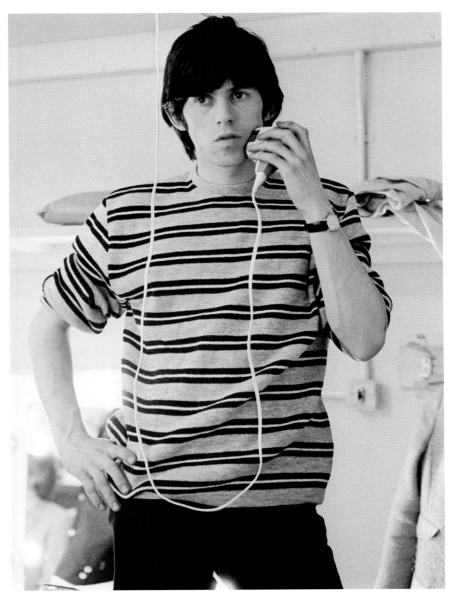

A Stone in stripes, in a simple T-shirt and sporting the ubiquitous Beatles haircut.
1963   Guitarist, Keith Richards, of *The Rolling Stones* shaving, using an electric razor.

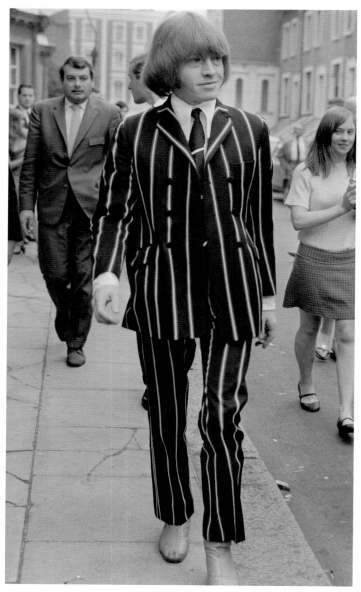

Natty but nice, a striped sixties suit.
1967 *Rolling Stones* Brian Jones leaving a London courthouse.

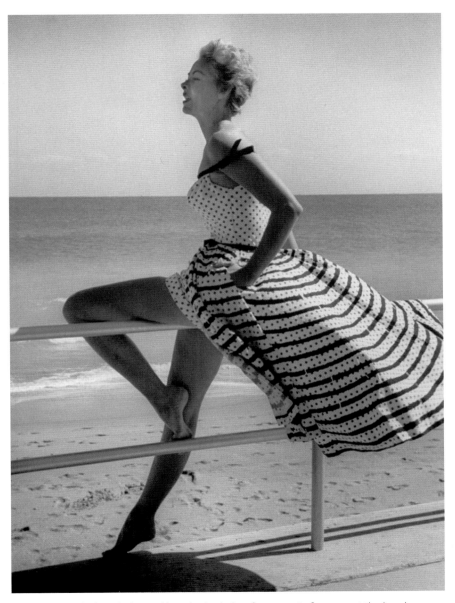

Blowing in the wind, casual but classic clothes for a smart afternoon at the beach.
1955   A model with a spotted swimsuit and striped overskirt, Miami, Florida, USA.

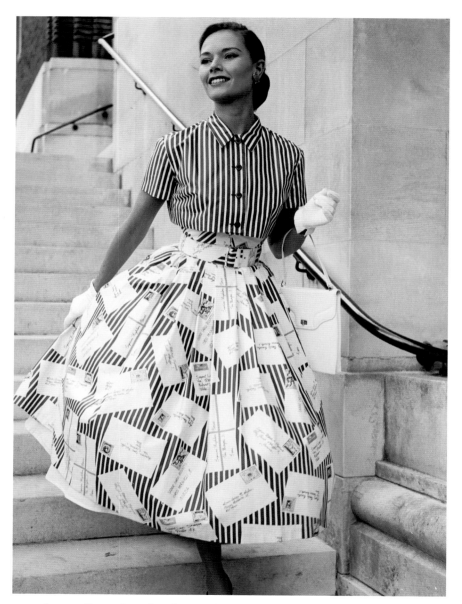

A post-office perfect print of stamped envelopes on stripes, very *Festival of Britain*.
1957 Tripping down the stairs wearing a summer frock in full-skirted Fifties fashion.

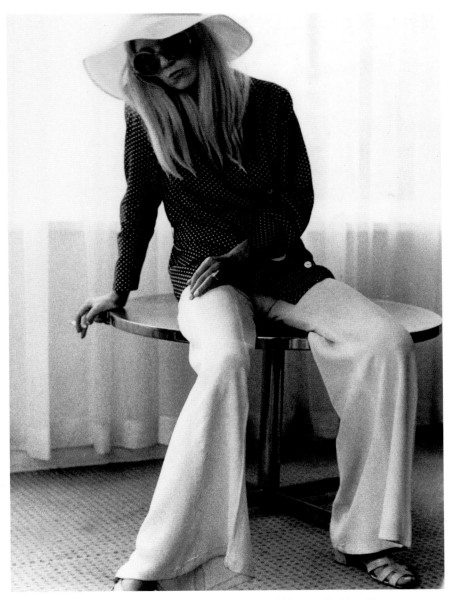

Oh so cool, in big shades and a floppy hat, a spotted blazer and wide white loons.
1969. Anna Wohlin, girlfriend of *Rolling Stones* Brian Jones at the time of his death.

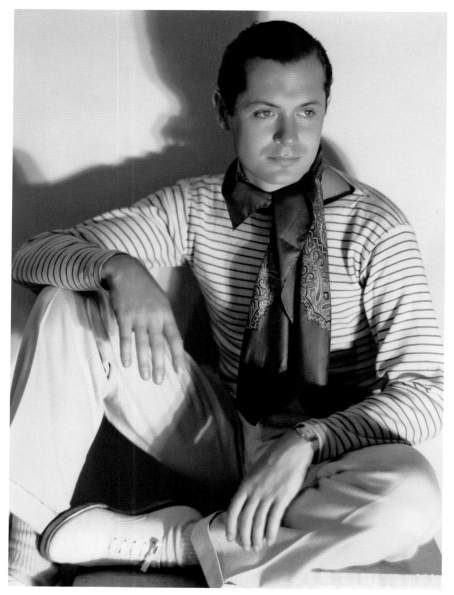

Cinema heart throb, coolly casual in flannels, and photographed in chiaroscuro.
1935   American actor, Robert Montgomery, in a striped sweatshirt and a silk scarf.

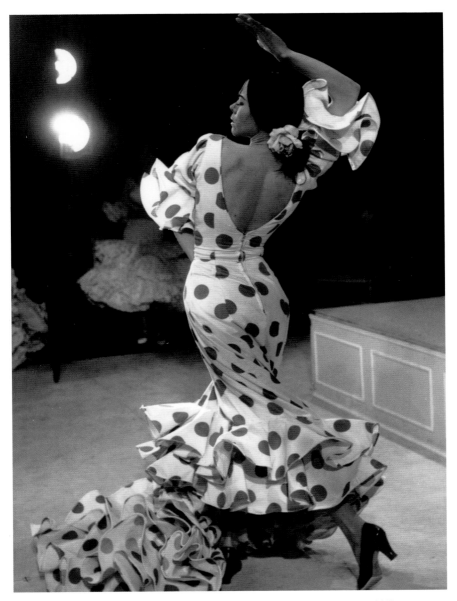

Strutting her stuff, with classic curves, in an enormous dress with acres of frills.
1964 Manuela Vargas in *The Tigress of the Flamenco*, Vaudeville Theatre, London.

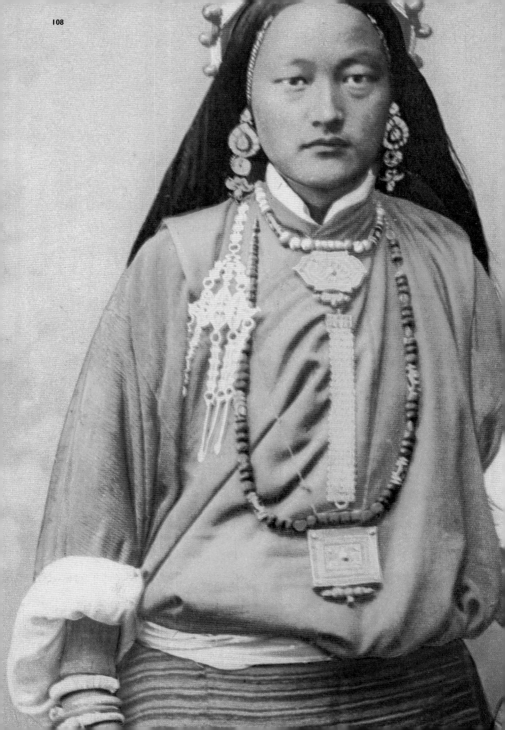

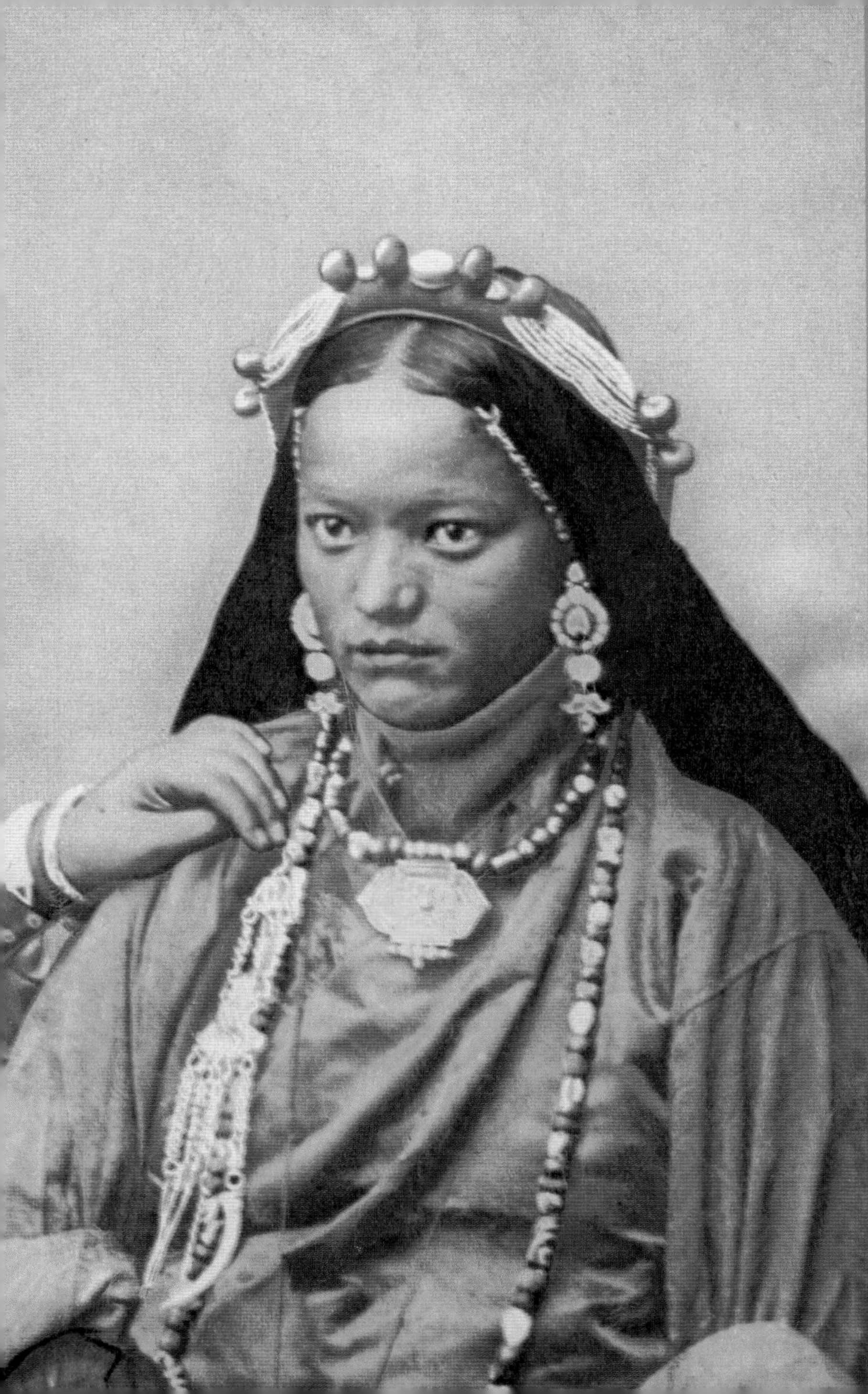

EXOTIC INFLUENCES

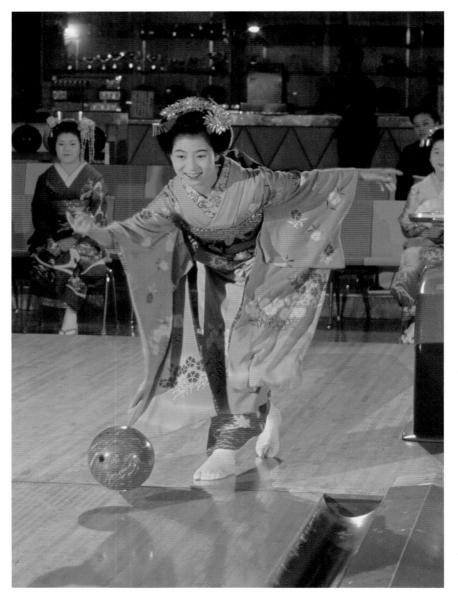

Sumptuous silk, with hand-painted flowers, in shades of sea green and peach.
1964   An apprentice geisha, in a kimono and full make-up, bowling, Kyoto, Japan.

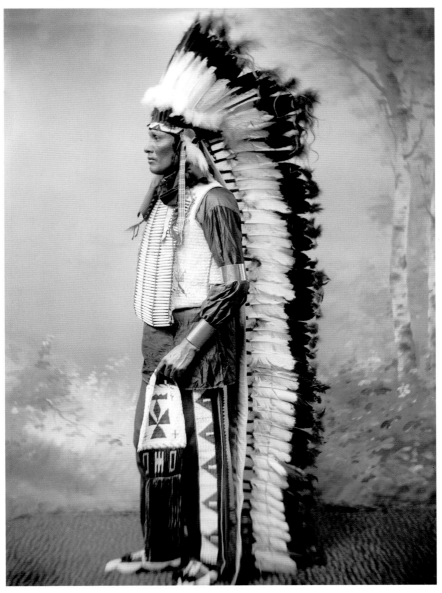

Leggings and moccasins, embroidered with porcupine quills, and eagle headdress.
1900   Sioux Indian warrior dressed for a gala occasion, South Dakota, USA.

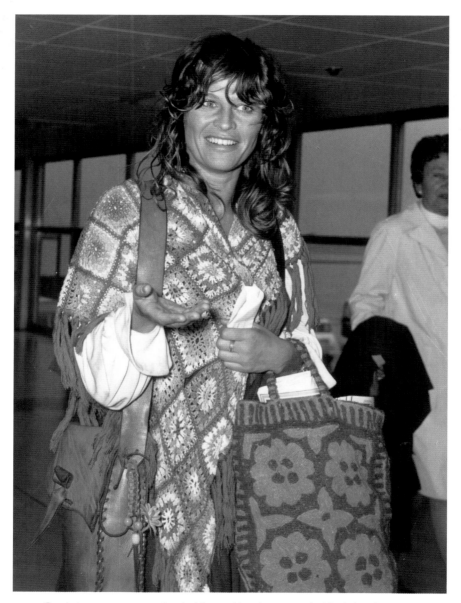

Crochet queen, a granny shawl with matching shopper, and a hippie handbag.
1971   British actress, Julie Christie, on her way to play Lara in *Doctor Zhivago*.

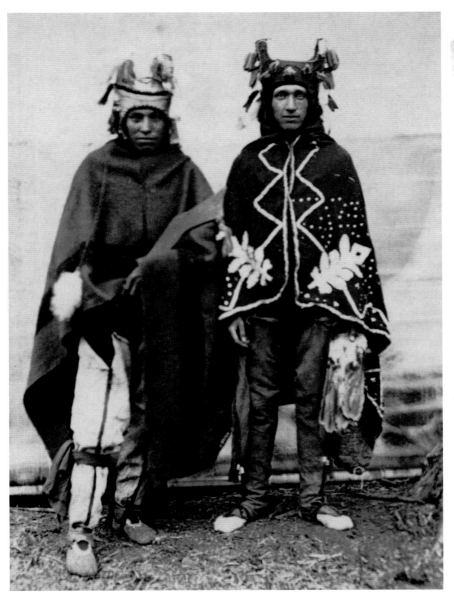

Caped crusaders, all rugged-up and embroidered, and headdresses with horns.
1874 Portrait of 'Wa-Geo-Hau-Ta' Great Thunder Chief, men in ceremonial attire.

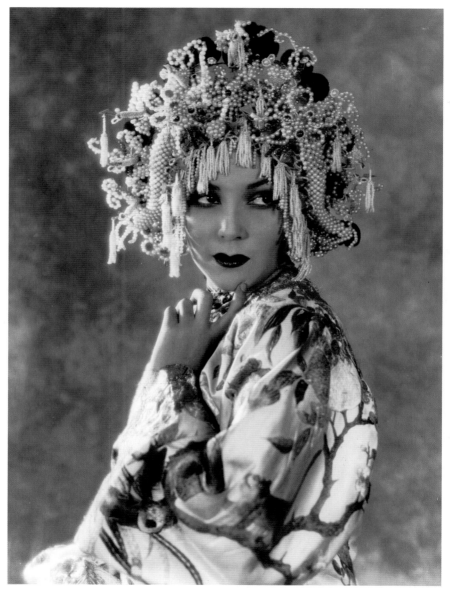

Decorated like a dream, pearls slithering snakes, tiny tassels and a rich robe.
1930   Mexican actress, Dolores del Rio, wife of the MGM director, Cedric Gibbons.

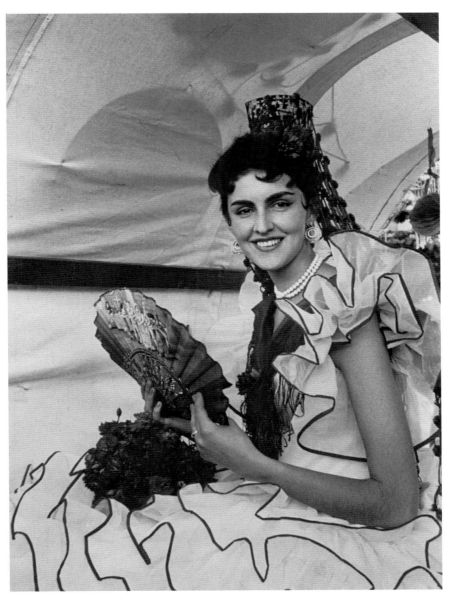

Flamenco finery, a fabulous smile, frills, flowers, a fan, lace mantilla and all.
1959   A Spanish señorita participating in an international beauty contest.

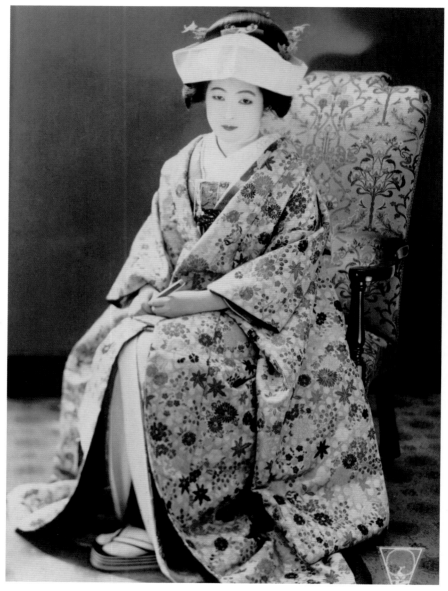

China-doll chic, an elaborate ceremonial kimono lends a certain stillness.
1900 A Japanese woman on an upholstered chair wearing traditional clothing.

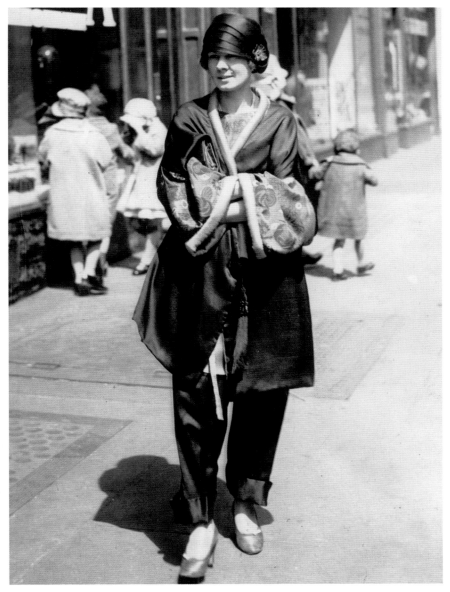

Anything Oriental, fashionable in the Twenties, but worn in a Western way.
1924 Jean Wilson wears Japanese pyjamas at an Easter parade, New York, USA.

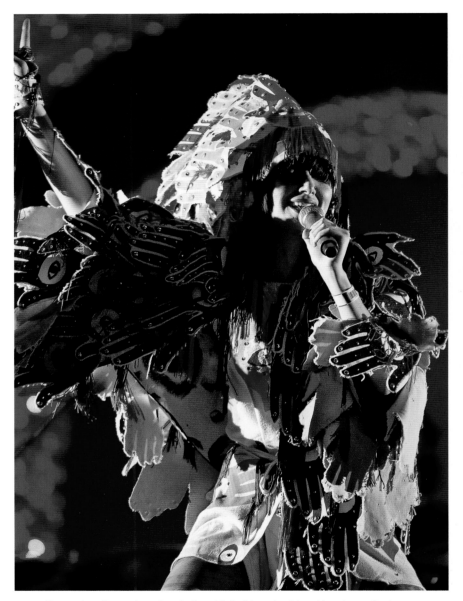

Dressed-up like an American Indian chief, with embroidered hands, not feathers.
2009   Karen O of the *Yeah Yeah Yeahs* at the Lollapalooza festival, Chicago, USA.

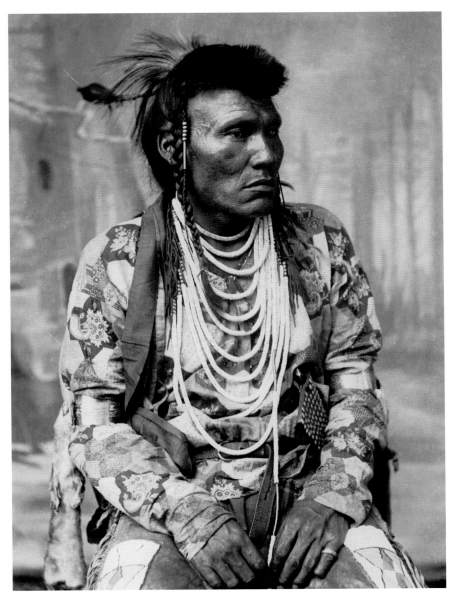

Regal in ritual robes, a big bone necklace, flowered shirt, with feathers and plaits.
1891   A portrait of Omuxistoan from Tsuu T'ina, Sarcee, Alberta, Canada.

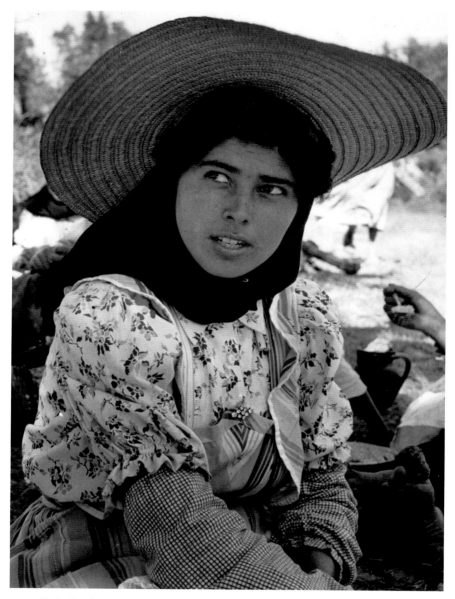

Sheltering from the sun, in scarves, a straw cartwheel-hat, and flowered shirt.
1955 A migrant worker employed in the rice fields of Portugal.

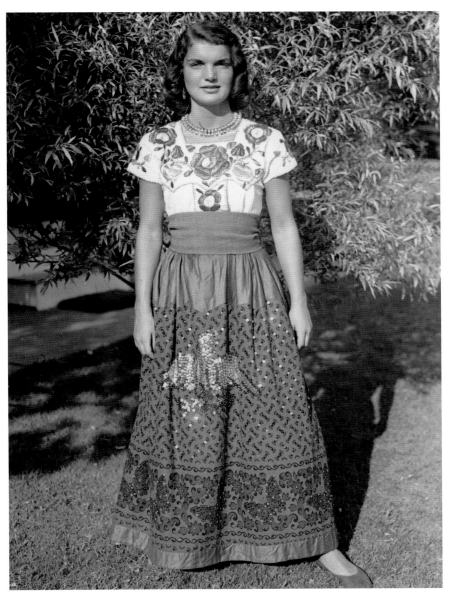

Tyrolean trends, a white, flower-embroidered blouse worn with a long skirt.
1949 Jacqueline Bouvier (Jackie O) at twenty years old, Long Island, New York.

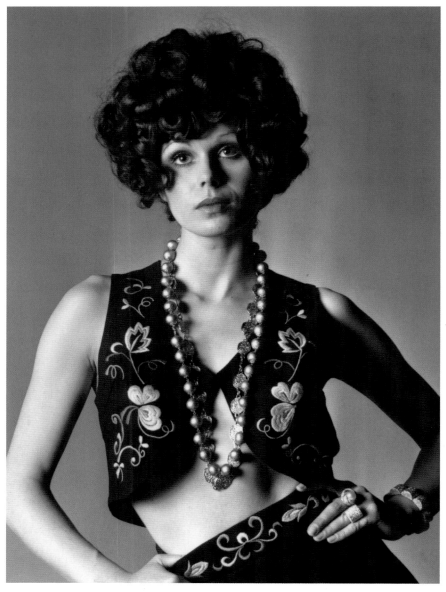

Sixties style, an embroidered waistcoat, flared trousers and bubble-cut hairdo.
1968   Joanna Lumley, the 'Bond' girl and star of the TV series *The Avengers*.

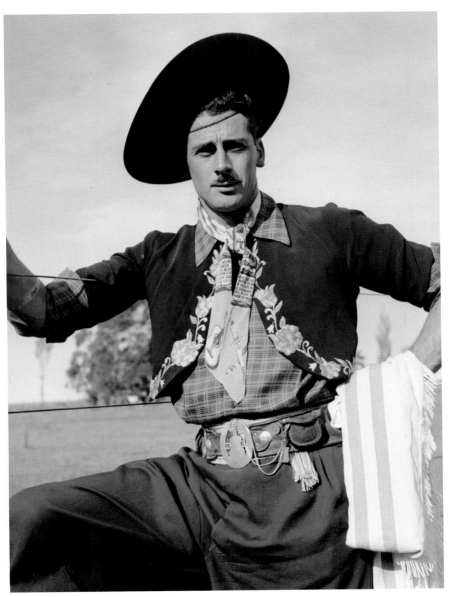

Macho man, a flowered jacket, checked scarf and skirt, and best black hat.
1955 A gaucho from Rosario, Uruguay, dressed in his best for a day at the rodeo.

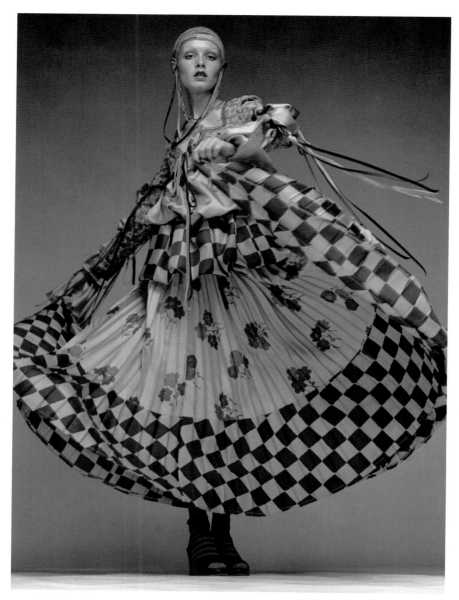

Whirling dervish dress, a glorious cacophony of prints, checkerboard and floral.
1970 Twiggy in a dress designed by Bill Gibb for the premiere of *The Boy Friend*.

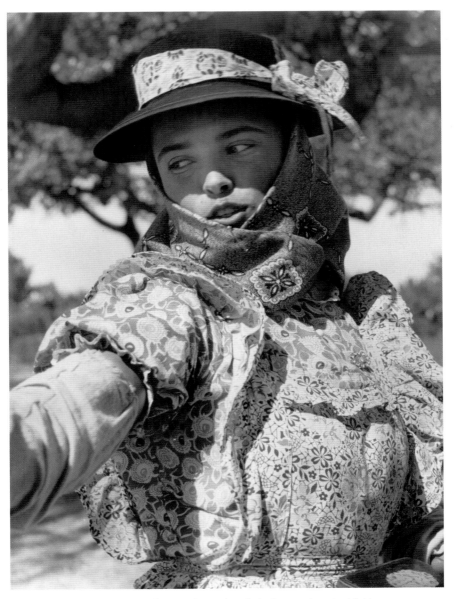

Covered-up in cotton, print on print, such style in the sun-drenched fields.
1955 A field worker in traditional Portuguese dress.

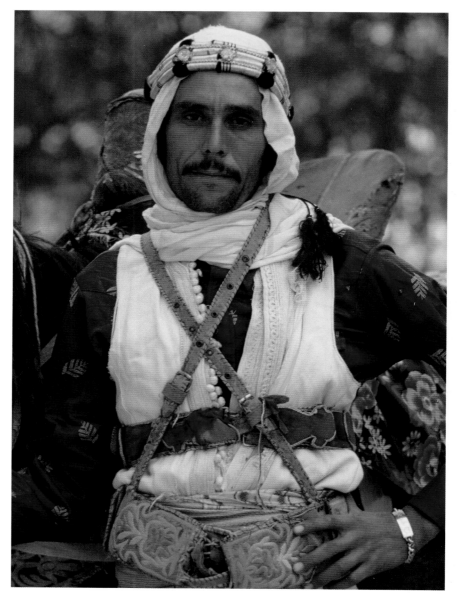

Very *Lawrence of Arabia*, complete with bandoleer, embroidered belts and all.
1980   A desert tribesman in brightly coloured traditional dress, Tunisia.

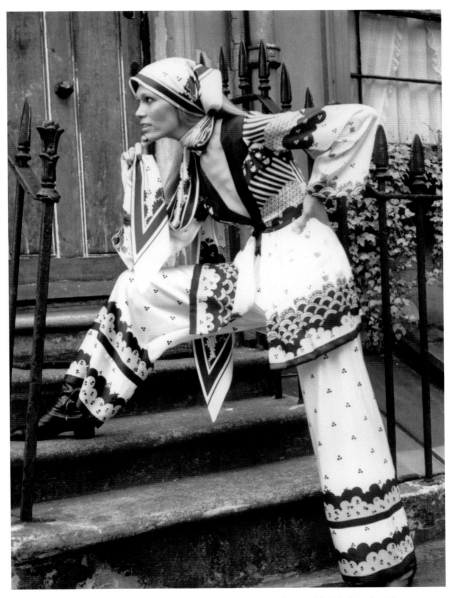

Difficult to miss, a matching scarf, jacket and trousers in graphic black and white.
1968 A model in a satin trouser suit by Ossie Clark and Alice Pollock, London.

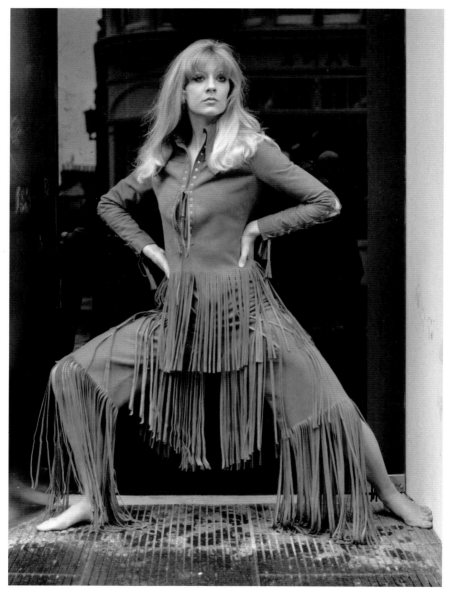

Hiawatha style, suede shirt and gaucho trousers, with an abundance of fringing.
1969 Vicki Hodge in Ossie Clark and Alice Pollock, Quorum boutique, London.

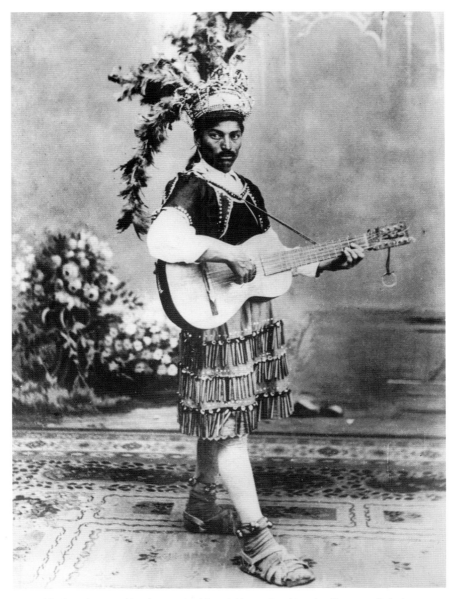

Manly and mustachioed, an embroidered skirt and waistcoat, with an exotic hat.
1920   A Mexican dancer and musician with his guitar.

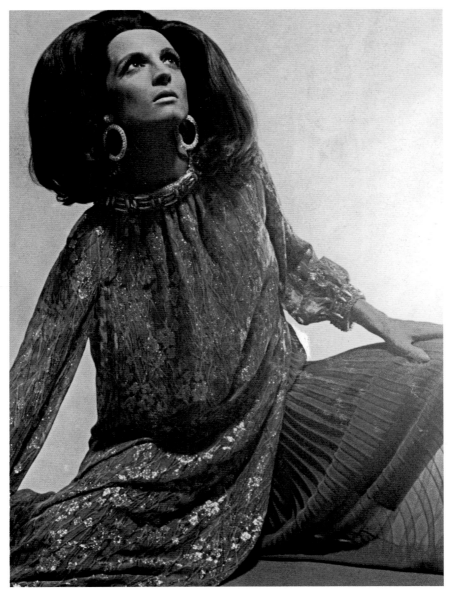

Turkish delight, brocade flowers and shoals of chiffon with huge hoop earrings.
1966   Italian designer Valentino's opulent tunic and pleated palazzo pants.

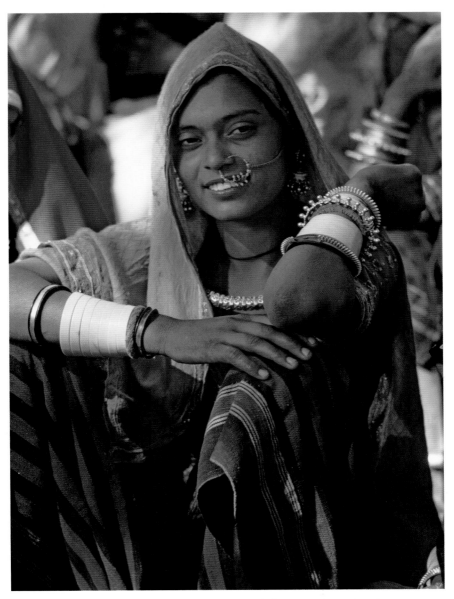

Exotically Eastern, armfuls of bangles in ivory and silver, nose ring and earrings.
1962 A woman wears her finery for a festival, Rajasthan State, India.

132

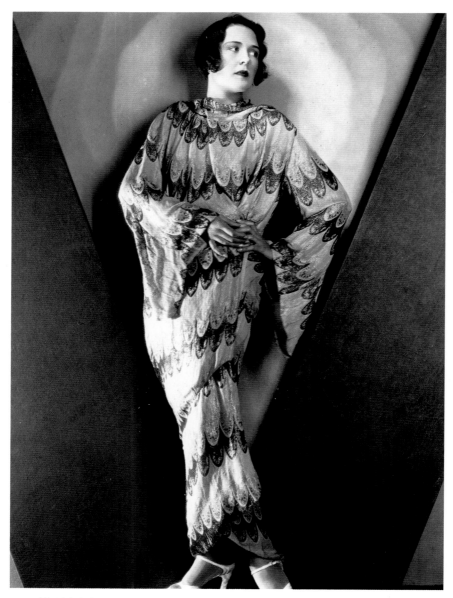

Exquisitely long and draped, trumpet sleeves, cowl neck and white sandals too.
1930   A woman models a turquoise lamé gown printed with peacock feathers.

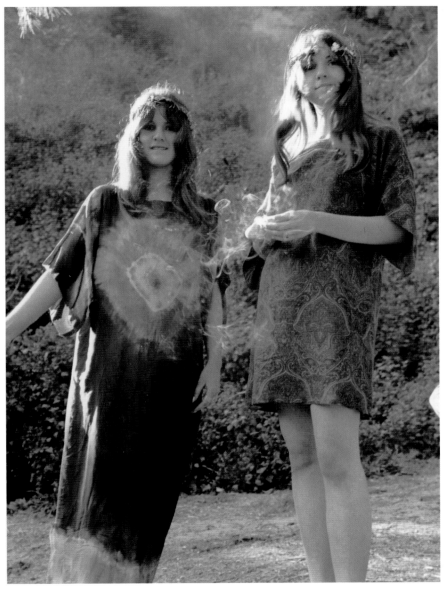

Flower power, batik or tie-dyed, short or long, daisy head-bands, anything goes.
1970 A photograph of two hippie girls dressed for summer in the park.

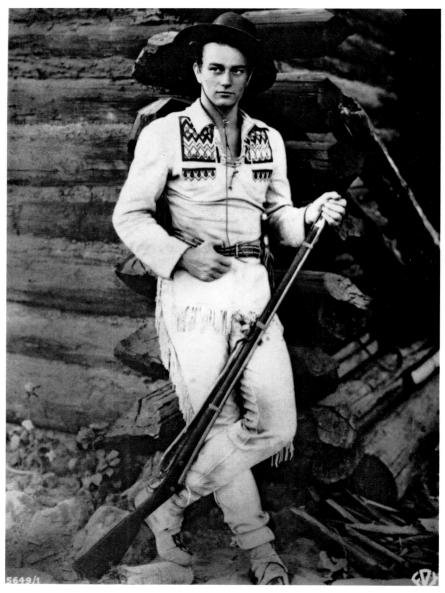

Brooding good looks, dressed in embroidered buckskins and a jaunty hat.
1930   American actor, John Wayne, stars in *The Big Trail*, his first leading role.

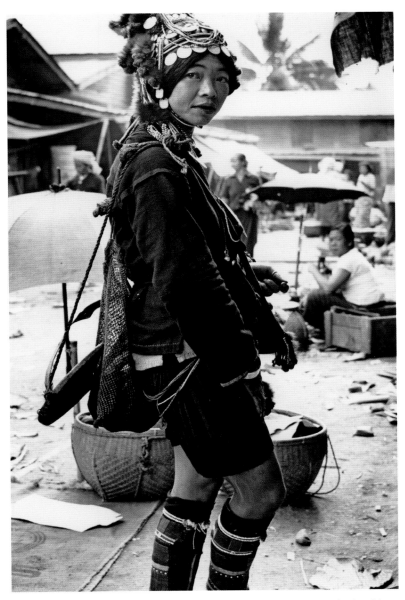

Dressed for best, decorated with bright beads, coins, trinkets, and tufts of fur.
1950 A girl from the Ekor Hill tribe at Mae Sai in northern Thailand.

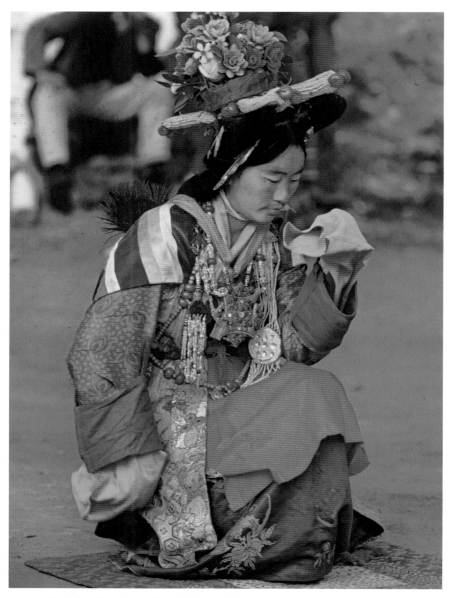

A fresh floral hat, bags of beads, fabulous fabrics, all make for a very special day.
1973   A Nepalese woman in a brightly-coloured costume kowtows on a small mat.

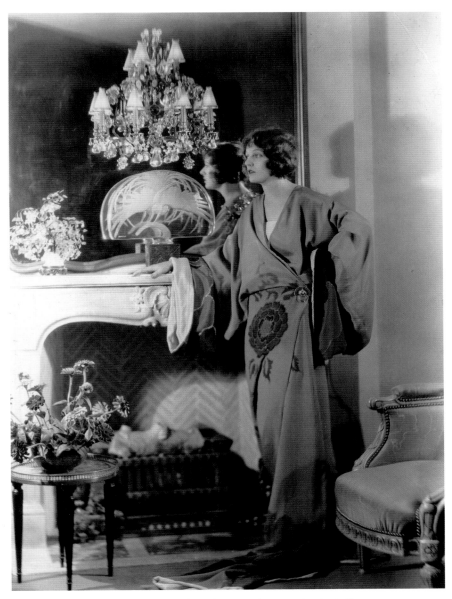

Champagne chic, very at-home in a glamorous, Japanese-inspired, silk gown.
1926   Hollywood film star, Corinne Griffith, who appeared in *Lilies of the Field*.

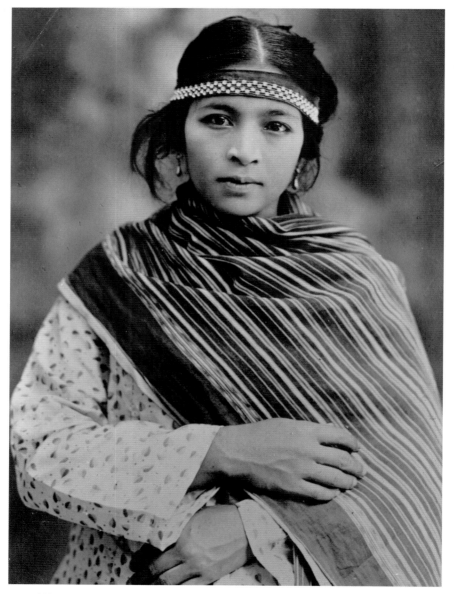

Woven textiles, bright eyes, bright stripes and a hippy headband, all beautiful.
1940   A portrait of an Indonesian woman in native dress of sarong and shawl.

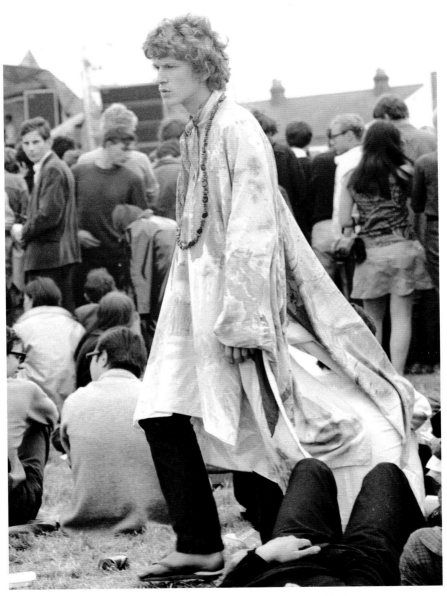

Golden boy, chill-out man in Rajasthan robes, jeans, beads and flip-flops.
1967 A youth in the crowd at a hippie festival in Windsor, England.

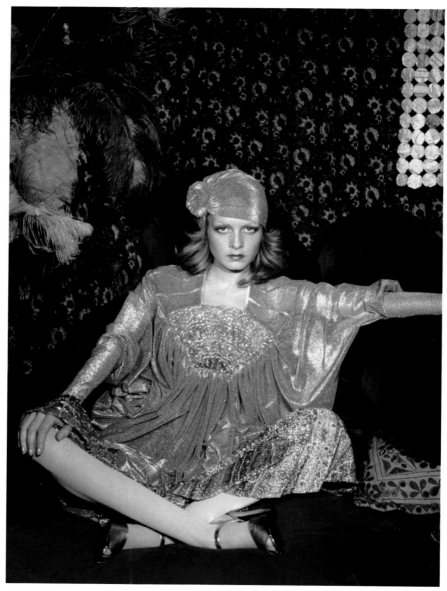

Exotic but English, Indian-inspired batwing dress in peach lamé and Liberty print. 1972 Model, Twiggy, in an exotic tent at boyfriend, Justin de Villeneuve's, house.

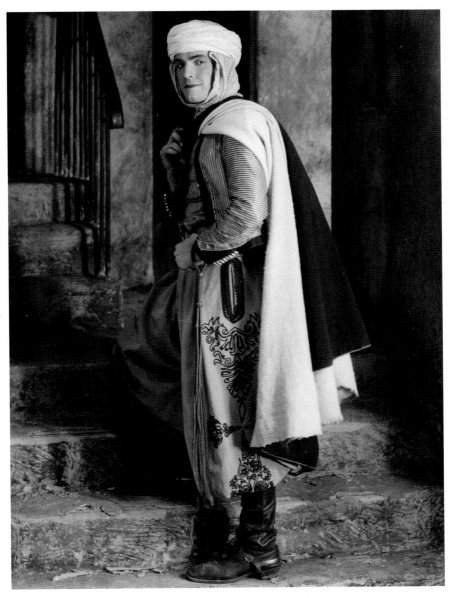

Cutting a dash, a desert drama, with a cloak, turban, boots but no camel.
1924 Mexican/American actor, Ramon Novarro, stars in the silent film *The Arab*.

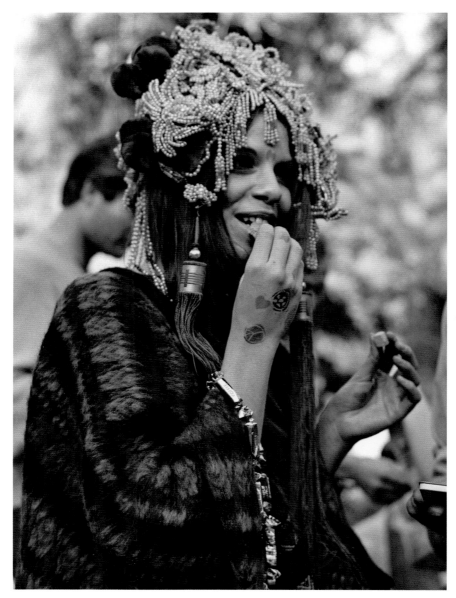

Worldwide influences, a pearl headdress from Indonesia and an outfit from India.
1967 Hippies gather for a celebration of peace and love, Los Angeles, California.

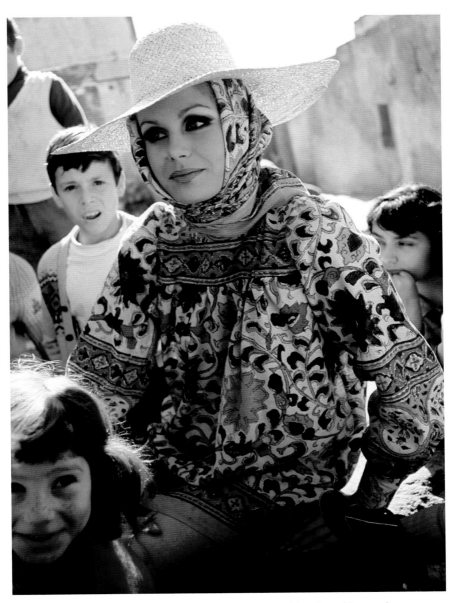

Colourful and characterful, block-print, bright chintz mini and matching scarf.
1968   British actress, Joanna Lumley, modelling a fashionable Sixties dress.

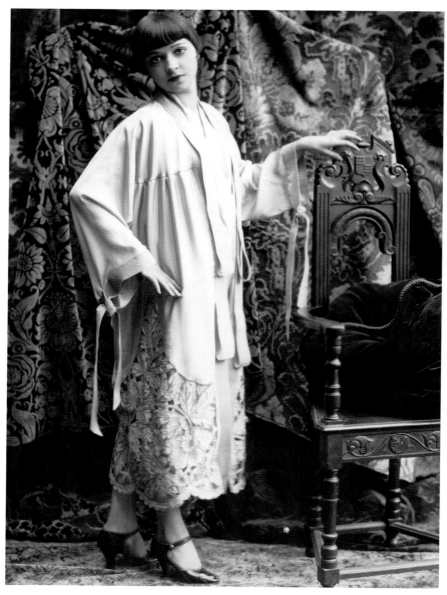

Fashionably French, with rose découpage work on the skirt and velour ribbons.
1925 An embroidered blue tea-gown, designed by Madeleine Fontenay.

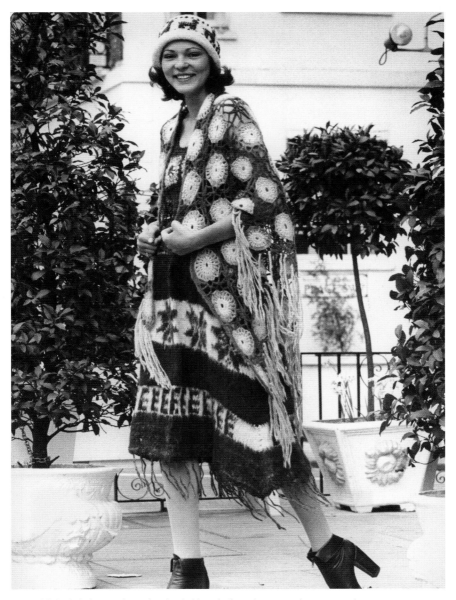

Kinky knitting, an Aztec-inspired skirt, platform boots, and a tea-cosy hat.
1974 A model wearing a woollen dress, worn with a big crocheted shawl.

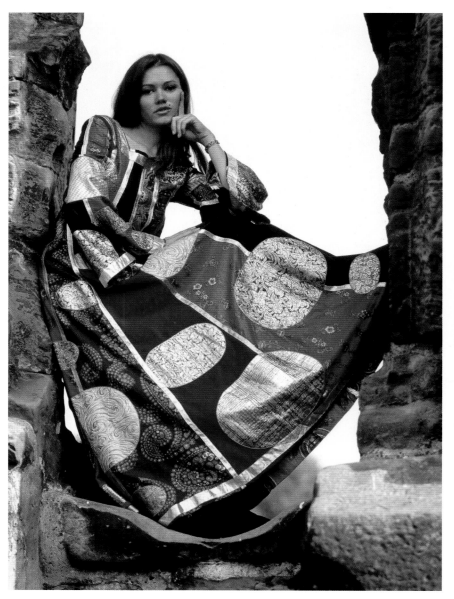

Patchwork and appliqué, beribboned and bedecked, the brave and the beautiful.
1970 A model in a multi-coloured maxidress, perched between pillars.

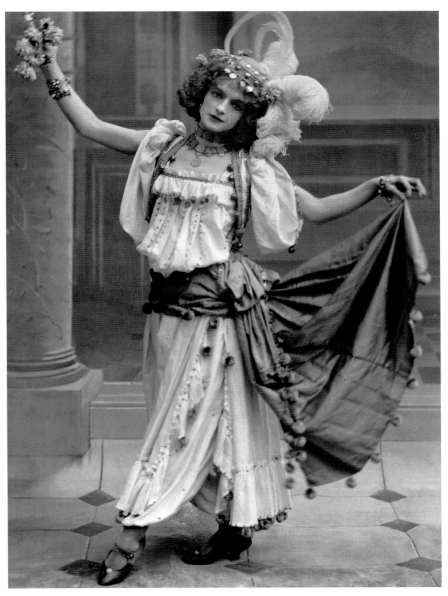

Dancing girl for your delectation, in egret feathers, pom-poms and tasteful tassels.
1898   Cabaret artist, Blanche Vaudon (queen of the cigarette card), in costume.

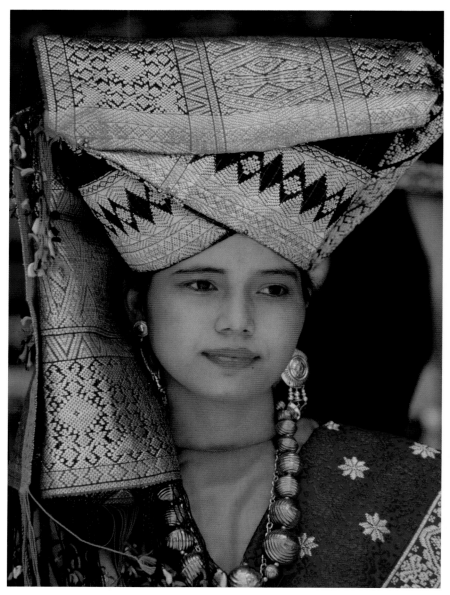

All that glistens is gold, cloth of gold, gold earrings and a heavy gold necklace too.
1990   A girl wearing an ornate headdress in traditional style, Java, Indonesia.

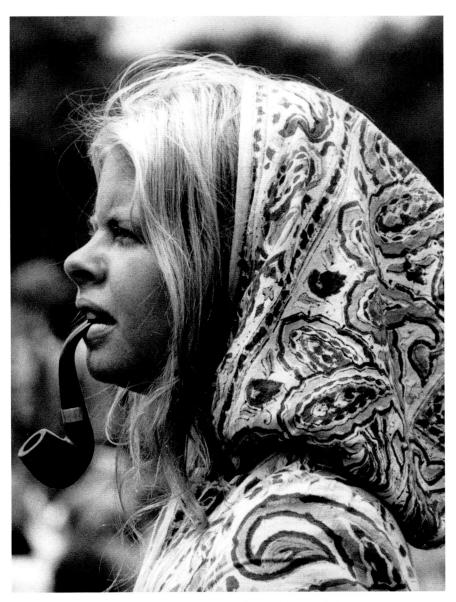

Summer in the city, sultry and smoking, wearing a paisley, hooded caftan.
1970   A blonde woman with a pipe in her mouth, Hyde Park, London.

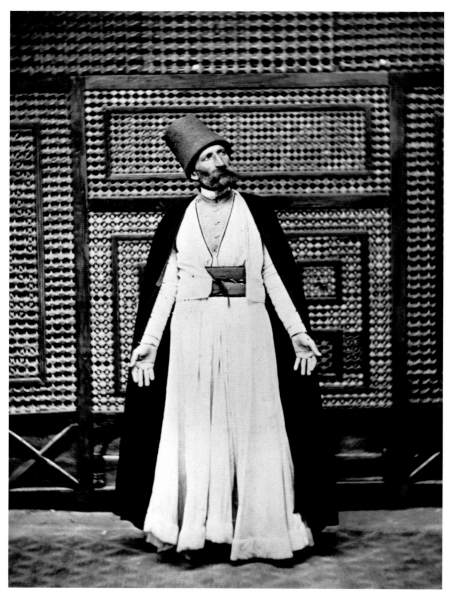

Religious robes with a clerical cape, a fine beard and a flower-pot hat.
1878   A portrait of a Dervish, Mohammedan friar.

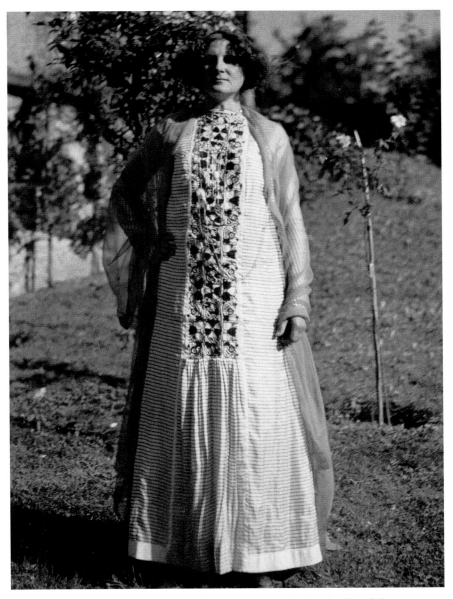

A painterly palette, a jade green chiffon coat over a striped, embroidered dress.
1910   Emilie Flöge, a friend of artist Gustav Klimt, at Atter Lake, Upper Austria.

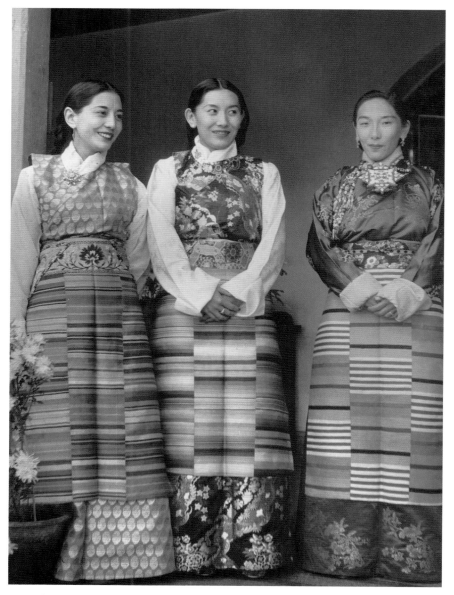

Ceremonial and very correct, in classic costumes woven in florals and stripes.
1959 Three women from Sikkim, the northern Indian state bordering with Tibet.

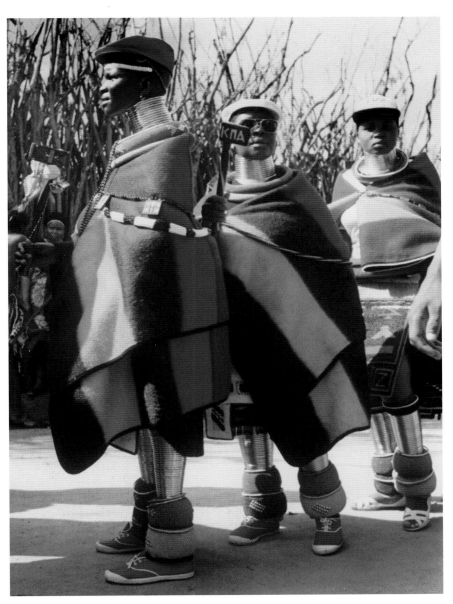

Blanket girls, in bright stripes and towering ringed necklaces, and plimsolls too.
1986   Giraffe women during King Mswati III coronation, Mbabane, Swaziland.

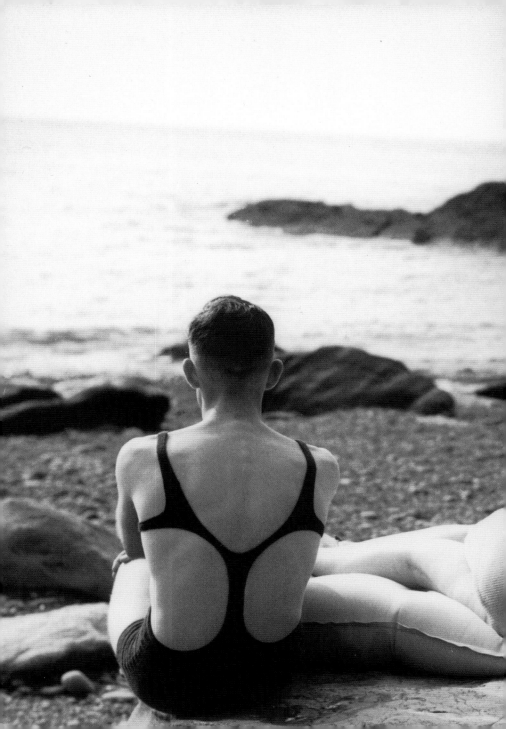

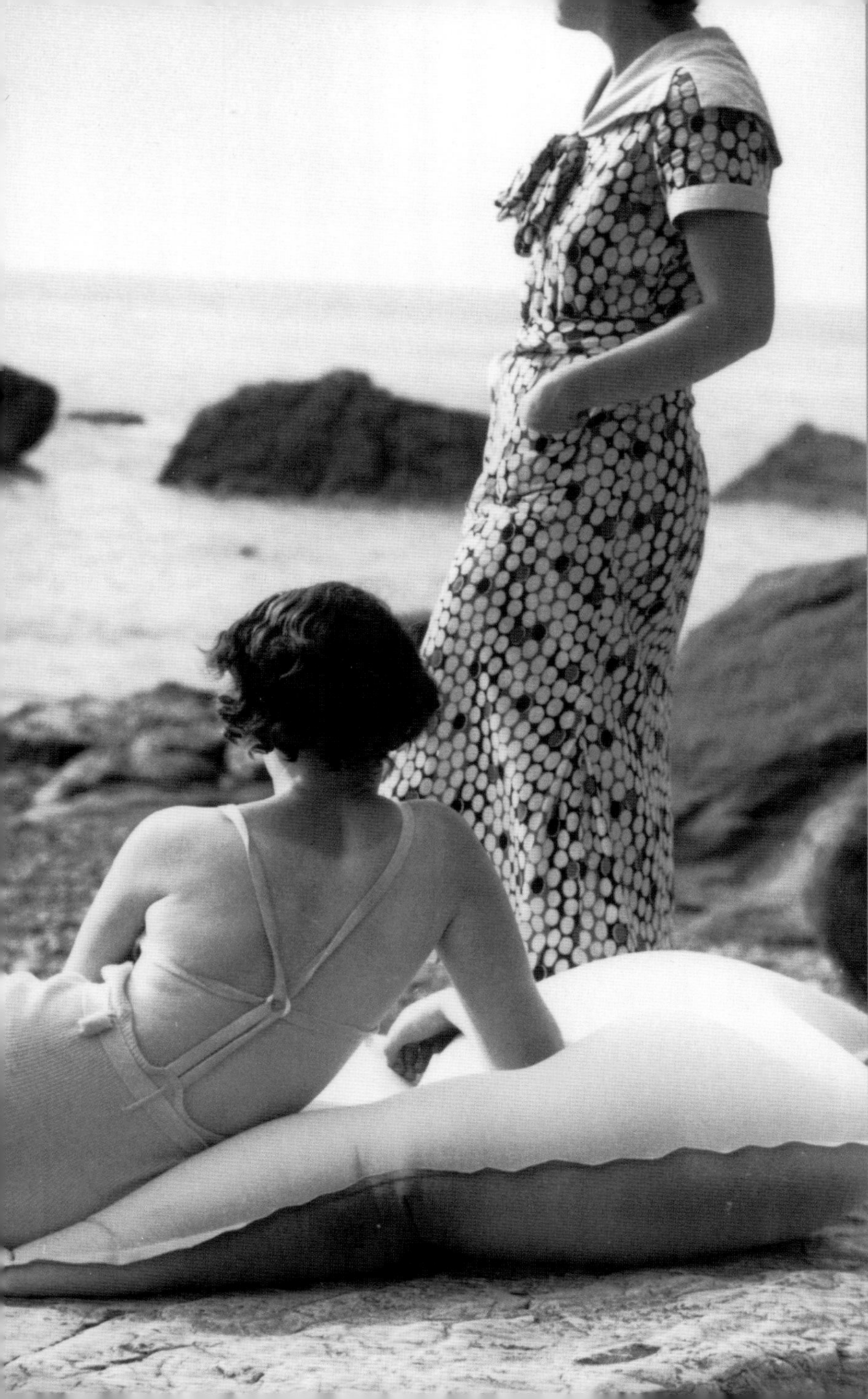

POOLSIDE TO SEASIDE

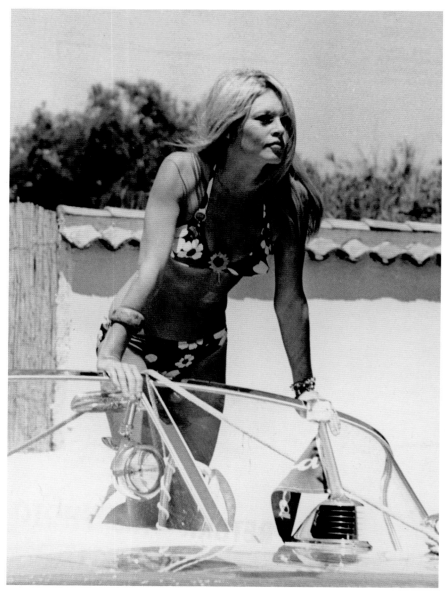

A fine figure of a woman, itsy-bitsy floral bikini, and bangles, sum up the Sixties.
1968   French actress, Brigitte Bardot, on a boat, *La Madrague*, St. Tropez, France.

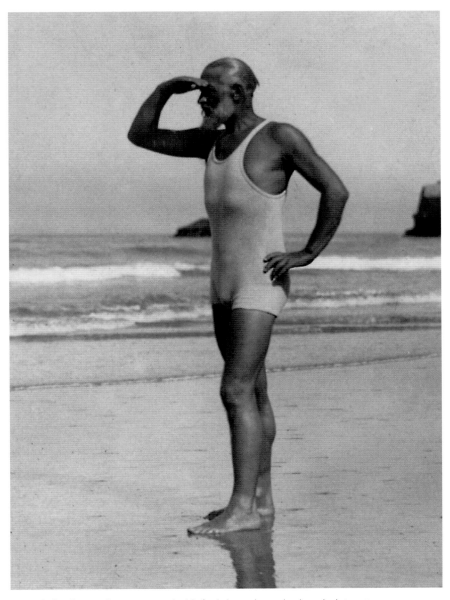

A fine figure of a man, tanned with finely honed muscles, in a singlet costume.
1929   Kees van Dongen, Dutch painter, on the beach, Biarritz, France.

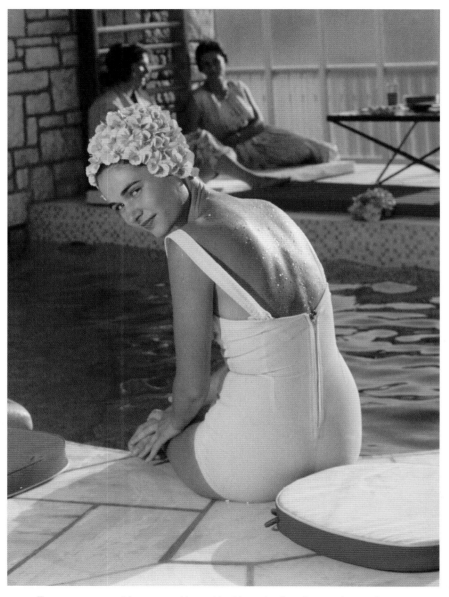

Flower power, a rubber cap and boned bathing suit, all set for a serious swim.
1961 Young women by the Canellopoulos penthouse pool, Athens, Greece.

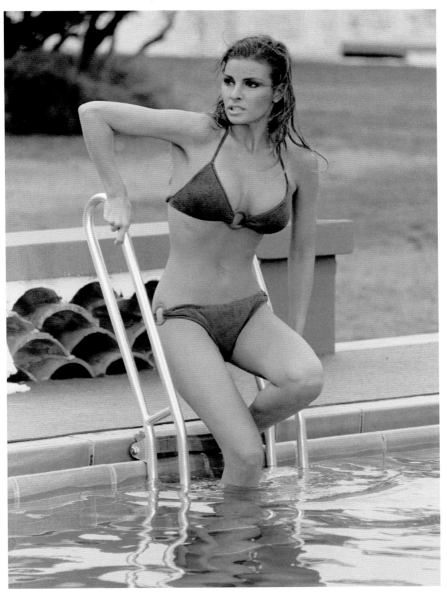

Pneumatic and ready for action, chilly dipping in a tiny bikini, all for art's sake.
1968   American actress, Raquel Welch, during the filming of Lady in Cement.

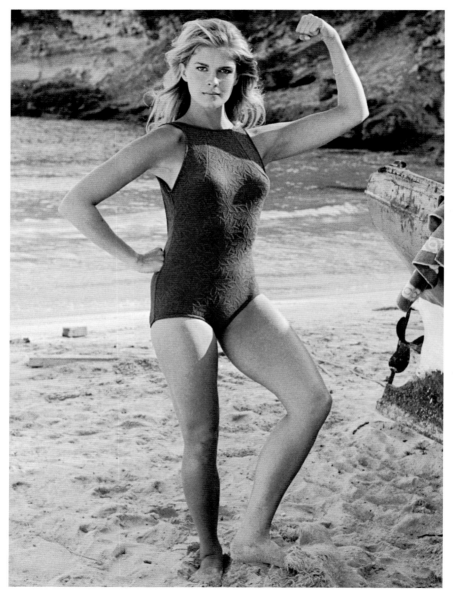

Pumping iron, in a perfectly-cut swimsuit, slash-necked, and with tousled hair.
1968   American actress, Candice Bergen, strikes a pose on a beach.

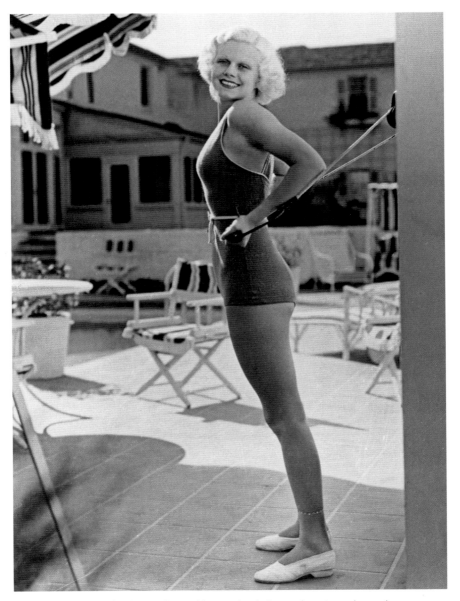

Fitness for the fainthearted, stretching out in a halter-neck costume, in wool.
1933   American actress, Jean Harlow, exercising with weighted pulleys.

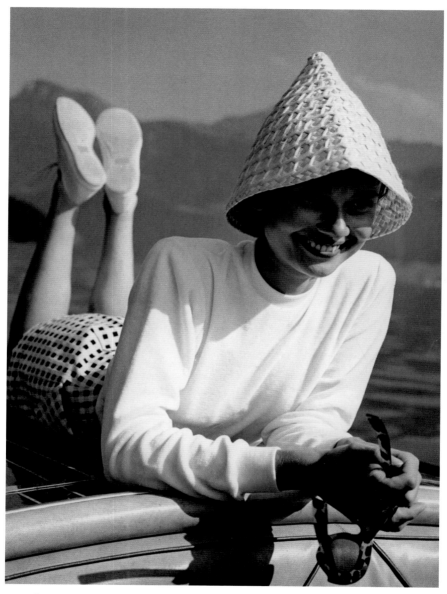

Beautiful on a bateau, a woven conical hat, white sweatshirt, and big, big shades.
1950 Belgian-born, American actress, Audrey Hepburn, on a lake in Switzerland.

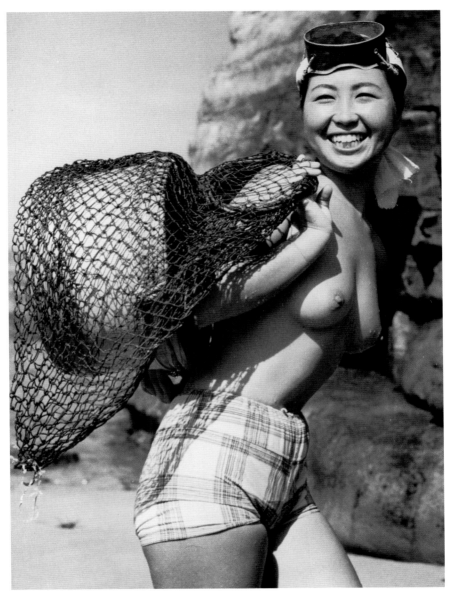

Very short shorts, in madras check, goggles, a basket, and not much else.
1959 A diver collecting seaweed near the fishing village of Onjuku, Chiba, Japan.

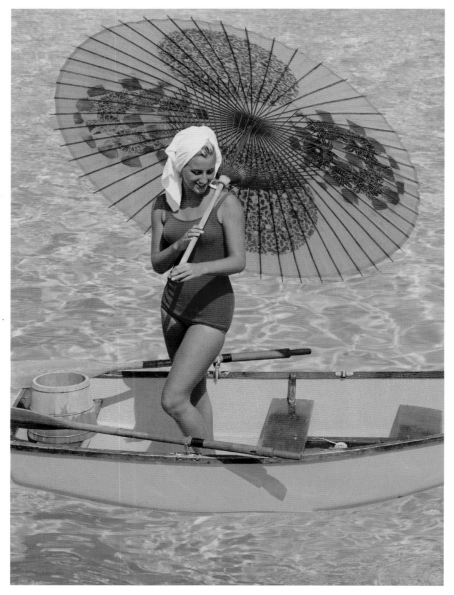

Bright light, sun city, a paper parasol shades a perfectly plain crimson swimsuit.
1960s   A woman in rowing-boat watches a man snorkelling.

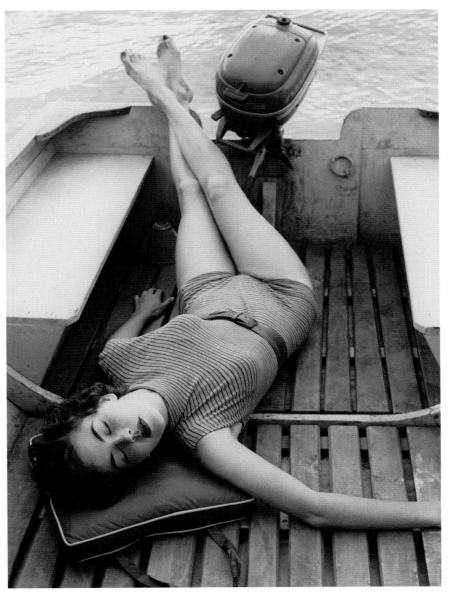

Posing in a little jumpsuit, striped and belted, and with painted toe nails too.
1955   A young woman, wearing a one-piece beach outfit, napping in a motorboat.

166

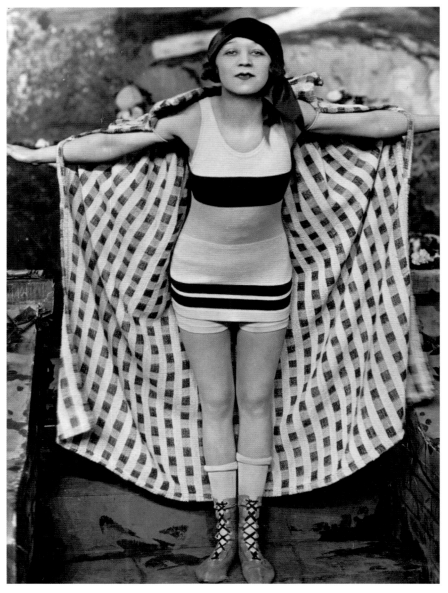

Caped crusader, in a checkerboard wrap, a striped swimsuit and lace-up boots.
1925   English actress, Binnie Hale, in *No, No Nanette*, at the Palace Theatre.

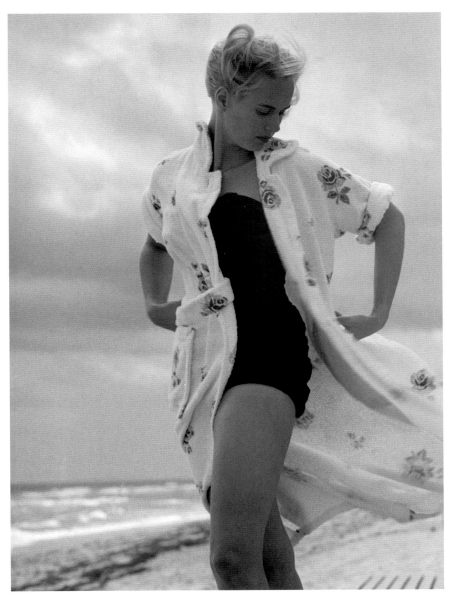

Stormy seas, pop on a pretty white cotton shirtdress, printed with roses.
1955 Socialite, Patsy Pulitzer, covering up on Palm Beach, Florida, USA.

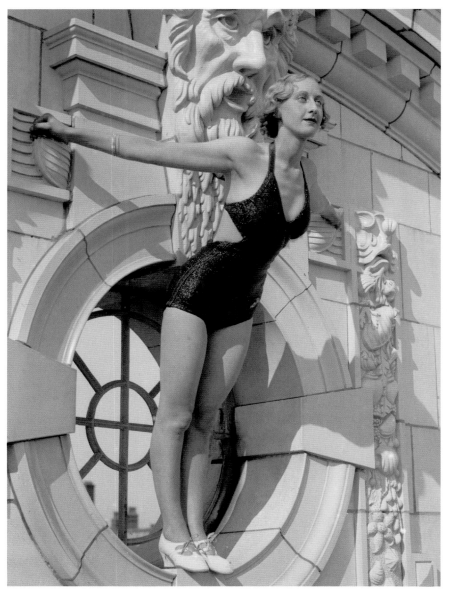

Performing arts, a sparkly swimsuit with a halter neck, and little white pumps.
1936 A live figurehead posing in front of stonework, Blackpool, England.

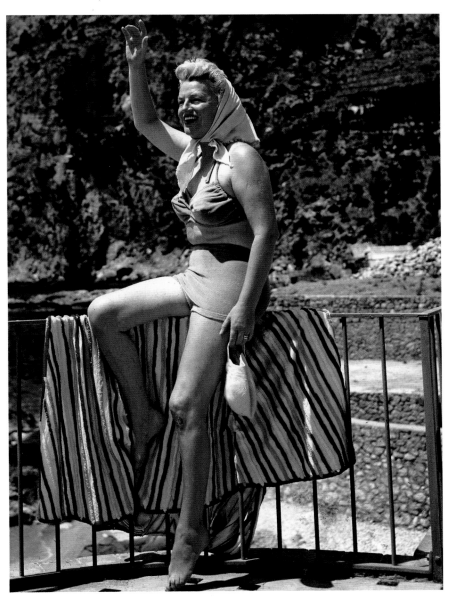

Hallo sailor, a denim blue, two-piece costume, and a headscarf against the sun.
1947   English variety artist and singer, Gracie Fields, on the Isle of Capri, Italy.

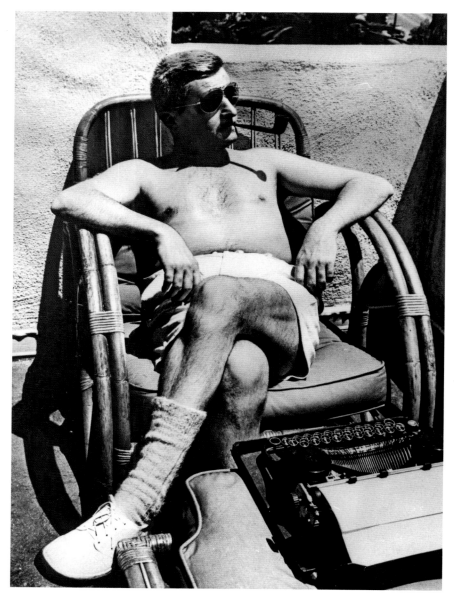

Musing mood, in aviators, colonial style socks and shorts, with typewriter too.
1942   American author, William Faulkner, sunbathes, Hollywood, California.

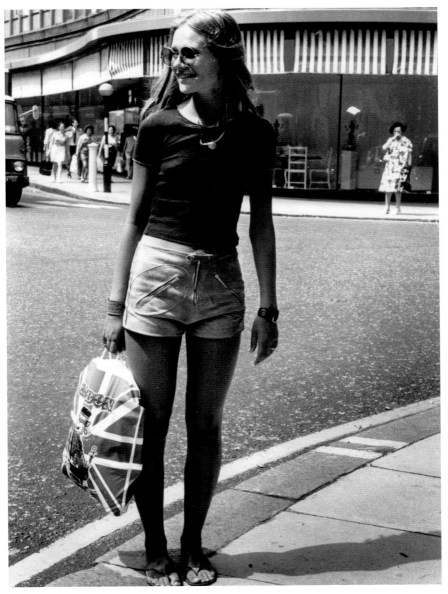

Holiday mode, you wear short shorts and a short shirt, and flip-flops too.
1971   Model, Birgitta Ekström, wearing a cotton T-shirt and suede hot-pants.

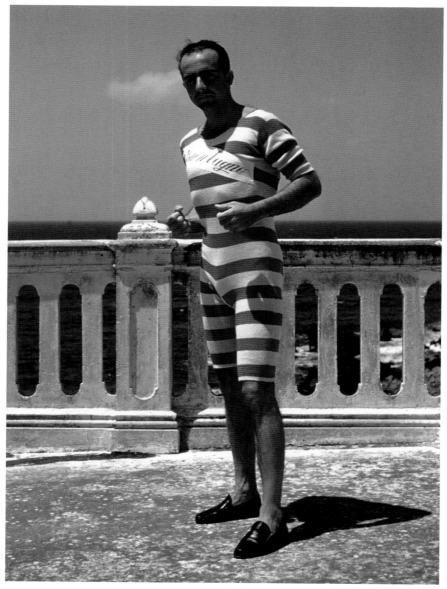

Fighting fit, in a red and white wide striped costume, and gorgeous Gucci loafers.
1954 Prince Lillio Sforza Ruspoli wearing a vintage swimsuit in Sicily, Italy.

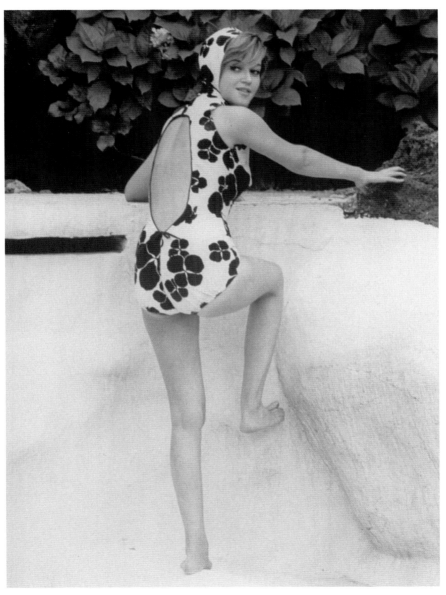

Keyhole class, an unusual hooded swimming costume with big black blooms.
1965 Julia Elvira, a producer's daughter, wearing a bathing suit by Rita Tillistt.

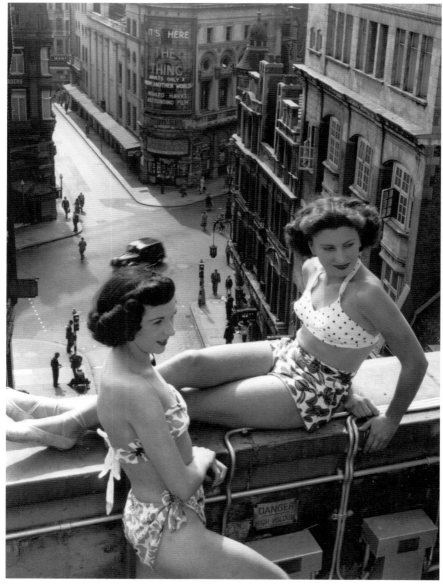

Summer in the smoke, a home-made bikini, and floral shorts with a spotted bra.
1953 Two women in swimwear soak up the sun on a rooftop in Piccadilly, London.

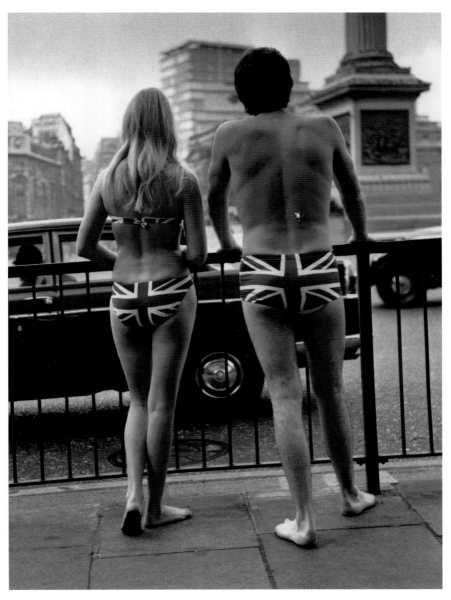

Summer in the square, *Rule Britannia* in very small bathers, flying the flag.
1969 Two models in Union Jack swimwear, Trafalgar Square, London.

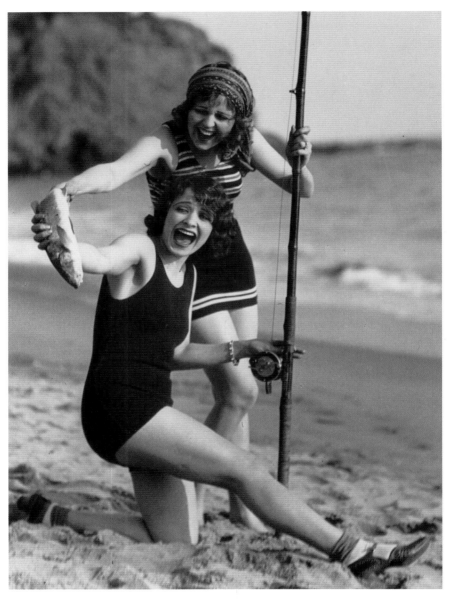

Fishing for compliments in woolly swimming costumes, with socks and shoes.
1928 Two flappers on a beach with a rod and tackle, and their catch.

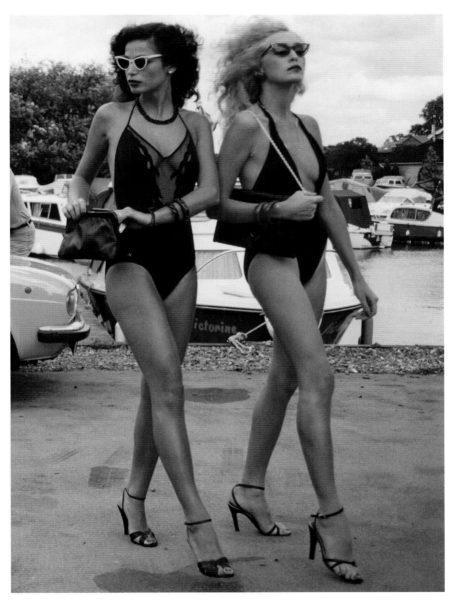

More nightclub than marina, in sexy swimsuits, stiletto sandals and sunglasses.
1979 Two young women in swimwear fail to catch the eyes of a group of men.

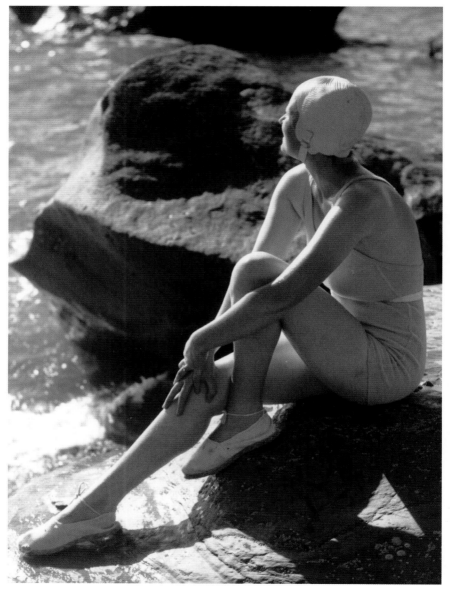

Olympic aspirations, in a simple swimsuit, sensible cap and plain espadrilles.
1930 A woman sits on a rock gazing out to sea.

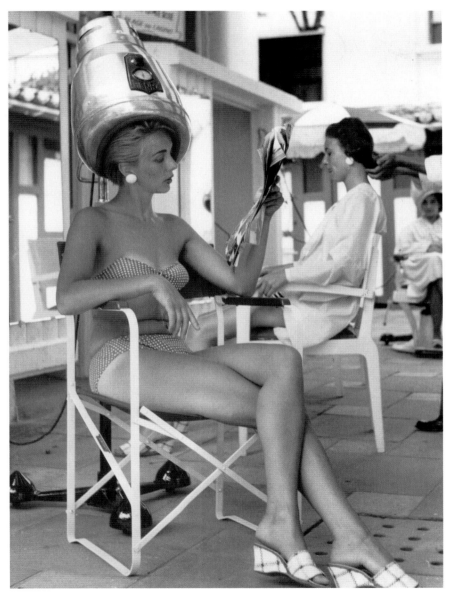

Gorgeous while grooming, hot stuff at the hairdressers, in a checked bikini.
1955   A model at an outside salon in Juan-les-Pins, Cote d'Azur, France.

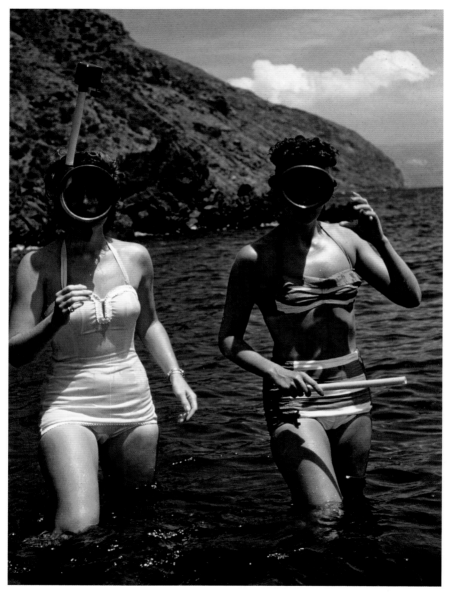

Ocean-going, in sunshine yellow and nautical stripes, crisp colours for cruising. 1954 Two young women going snorkelling.

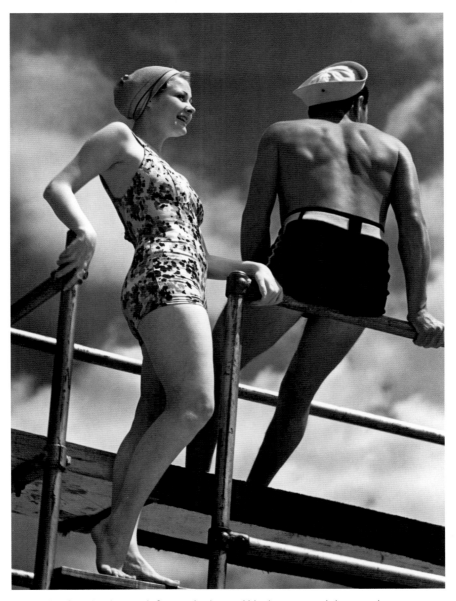

High fliers, her in stretch flowered nylon, and him in natty naval shorts and cap.
1950s   A couple on a diving platform, USA.

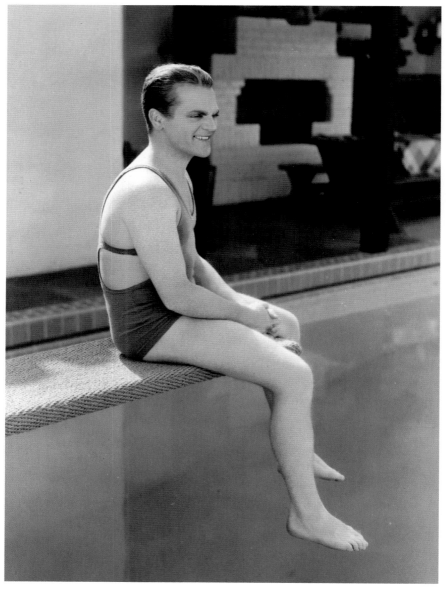

Tough guy chilling out, small but perfectly formed, in an all-in-one bathing suit. 1930s American actor, James Cagney, sitting on a diving board.

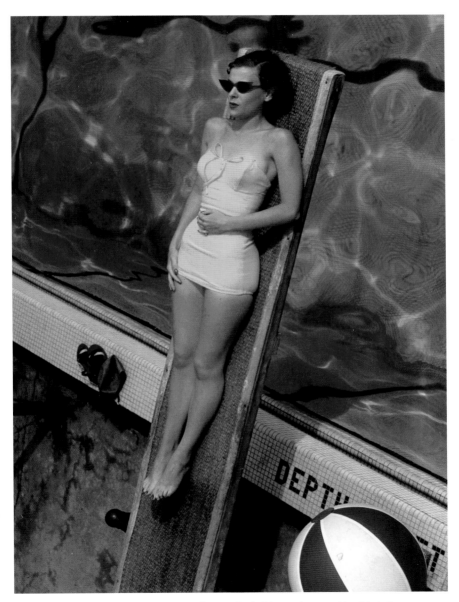

Flat out and laid back, in canary yellow and suitable sunglasses, with a big ball.
1950s   A woman wearing a swimsuit relaxing at the poolside.

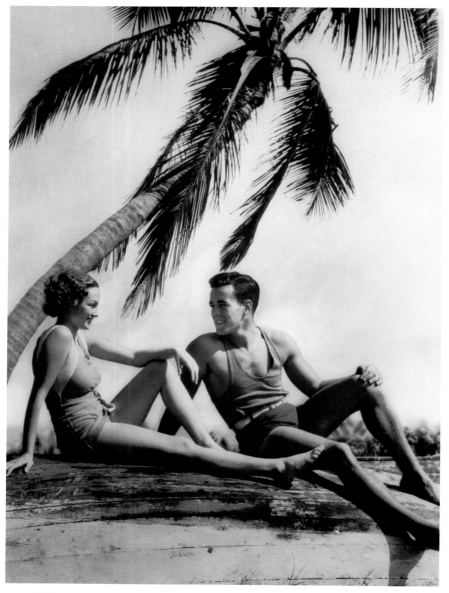

Flirting under the foliage, his and hers swimming gear before the luxury of Lycra.
1920s   A couple under a palm tree, Florida, USA.

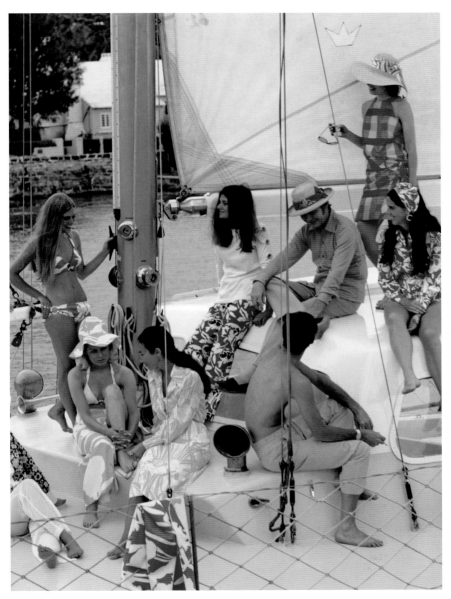

Bright, beautiful people, in yellow and pink playful prints, with perfect panamas.
1970   A group of colourfully dressed holidaymakers on a yacht, Bermuda.

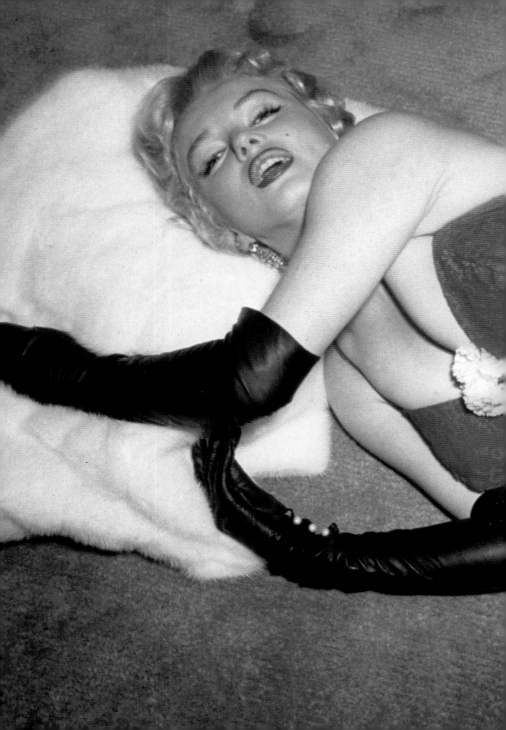

FUR TOO FAR

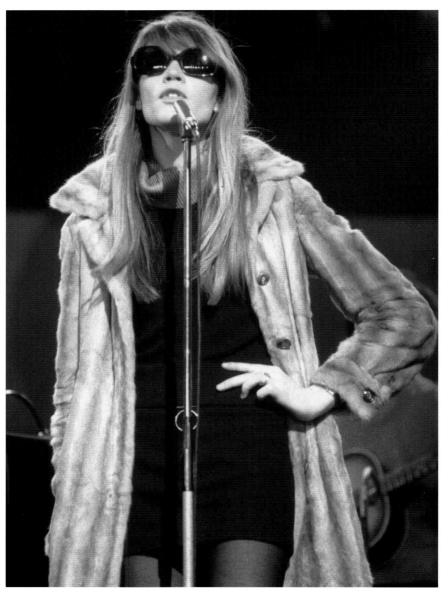

Maxi over mini, an ankle-length coat over a little black dress, very Sixties.
1965 French singer, Françoise Hardy, wearing sunglasses and a long fur.

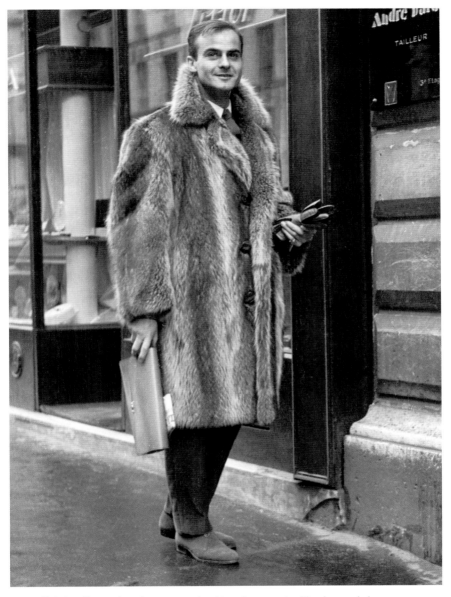

Slightly self-conscious, in a square-shouldered overcoat, with a bag and gloves.
1958   A man modelling a Canadian marmot coat by Parisian tailor, André Bardot.

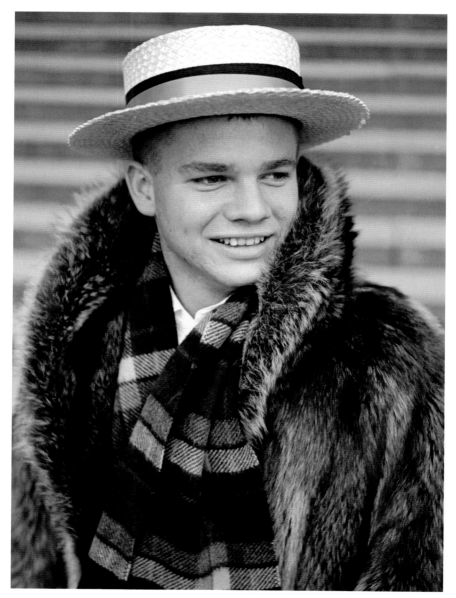

Curious contrasts of fur and panama, winter and summer, and a plaid scarf too.
1940 An undergraduate in a raccoon coat with a college hat, Princeton, USA.

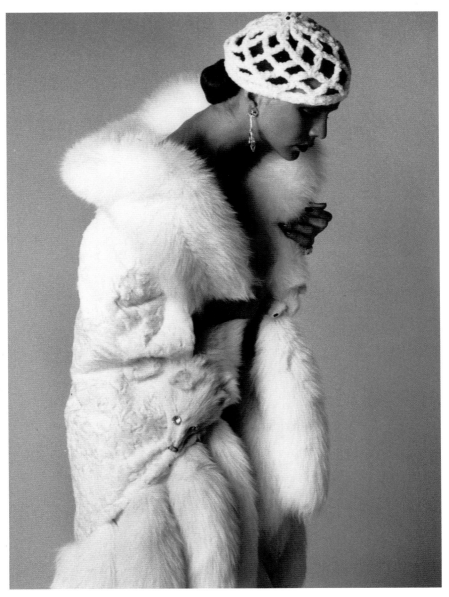

Winter wonderland, in ice white, with a crocheted cap and diamond earrings.
1976 A white astrakhan cape with a fox collar and tails, Christian Dior, Paris.

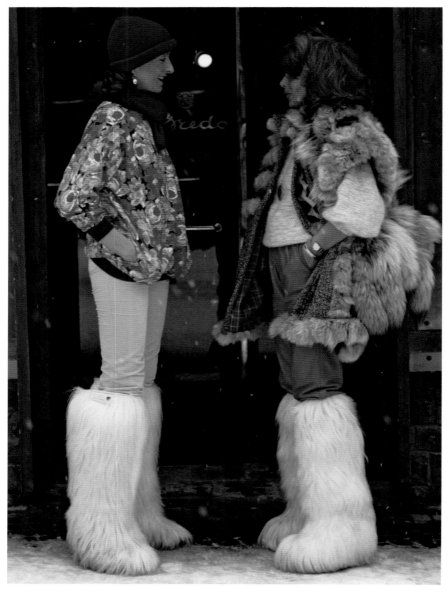

Ski style, enormous furry boots, an enveloping fox waistcoat or a print jacket.
1982   Isa Genolini and Marie Antonia, at the ski resort Cortina d'Ampezzo, Italy.

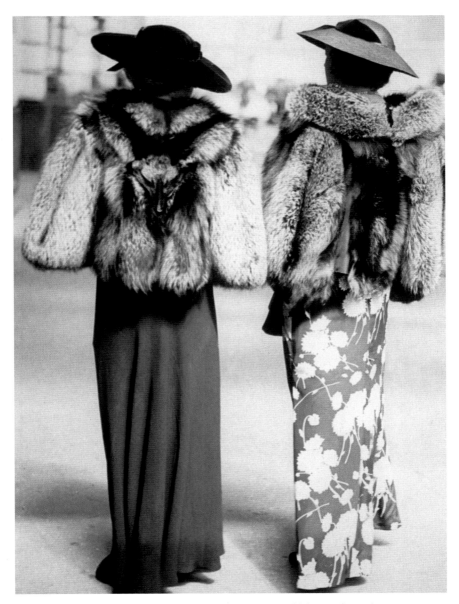

Fox fur jackets, heads and all, worn over long gowns with hats, quite curious.
1936 Two ladies wearing very similar outfits, waiting for a train to Ascot races.

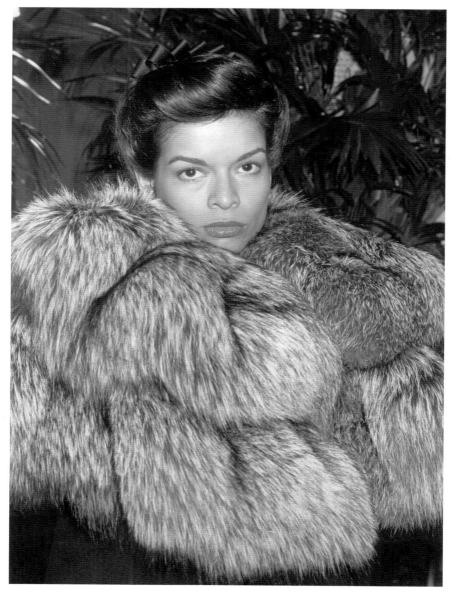

Hot stuff, all covered up and cosy in furlongs of fox fur, at a fashion show.
1977   Bianca Jagger, wife of *Rolling Stone* Mick, Christian Dior couture, Paris.

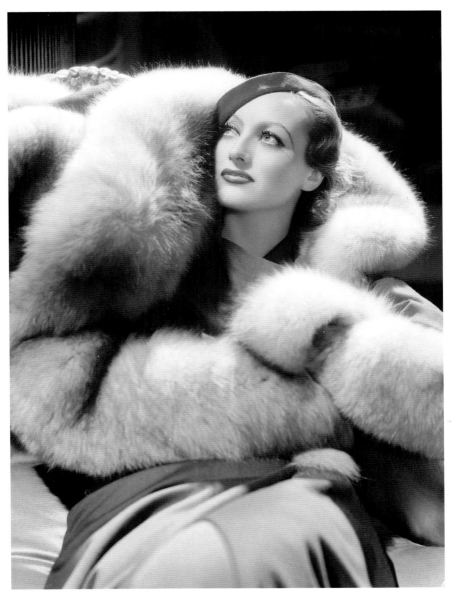

Cinema siren, in a fox fur stole, over a long satin dress, worn with a jaunty beret.
1932 American actress, Joan Crawford, in the title role of the film *Letty Lynton*.

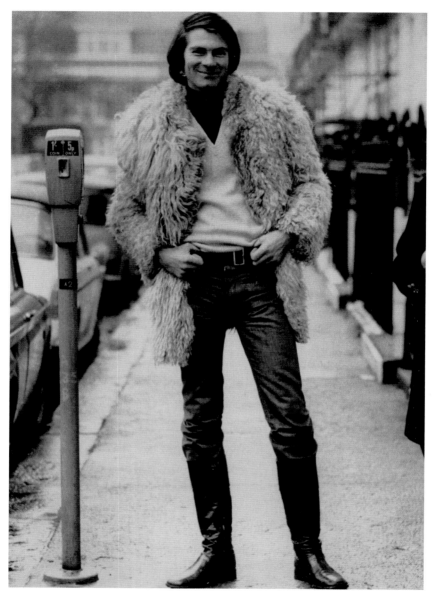

London life, wearing lean pants and Cossack boots, with a trendy shaggy coat.
1972 Designer, James Clifton, in a Mongolian sheepskin jacket and jeans.

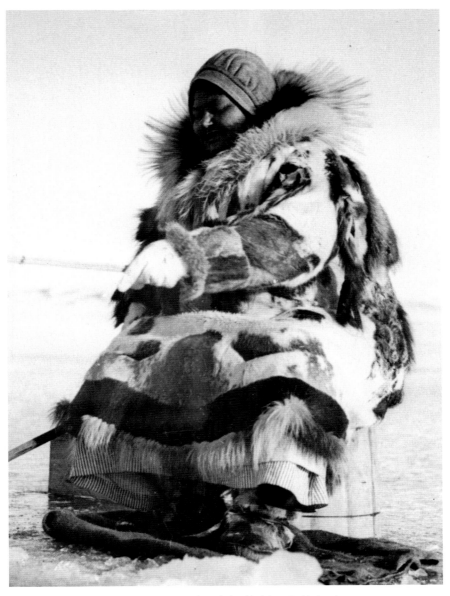

A patchwork of skins gives a certain style in this inhospitable landscape.
1950 A native woman fishing on the tundra through a hole in the ice, Alaska.

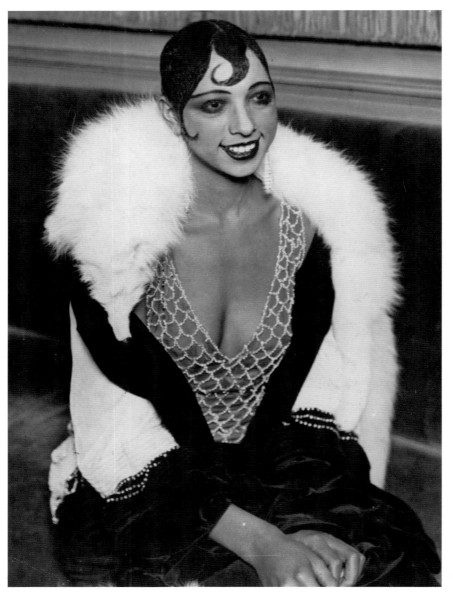

Gamine and gorgeous, with a Twenties Eton crop and a fine bonne pointe.
1928   American-born entertainer, Josephine Baker, became a French citizen.

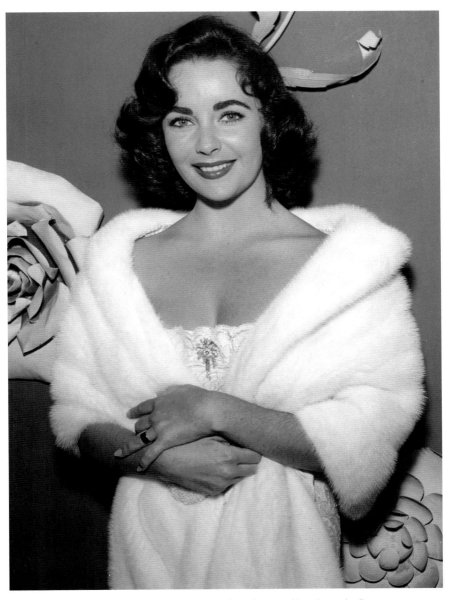

Pure and perfect, in a white mink wrap, a lace dress, and lovely scarlet lips.
1956   British-born actress, Elizabeth Taylor, at the premiere party for *Moby Dick*.

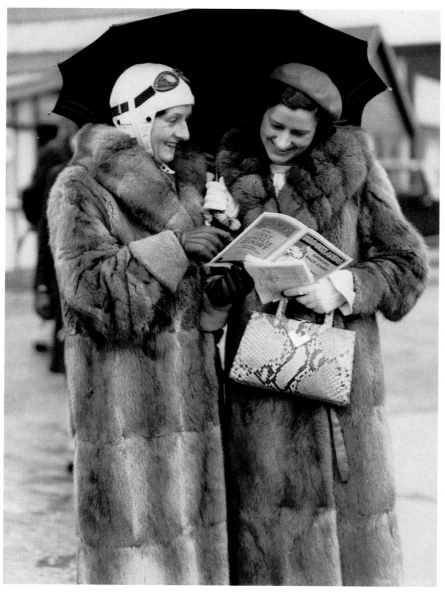

Sheltering from the weather in sensible furs, with an aviator helmet or a beret.
1936 Motor racing fans during the Easter Monday meeting at Brooklands, England.

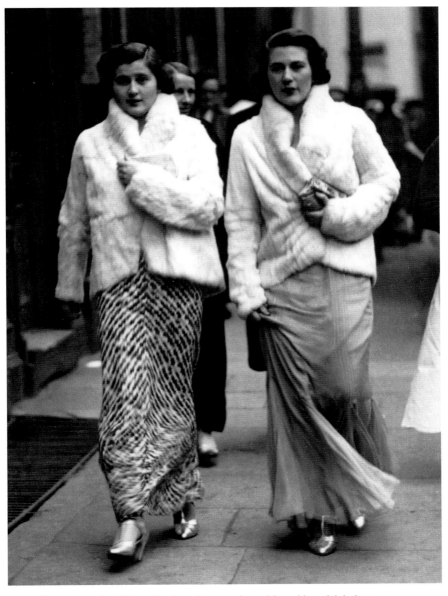

Opera-goers in chiffon with silver shoes, and matching white mink jackets.
1937 Society ladies at the opening night of *Otello* in Covent Garden, London.

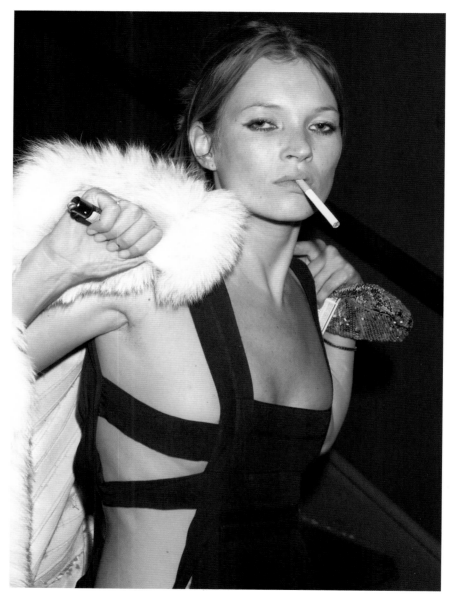

Cigarette chic, in a black bondage dress, with a white fox wrap for warmth.
2002   Model, Kate Moss, at photographer Mario Testino's exhibition, London.

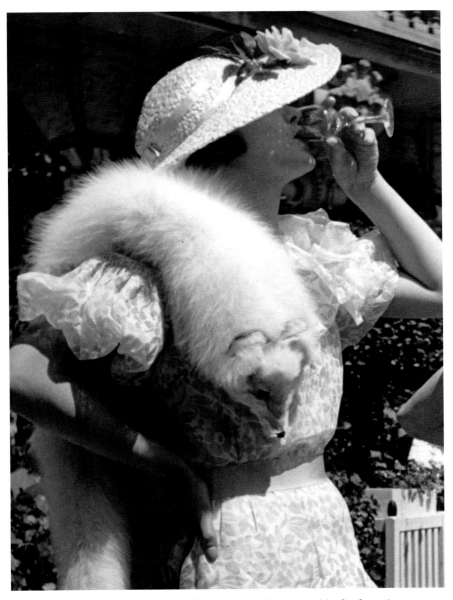

Champagne chic, in a floral frock, flowered straw hat and a white fox fur stole.
1934   A lady at a racecourse, taking refreshment, in a fashionable dress.

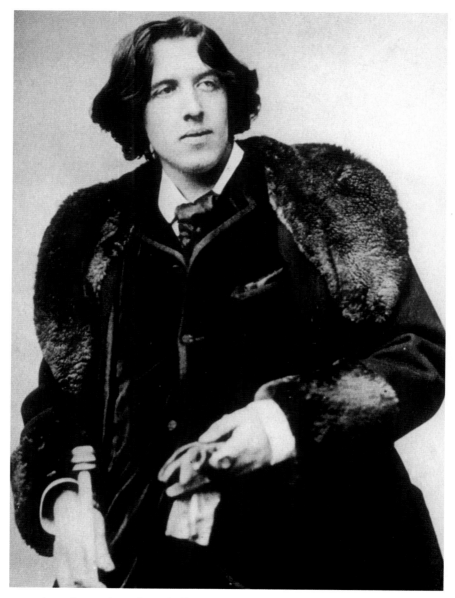

A poetic pose, in a velvet suit, silk cravat, fine cane and leather gloves.
1885   Irish-born author and critic, Oscar Wilde, wearing a fur-trimmed coat.

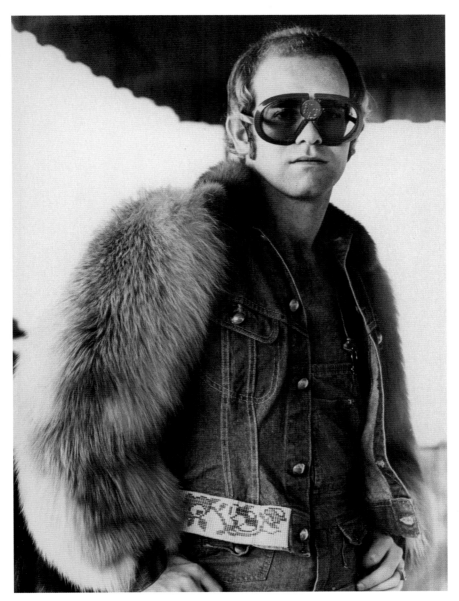

Pop perfect, a denim jacket and dungarees, with his huge signature sunglasses.
1974   British singer, Elton John, hanging out in Hollywood, wearing a fur jacket.

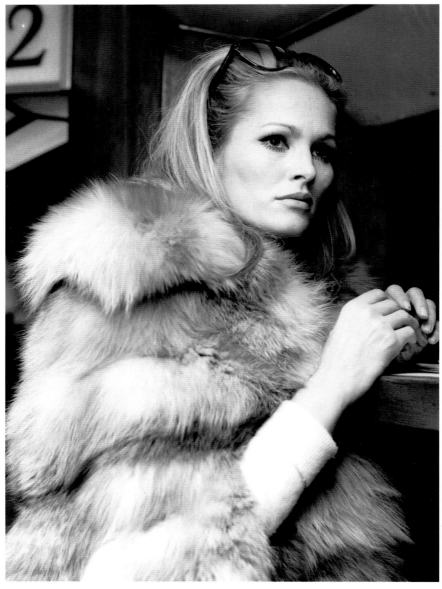

Dressed to kill, Bond-girl lovely in a fluffy, fur jacket and serious spectacles.
1968   Swiss film actress, Ursula Andress, snapped at Heathrow Airport, London.

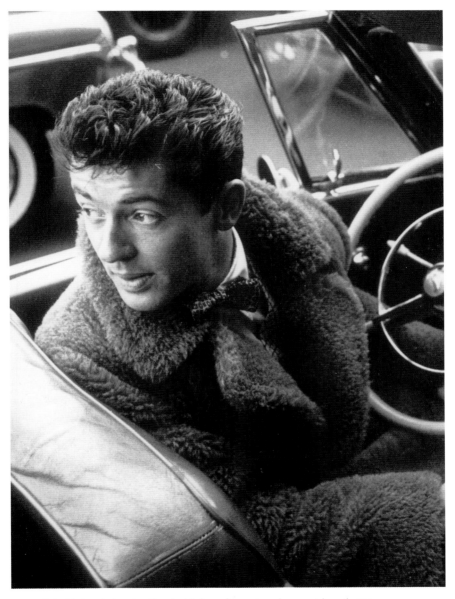

A teddy boy hair cut, with a teddy bear fur coat, and a smart bowtie too.
1955   American film star, Farley Granger, outside the Plaza Hotel, New York.

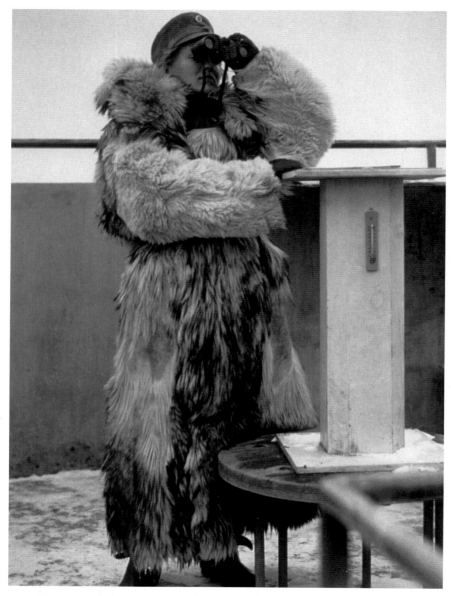

Wolf woman, a hefty fur coat on the frozen wastes, during the Russo-Finnish Civil War. 1940   A member of Finland's famous women's army, Lotta Svärd, on the lookout.

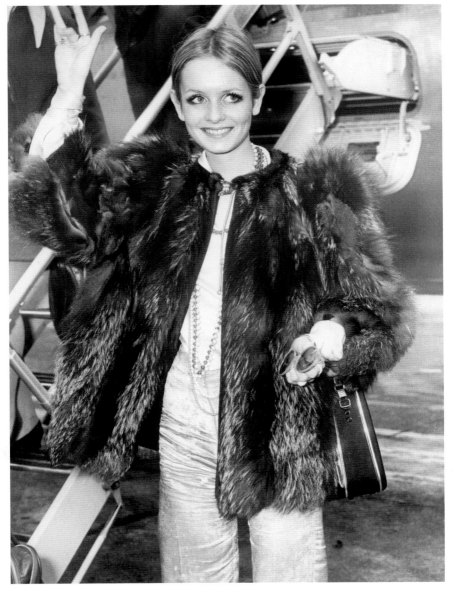

Famous in fur, a tufted fur and leather jacket, wards of the British chill.
1967 British model, Twiggy, arrives at Heathrow Airport after a trip to Japan.

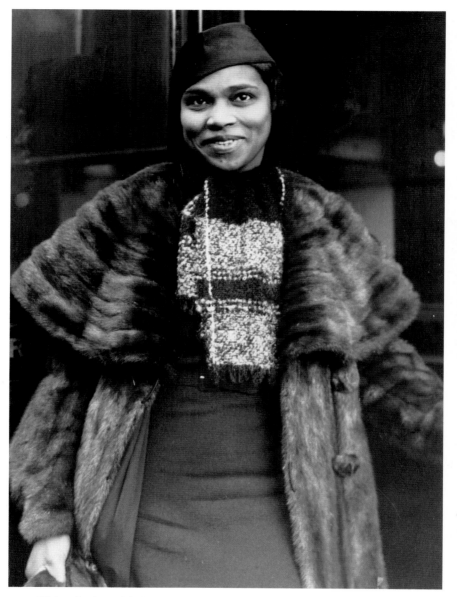

Divine diva, in a mink shawl-collared coat, and a perky little cap.
1936   American opera singer, Marian Anderson, in London for a concert.

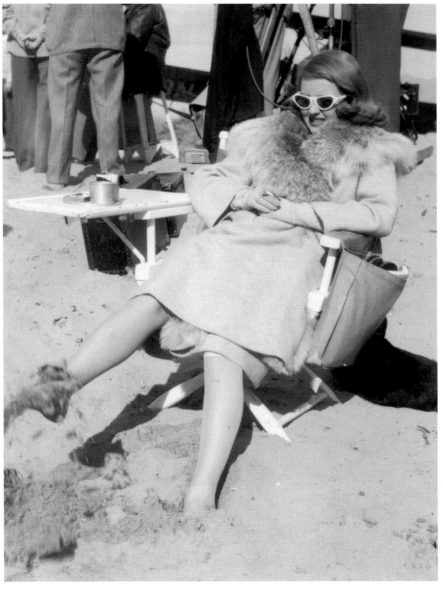

Fabulous in fur, on a film set in the desert, sunglasses, stockings and gloves.
1941   American actress, Bette Davis, in The Bride Came C.O.D., California, USA.

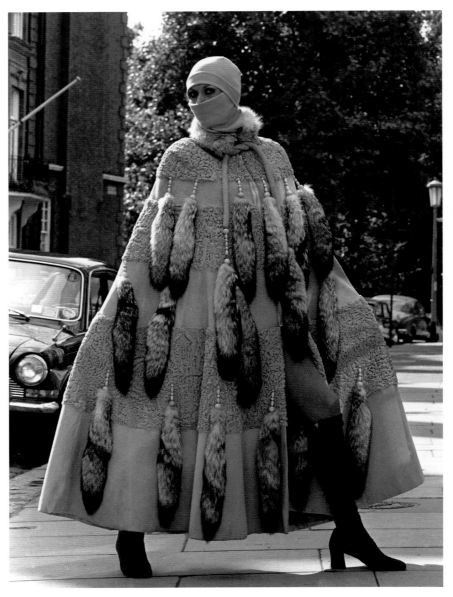

A curious camouflage, all covered up from head to toe in tones of stone.
1971   A beige cape of suede and sheepskin, with a fox collar and tails, London.

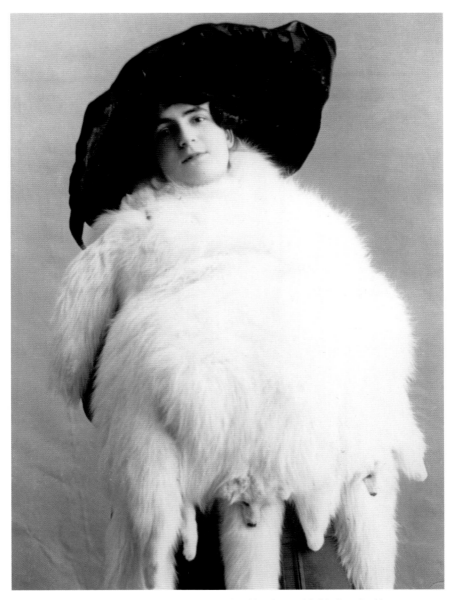

Dripping in fox heads, with a velvet cartwheel hat, in graphic black and white.
1912 Austrian pianist, Germaine Schnitzel, wearing a white fox fur wrap.

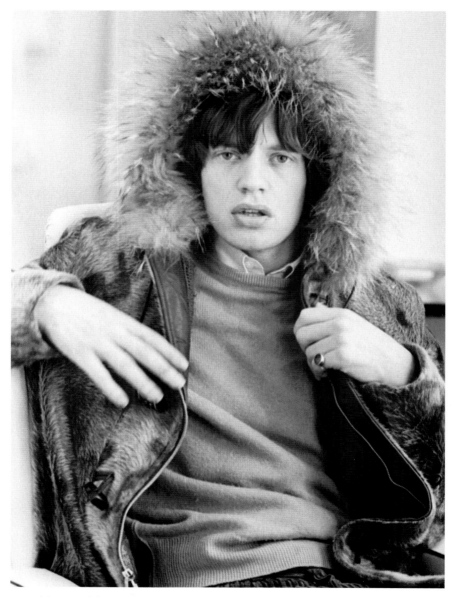

More mod than rocker, jumping Jagger chills out in an Army style anorak.
1964 *Rolling Stones* singer, Mick Jagger, pouting in a fur-trimmed parka.

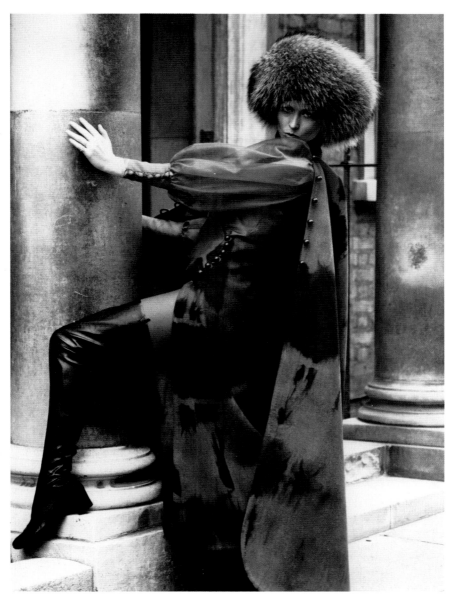

Cossac-inspired, marble-printed maxi and cape, with thigh boots and fox hat.
1970   A model in an outfit by Franka, a young Yugoslavian designer, in London.

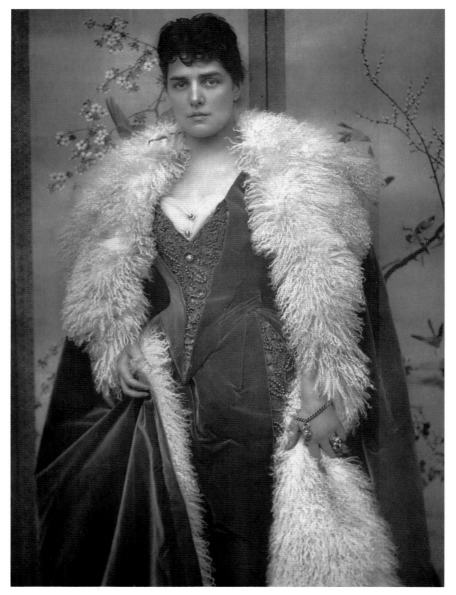

Statuesque and politically correct, in an impressive fur-lined velvet cape.
1888 Jennie Churchill, wife of Lord Randolph Churchill and mother of Winston.

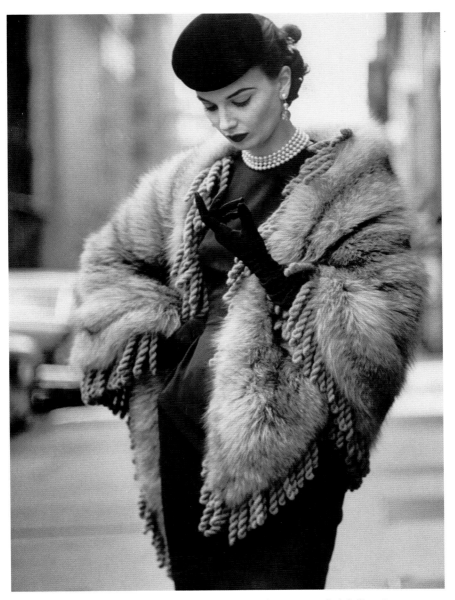

Elegance personified, in a little black dress and hat, with a tasselled, fluffy stole. 1952 A lady modelling a fringed shawl made of natural Norwegian blue fox.

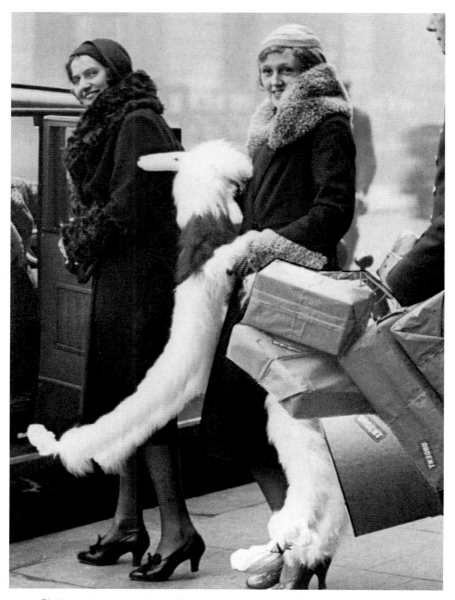

Christmas is a coming, dressed in cloche hats, fur-collared coats and court shoes.
1930 Women load their shopping into a car, Whiteleys department store, London.

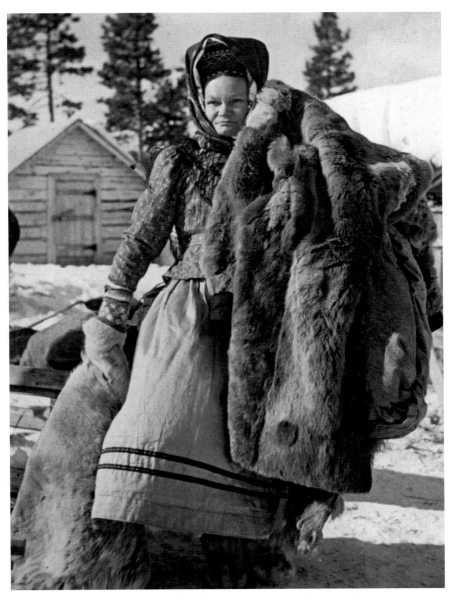

Snow scene, with shack, and piles of reindeer pelts for next season's fur coats.
1955   A woman dressed in a traditional costume, probably of Russian origin.

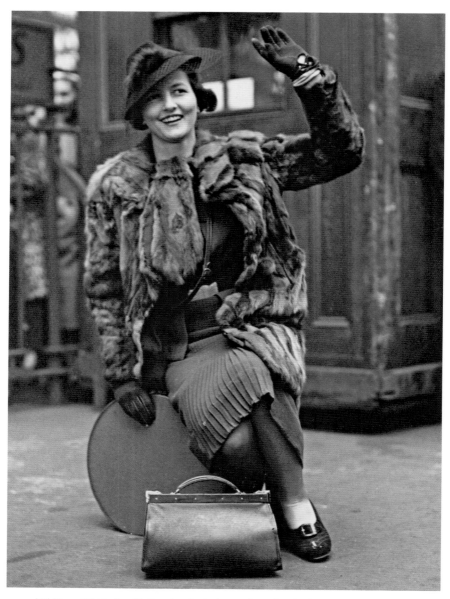

Waiting at Waterloo Station, in a fur jacket and scarf, and prim pleated skirt.
1937 Joyce Edwards, winner of Natal's Coronation Girl competition, in London.

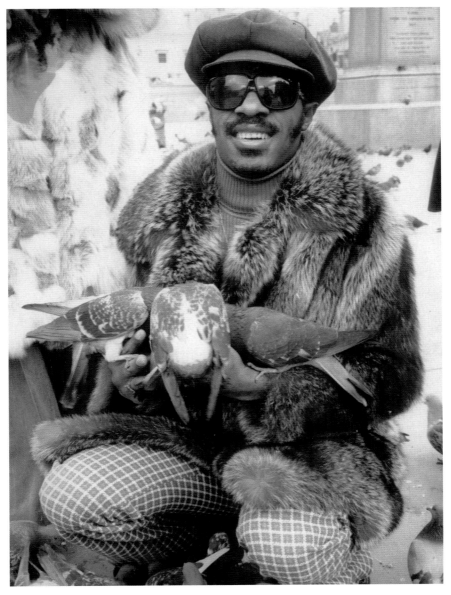

Soul brother, cool in a cap and shades, fox jacket and checked pants.
1974   American singer, Stevie Wonder, feeding the pigeons in Trafalgar Square.

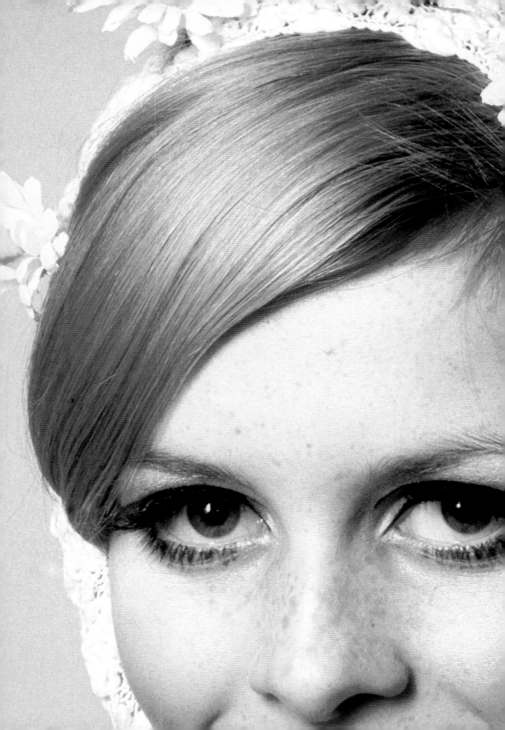

FLOWER POWER

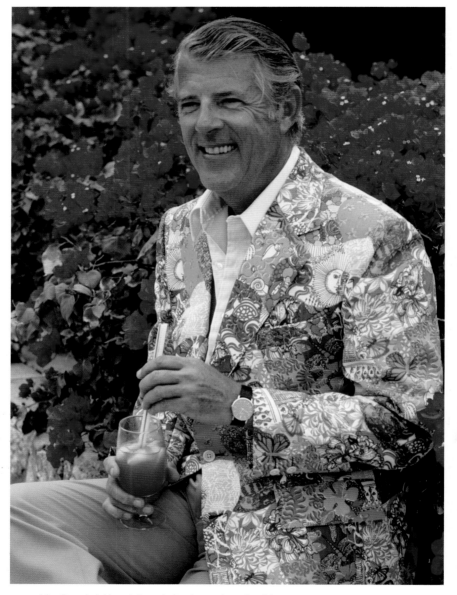

Hardly a shrinking violet, a jacket in patchwork, with grass green trousers.
1980   David Trapp on Windermere Island in the Bahamas.

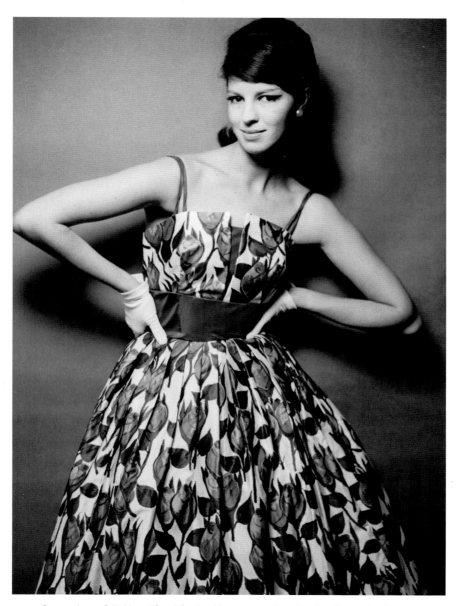

Sun seeker, a full-skirted floral frock with a cummerbund and polite white gloves.
1960   A photograph for *Vogue* magazine.

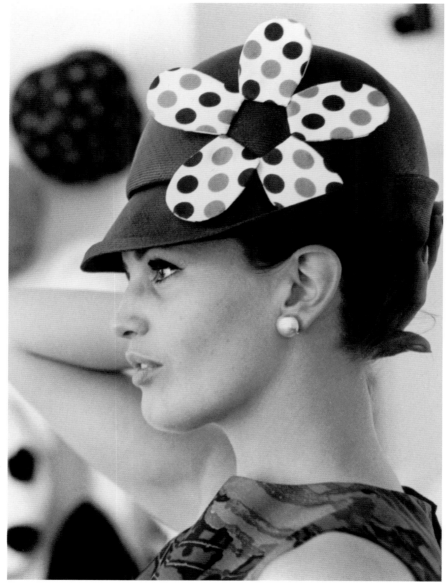

Headline news, a spotted flower appliquéd onto a jaunty cap.
1964   A hat by milliner, James Wedge, London (now a photographer).

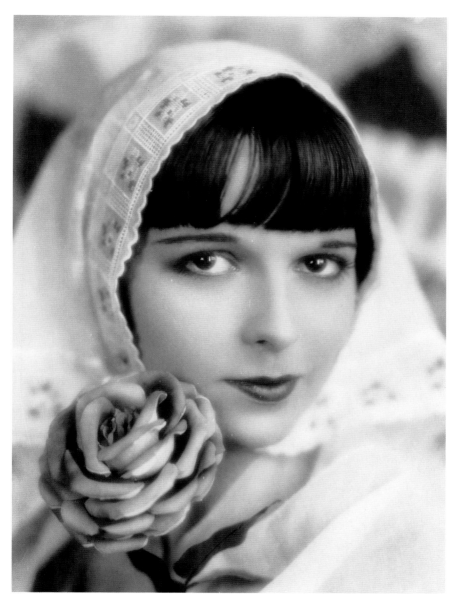

A rose is a rose is a rose, a white lacy scarf over her signature haircut.
1929   American actress, Louise Brooks, wearing a shawl and carrying a rose.

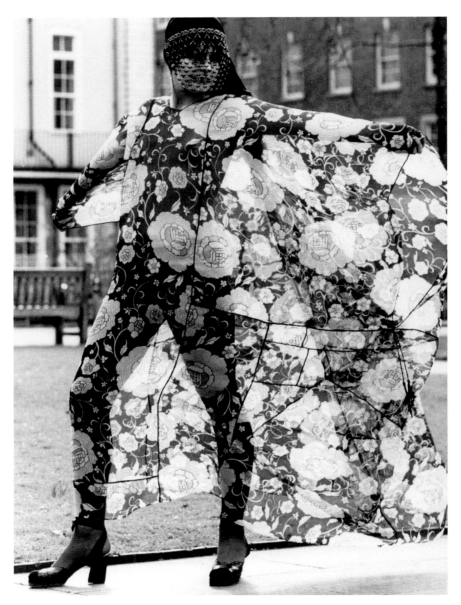

Giant blooms, fly away in a perfect print, worn with clumpy block-heeled shoes.
1971 A floral silk chiffon outfit with a beaded mask by Thea Porter, London.

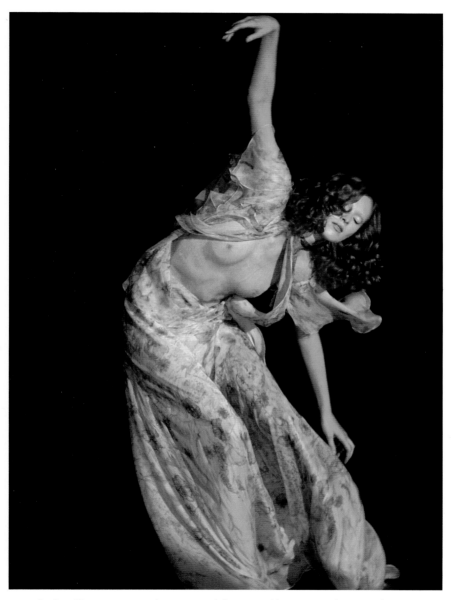

Isadora Duncan eat your heart out, swirling around in a pretty primrose print.
2003   A model at British designer Alexander McQueen's show in Paris.

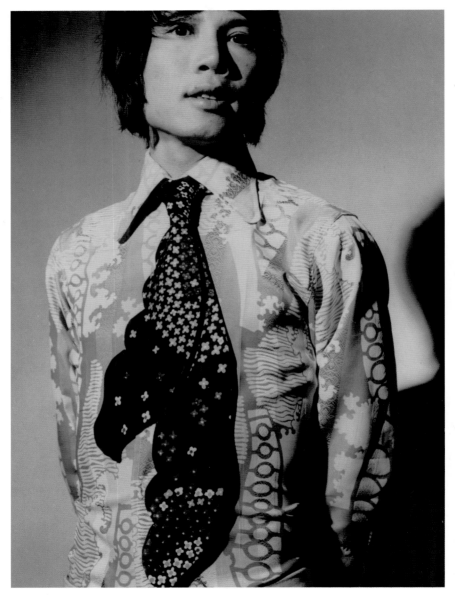

Seventies style, a scalloped-edge tie with shocking pink and white flowers.
1971   Designer, Eric Young, wearing one of his own creations, an unusual shirt and tie.

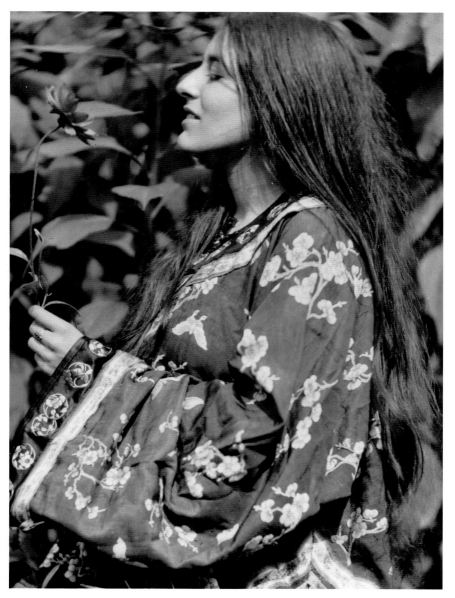

Exotic and Eastern inspired, a silk robe embroidered with delicate flowers.
1910 Portrait of a long-haired lady, possibly Miss Elaine Thomas, in a garden.

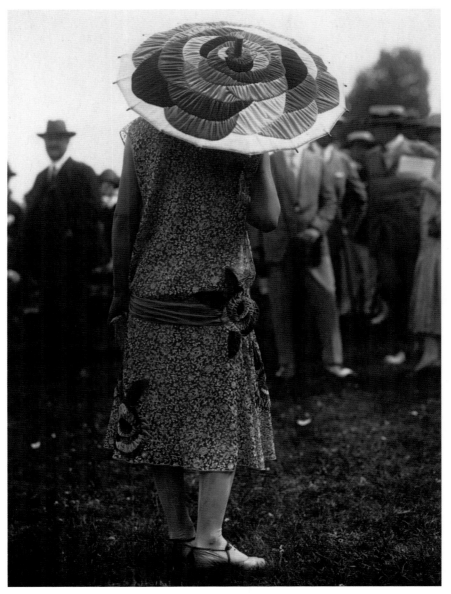

Shaded from the sun, a day at the races with a small, pretty parasol.
1925 A low-waisted dress with flower print and appliquéd flowers, Deauville, France.

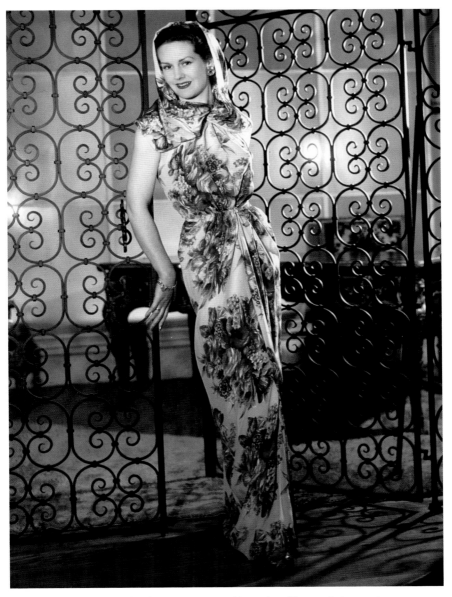

Cowled and draped, a glamorous gown, with a print of flowers in bouquets.
1950 An elegant mannequin modelling a long evening dress.

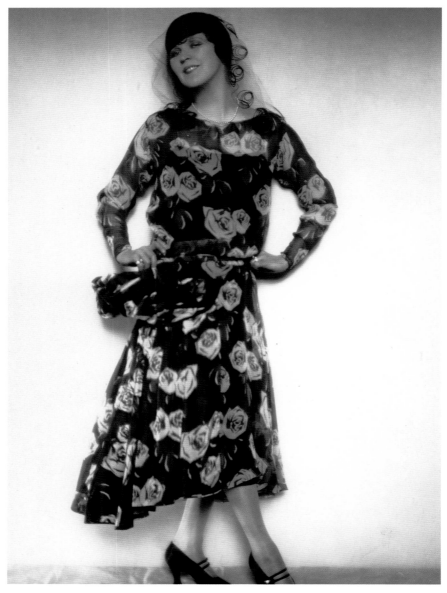

Beautiful in black, a stylized rose-print dress with an asymmetrical hem.
1930 Canadian-born actress, Margaret Bannerman, who later settled in Britain.

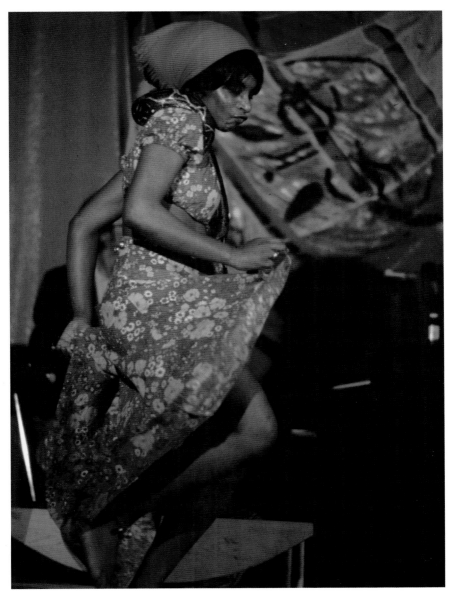

Beautiful and bright, tripping the light fantastic in sunshine yellow and orange.
1978 A woman dancing barefoot at the Mardi Gras celebrations in New Orleans.

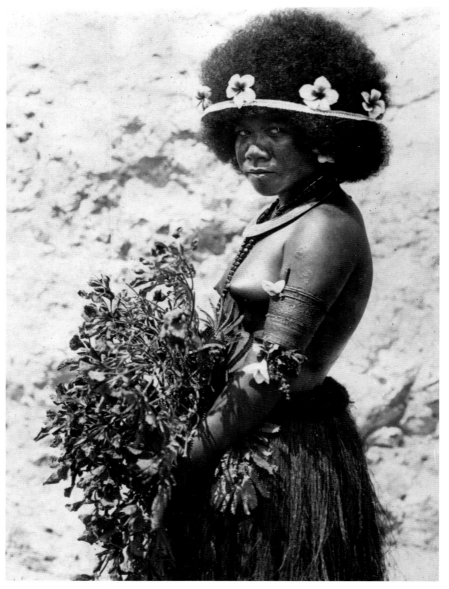

Big hair and a big bunch of flowers, worn with a grass skirt, dressed for best.
1930   A young woman at a ceremony on Kerowa Goaribari Island, New Guinea.

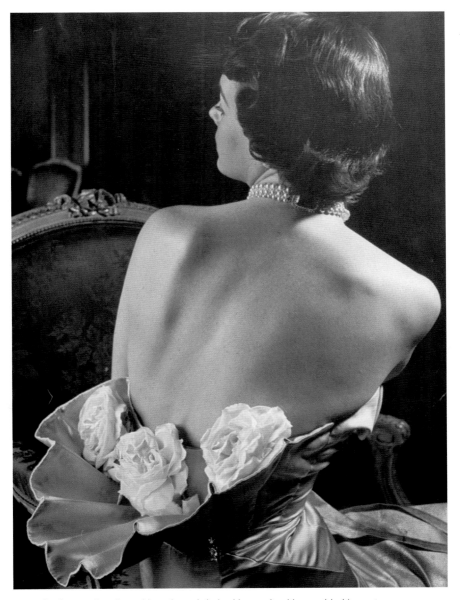

Back appeal, scalloped in satin and slashed low, exit with an added impact.
1949 A mother-of-pearl silk gown by Balmain with huge roses at the waist.

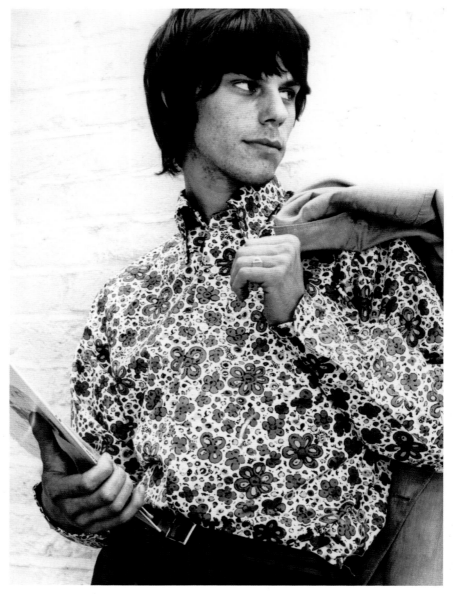

Top of the pops, a flowered, cotton shirt fit for cruising along the King's Road.
1966 Jeff Beck, with the British band *The Yardbirds*, in a shirt by John Stephen.

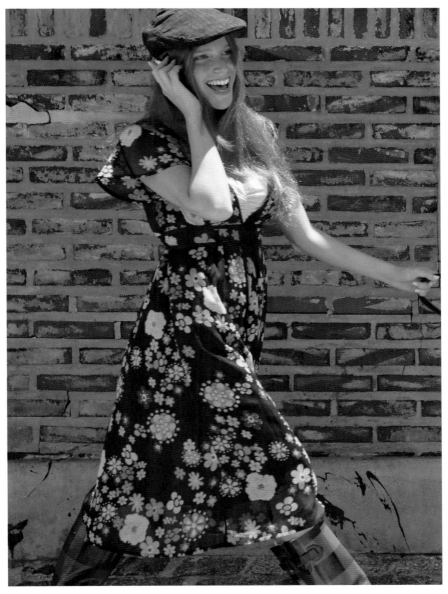

Curious combinations, bright flowers on a black background, with tartan boots.
2000   A girl, in a tweed flat-cap cuts a fabulous figure, chatting on mobile phone.

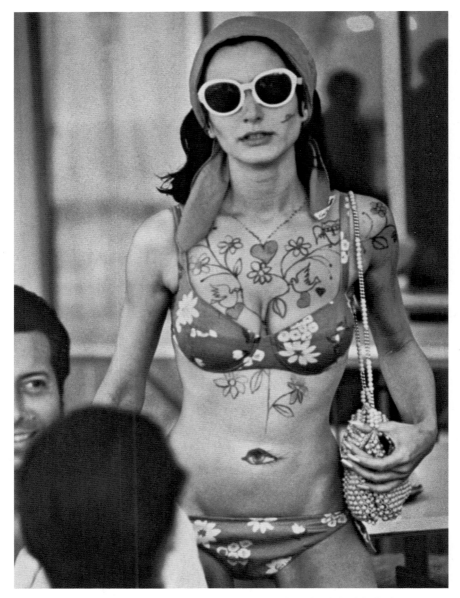

War-painted jetsetter, out on the town in a tiny bikini, scarf and sizeable shades.
1968   Spanish socialite and model, Nati Abascal, at the opening of a hotel casino.

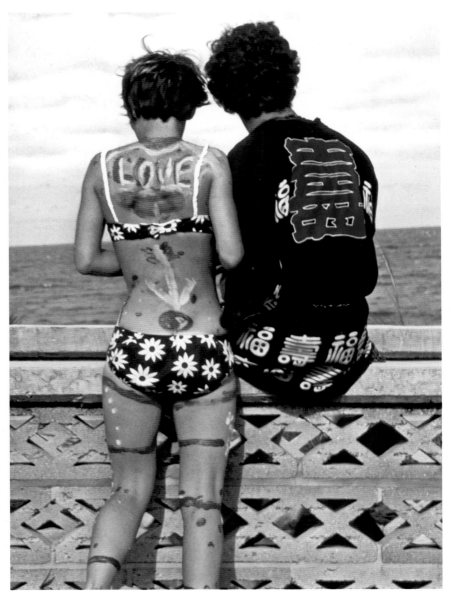

Daisies and Chinese symbols, sit side-by-side, love's young dream in body paint.
1967 A hippie couple looking out to sea along the beachfront.

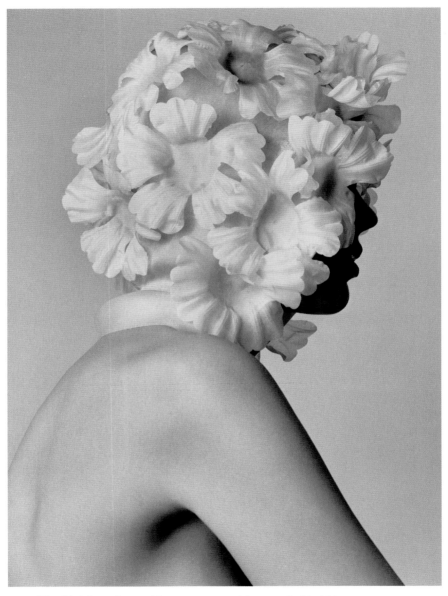

The third dimension, a white organza snood decorated with daisies.
1967   A hat by Jean Barthet, a Parisian who designed for films and the famous.

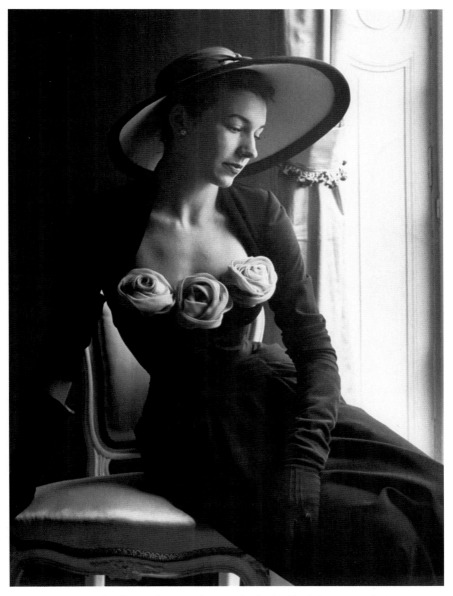

Attention to detail, a fine bonne pointe emphasized with plush roses, and a hat.
1947   A French opera singer, Denise Duval, wearing a Christian Dior dress, Paris.

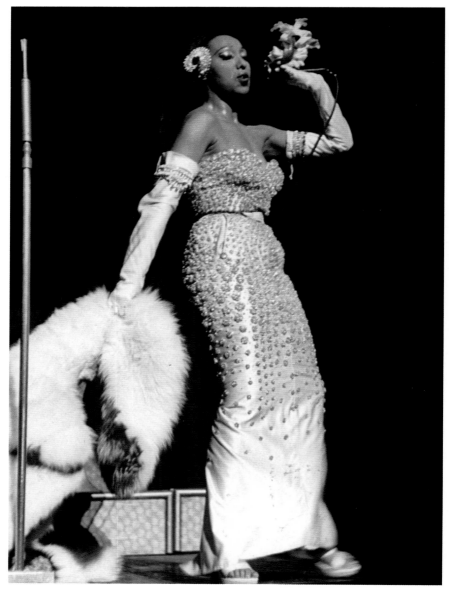

Soul sister, shimmying in white satin, appliquéd with flowers, and long gloves.
1951 Entertainer, Josephine Baker, in a gown by Christian Dior, on a USA tour.

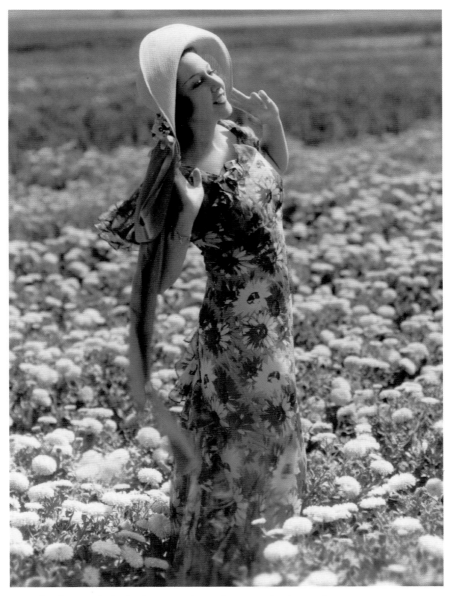

Sunflowers, singing in the sun and a star in a straw hat, happy times.
1950 The Broadway singer, Ethel Merman, in the Lompoc Valley, California, USA.

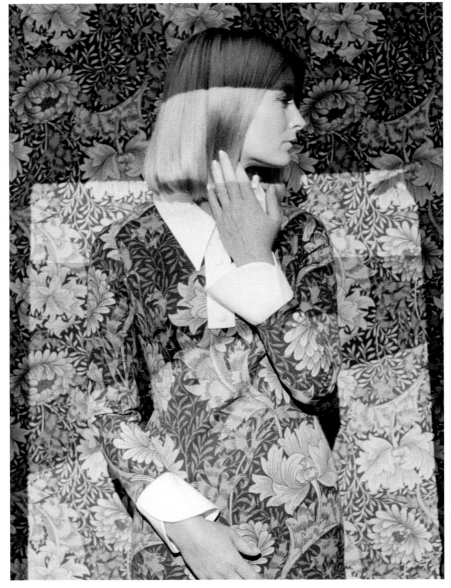

Chrysanthemum chic, with a white collar and cuffs, prim in print.
1966   A model, in a shirtdress, blends in with an identical background.

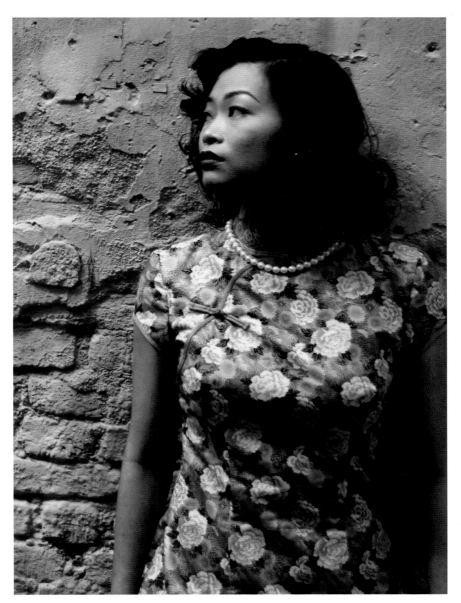

Chinese chic, in multi-coloured carnations, and a perfect string of pearls.
2009 A girl in a flowered cheongsam against a jade green wall.

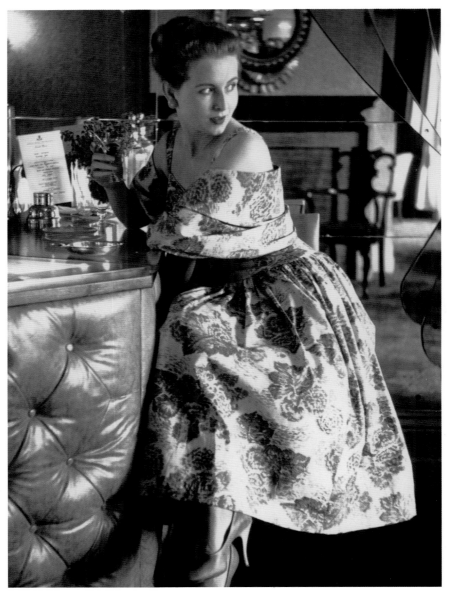

Cocktail chic, Fifties and full-skirted, with a matching shawl, and a chignon.
1956 *Picture Post* girl, Ann West, in a cocktail dress, Eastbourne, England.

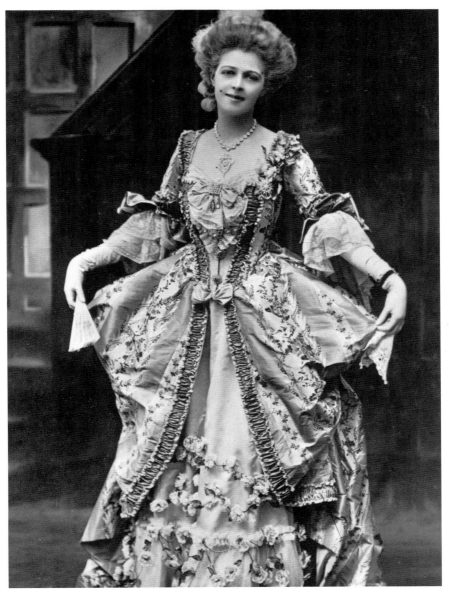

Powdered and bewigged, with bows and flounces of flowers, and a fan.
1909   Australian actress, Marie Lohr, in *The School For Scandal.*

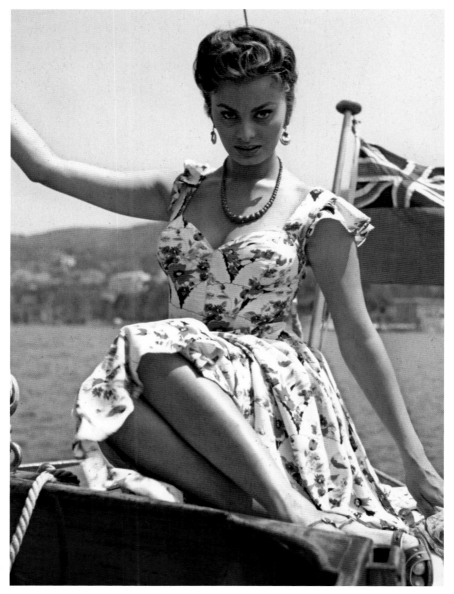

Cinema chic, in a boned, flowered summer dress, and a simple strand of coral.
1965   Italian actress, Sophia Loren, on a British boat.

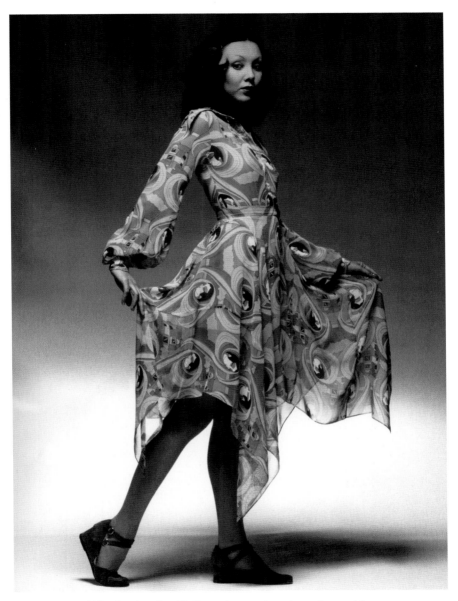

Swirling chiffon, in a handkerchief-hem dress, and suede, wedge sandals.
1971   Model, Marie Helvin, in an Art Deco print by Jeff Banks, England.

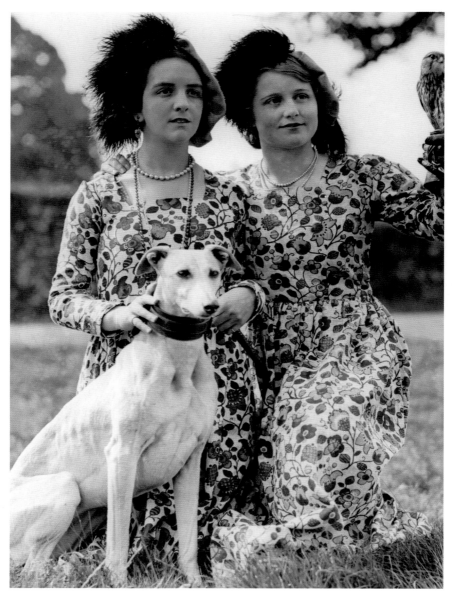

Seeing double, in flowered frocks with matching feathered hats and pearls.
1931 Girls with their greyhound and a falcon, wearing nearly identical outfits.

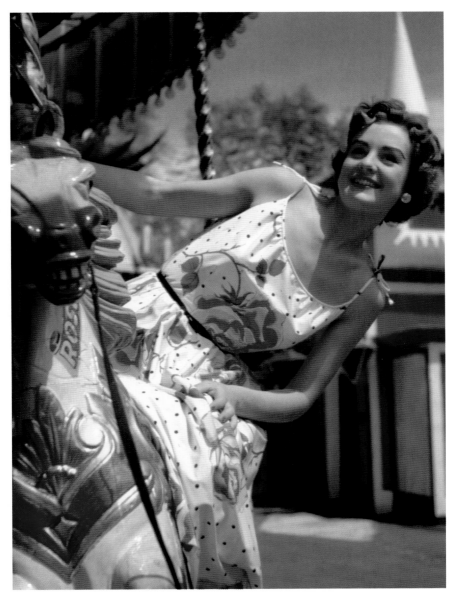

Fairground fashion, in crisp white cotton with a bold pink and green rose print.
1955 A girl rides a wooden horse on a carousel wearing a floral frock.

254

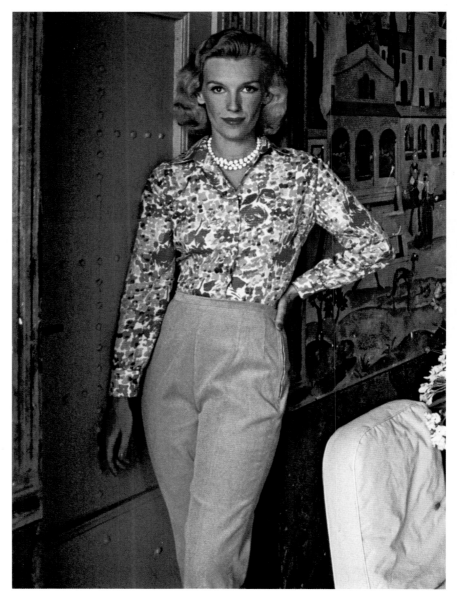

Social chic, slim mauve pants and a pretty flowered blouse, and pearls, of course.
1957 Viscountess Harriet de Rosière at Mougins, near Cannes in France.

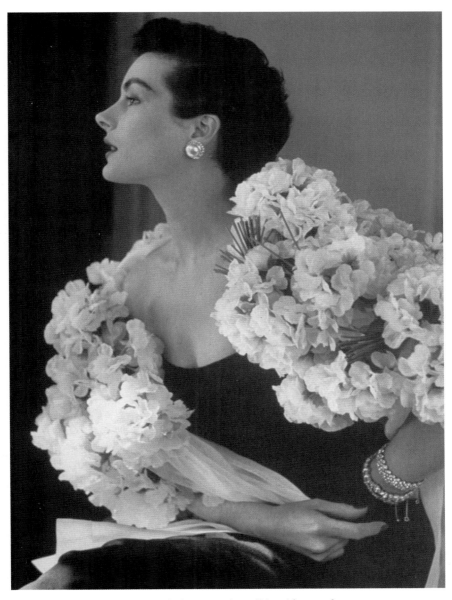

Bunches of flowers make a bolero more beautiful and frame a face.
1951 A model in profile wearing a little black dress with a white cape.

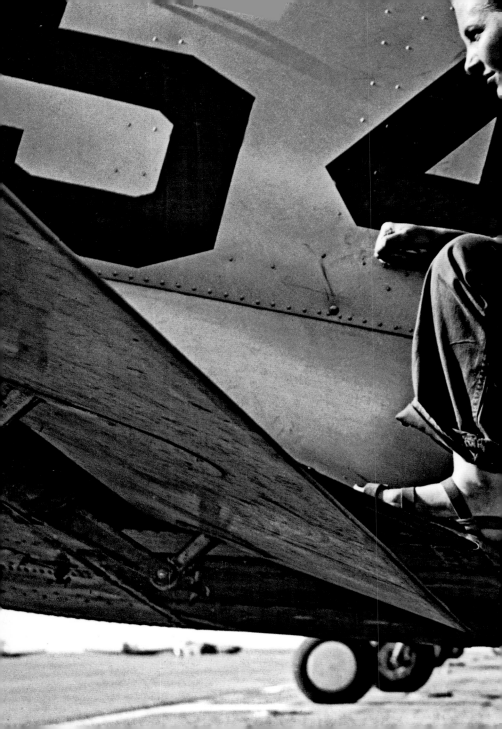

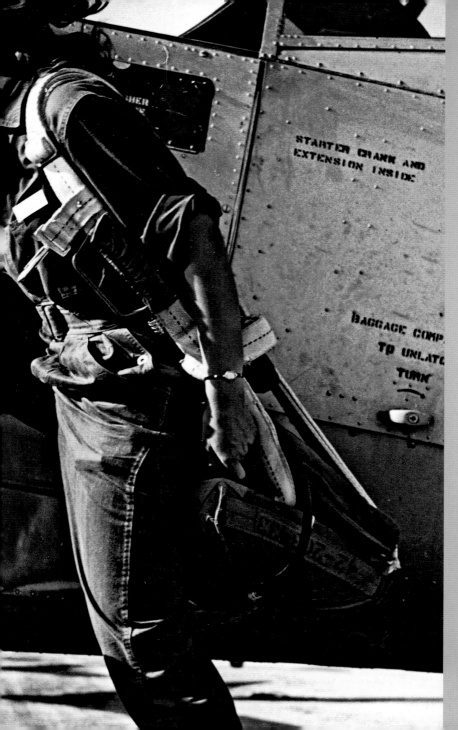

STARTER CRANK AND
EXTENSION INSIDE

BAGGAGE COMP
TO UNLATC
TURN

ALL IN ONE

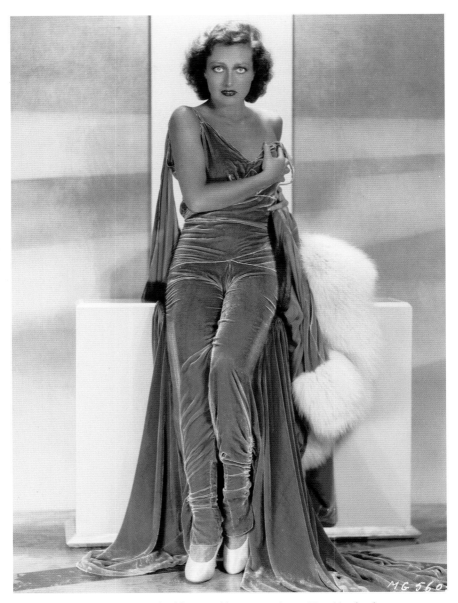

A vixen in velvet, a cat suit with a matching gown trimmed in white fox fur.
1930   American actress, Joan Crawford, wearing an off-the-shoulder suit.

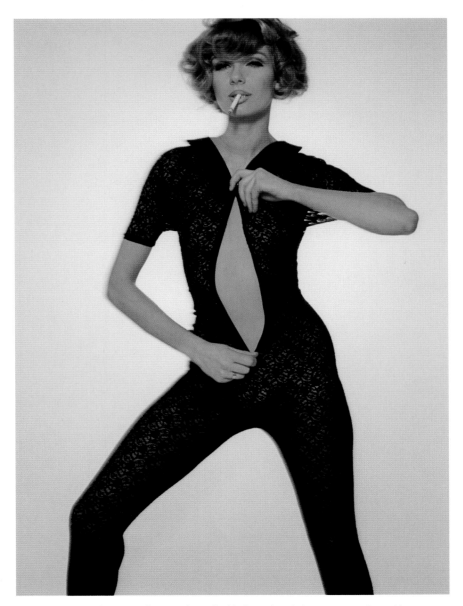

Lingerie looks, somewhat see-through, this foxy piece is best worn under a skirt.
1965 A model in a black lace, stretchy cat suit.

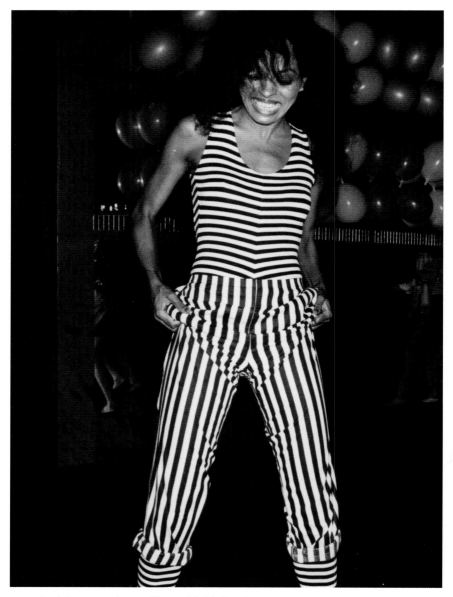

Soul sister, struts her stuff in graphic black and white stripes.
1983   American singer, Diana Ross, wearing an all in one with cuffed trousers.

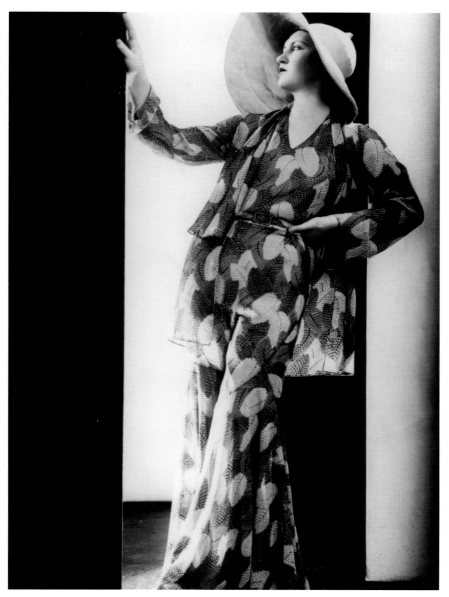

Super for the summer, lounging pyjamas in a pretty print with a matching jacket.
1928   A woman wearing a leaf-pattern trouser suit and broad-brimmed sun hat.

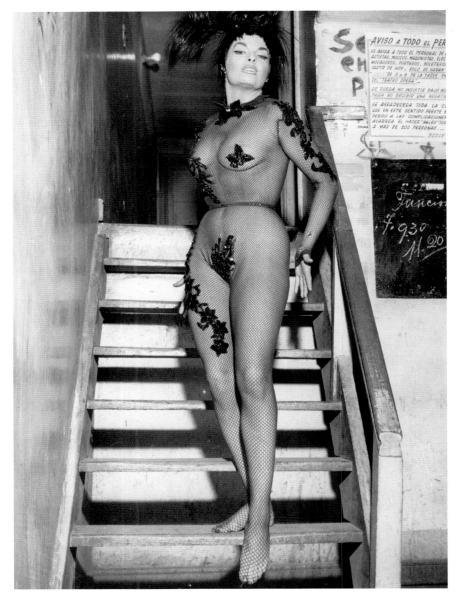

A fine figure of a woman, a net cat suit with a fig leaf preserving her modesty.
1955   A striptease artist backstage at the Opera House in Santiago, Chile.

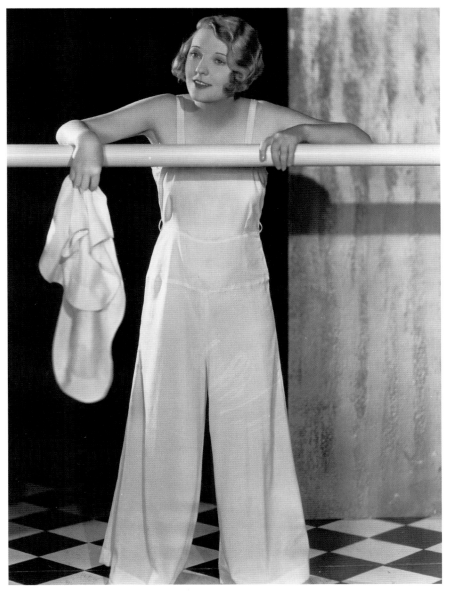

Divine in dungarees, crêpe de Chine with satin slippers and a little blond bob.
1931   British actress, Dorothy Mackaill, in *Party Husband* for Warner Brothers.

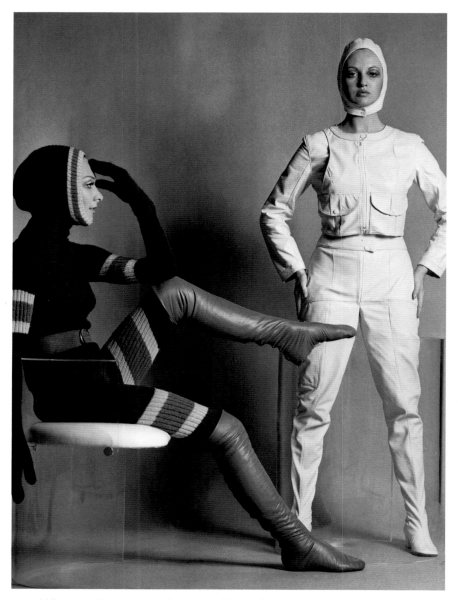

Winter woollies, top to toe in stripes with gauntlets and over-the-knee boots.
1968 Knitted cat suits designed and modelled by Shirley Belljohn (left).

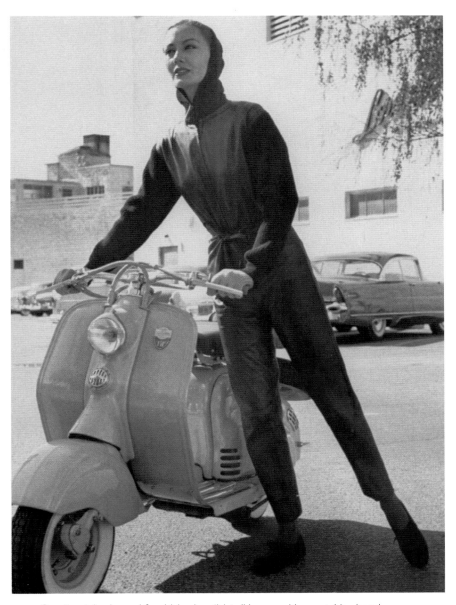

Scooter style, dressed for driving in a tight all in one with a matching hood.
1956   A woman modelling a jersey jumpsuit.

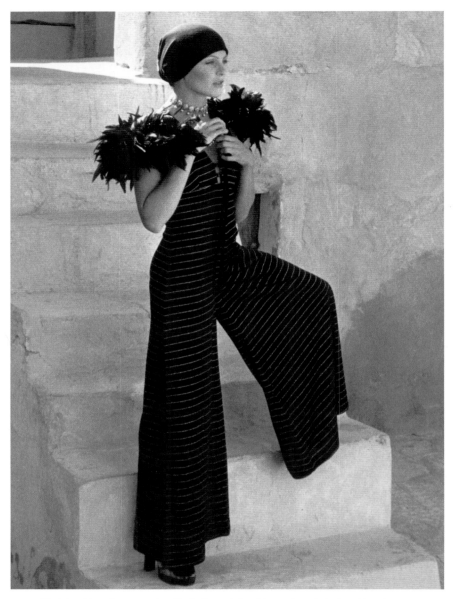

Pinstriped in palazzo pants, with feathered shoulders, a beanie hat and beads.
1973   A model wearing an all-in-one jumpsuit designed by Fernand Ledoux.

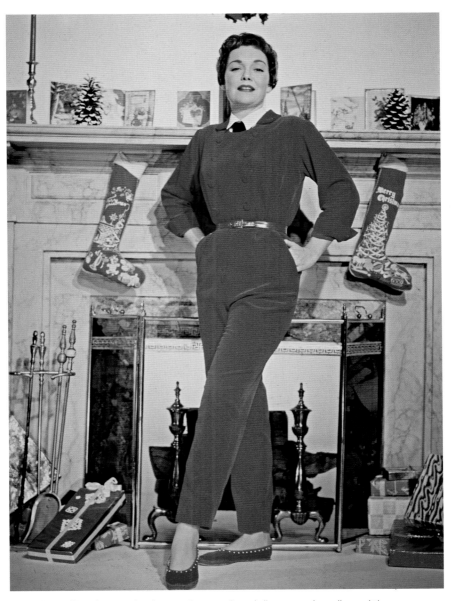

Santa Claus is a-coming, in a scarlet cat suit and slippers, and a collar and tie.
1955 American actress, Jane Wyman, at home, all ready for Christmas.

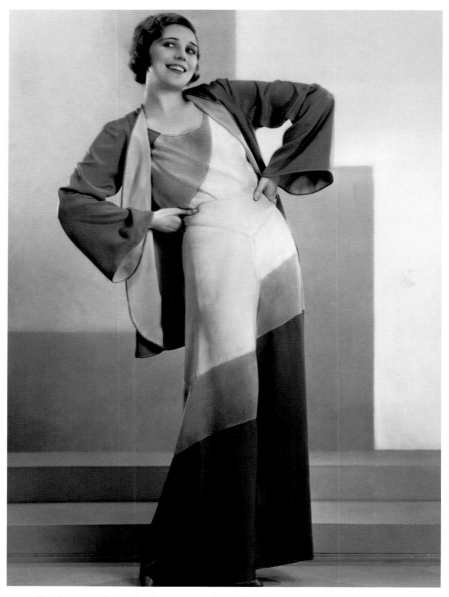

On the cross, diagonal stripes cut in crêpe with wide trousers and a long top.
1925   A model wearing a cat suit and a matching jacket.

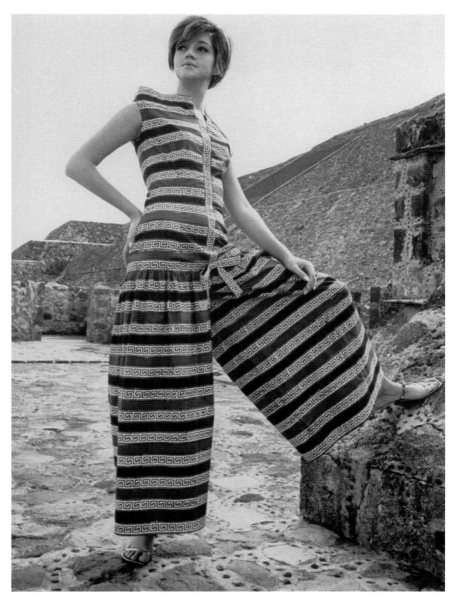

Horizontal stripes, Sixties style, a sleeveless all in one with a dropped waist.
1965   A model in an outfit designed by Rita Tillistt.

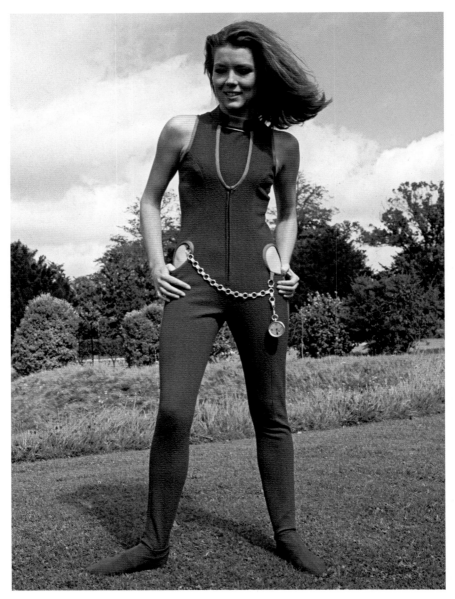

Purple prose, in a tight Lycra jumpsuit with cutouts at the hip, and a fob watch.
1966 English actress, Diana Rigg, in an episode of the TV series *The Avengers*.

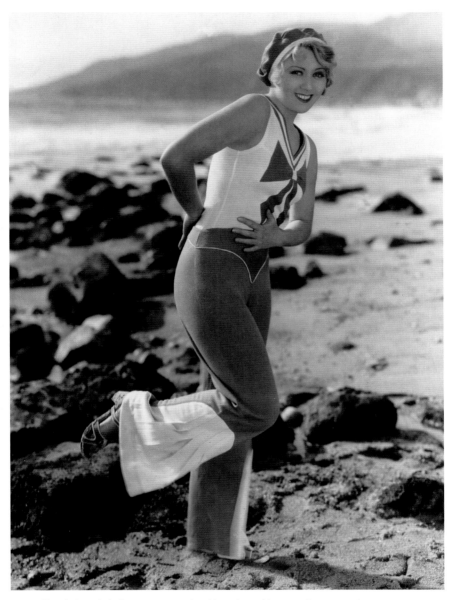

Blonde bombshell, a curvy cat suit with a pleated inset at the trouser bottoms.
1929   American actress, Joan Blondell, a whacky, wise-cracking Hollywood starlet.

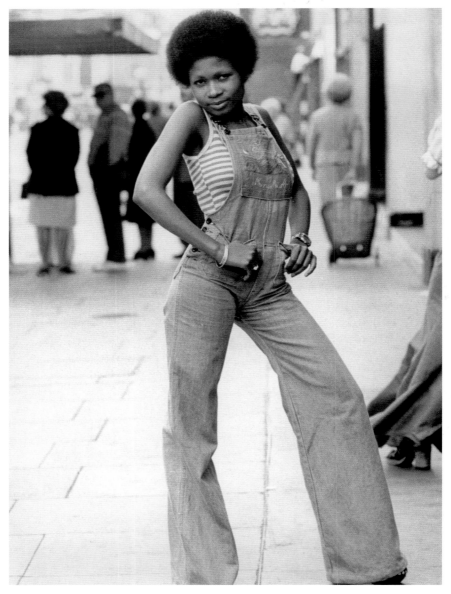

Funky chick, in denim bell-bottom dungarees, with a striped singlet and an Afro.
1973   Gloria Reynolds, a shop assistant in King's Road, London.

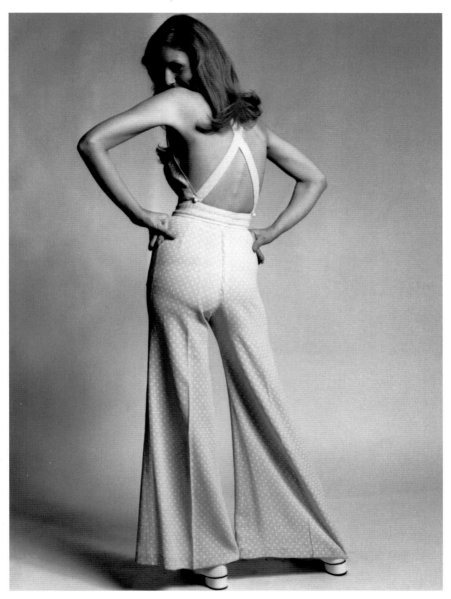

Back up, in very wide, woollen pants with a small shell-shaped bodice.
1969 A model wearing a halter-neck cat suit with crossover back straps.

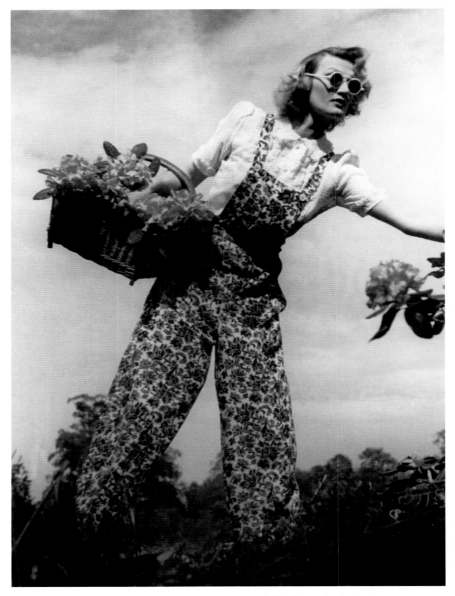

Little and large, dungarees with tiny flowers in a field of huge rhododendrons.
1941 *Clothes For A Coupon Summer*, picking flowers, dressed for the war effort.

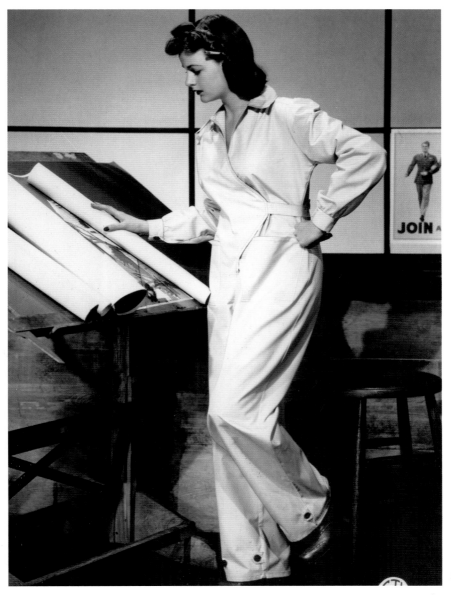

World War wear, crisp in white cotton with a classic rolled hair-do.
1943   A woman wearing coveralls examines designs on a drafting table.

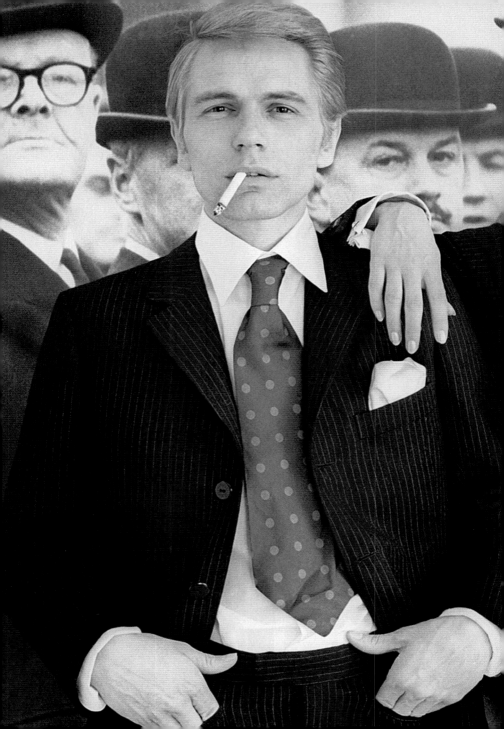

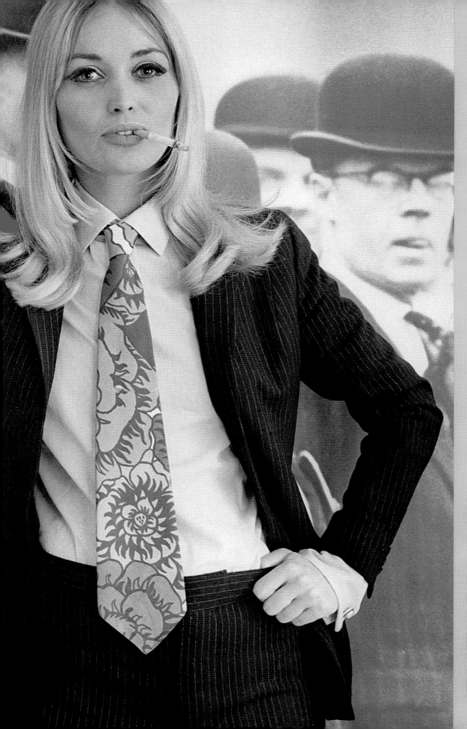

BUTTON UP

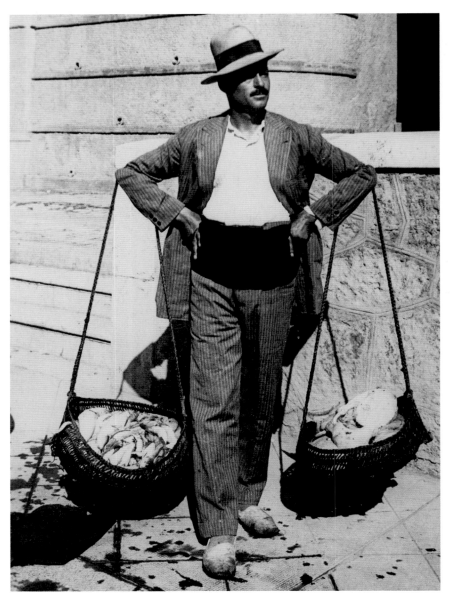

Hawking in the height of fashion, a cotton striped suit, shirt, sash and panama.
1930s   A man carrying baskets of fresh fish to sell, Malaga, Spain.

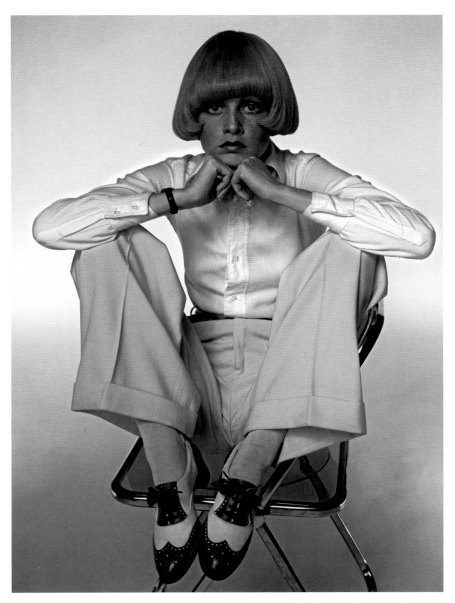

Co-respondents, chocolate and white leather brogues give that man/woman mix.
1972 Model, Twiggy, wears shoes made exclusively for her by George Cleverley.

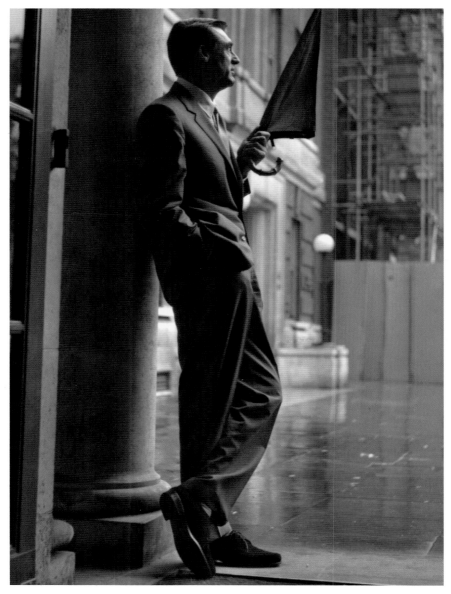

Standing in the rain, casual elegance personified in a tailor-made, two-piece suit.
1957   British-born American actor, Cary Grant, sheltering in a hotel porch.

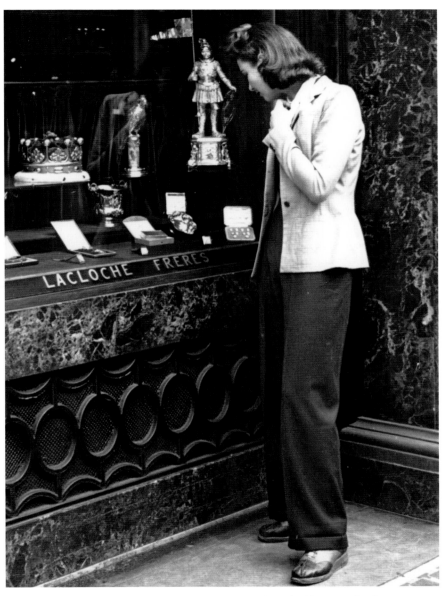

Shock of the new, manly tailoring was deemed to be quite bizarre at the time.
1941 A young French lady window-shopping, wearing the latest fashion of slacks.

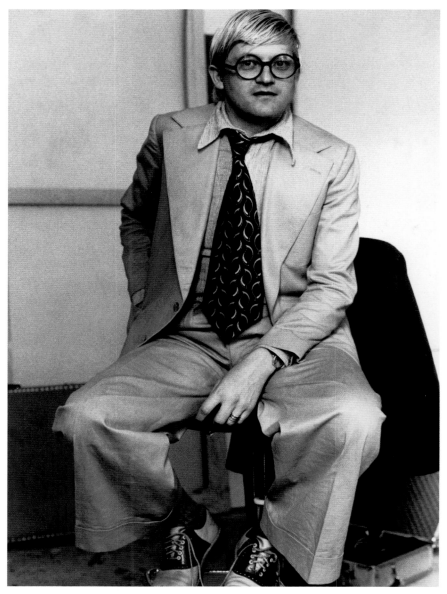

Suited with sneakers, and a kipper tie, with wearing his signature spectacles.
1975   English painter, David Hockney, away from his studio and swimming pool.

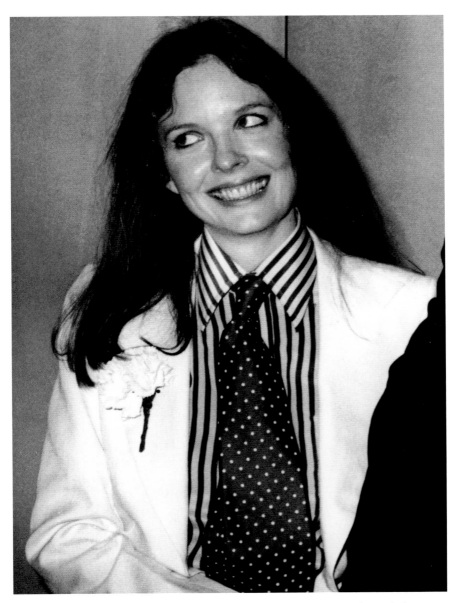

Annie-Hall inspired, in a striped shirt and a spotted tie, and carnation buttonhole.
1976 American actress, Diane Keaton, at the Academy Awards, Los Angeles.

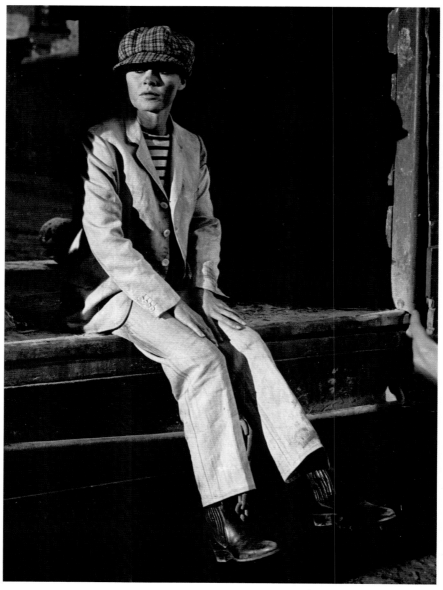

Baker-boy blues, in little laddish suit with a striped T-shirt and checked bonnet.
1965   French actress, Brigitte Bardot, filming Louis Malle's *Viva Maria* in Mexico.

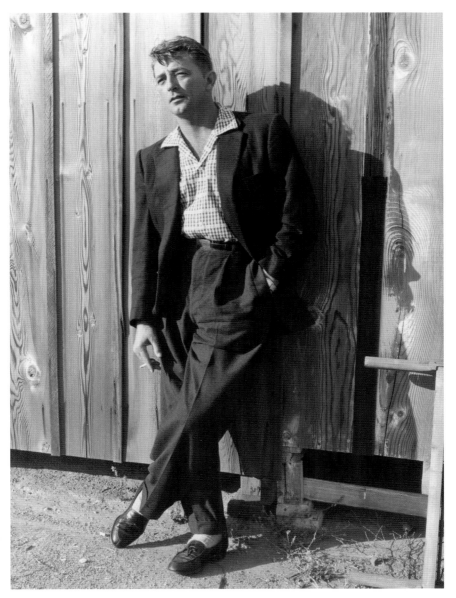

Rough and ready, a baggy-trousered suit with a casual checked shirt and loafers.
1945   American actor, Robert Mitchum, on set leaning against a wooden barn.

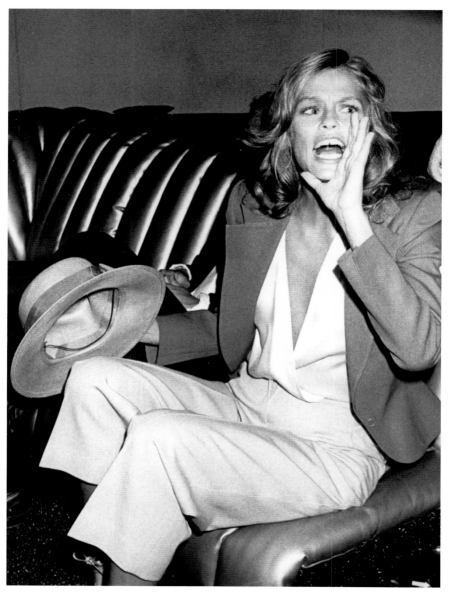

Just a gigolo, clubbing in a classic jacket and trousers, with a fedora in hand.
1978   American model and occasional actress, Lauren Hutton at Studio 54, USA.

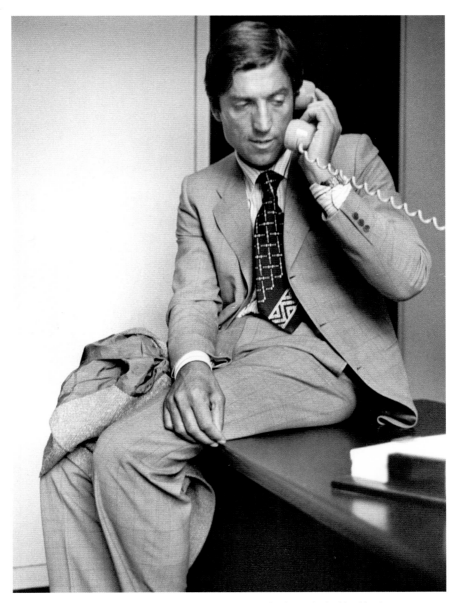

Well-connected, in one of his own single-breasted suits and a bold, wide tie.
1970 Nino Cerruti, an Italian tailor, famous for his mannish women's suits.

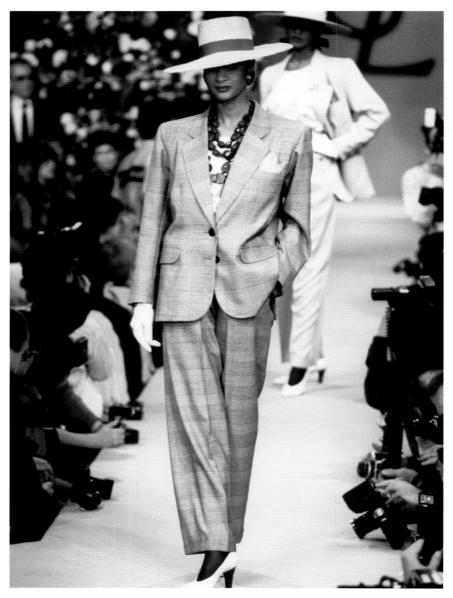

Squaring up, in a checked trouser suit with wide shoulders, and simple straw hat.
1989   A model on the catwalk at Yves Saint Laurent's Spring/Summer show, Paris.

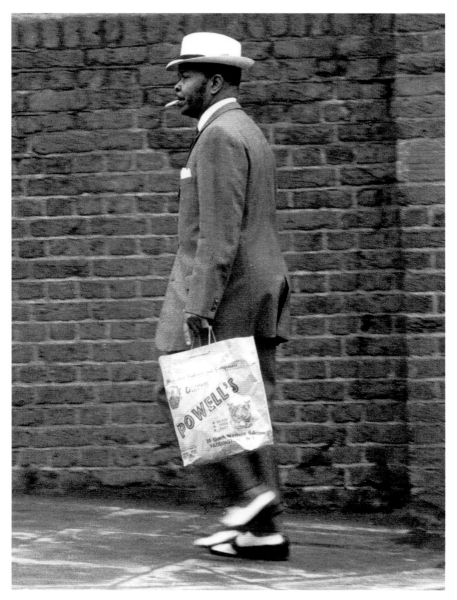

Sharp dressing, with a panama hat, two-tone shoes and a pocket handkerchief.
1968   A man in a zoot suit walking down the road, Notting Hill Gate, London.

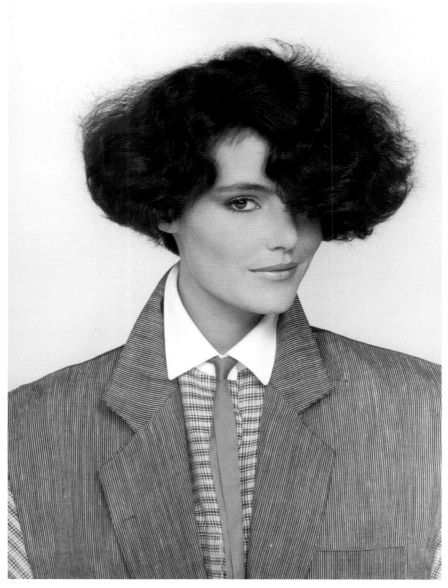

One-eyed wonder, a frizzy fantasy, with a sleeveless jacket and striped shirt.
1981   Styled by Parisian hairdresser, Patrick Ales, a cut held in place by a perm.

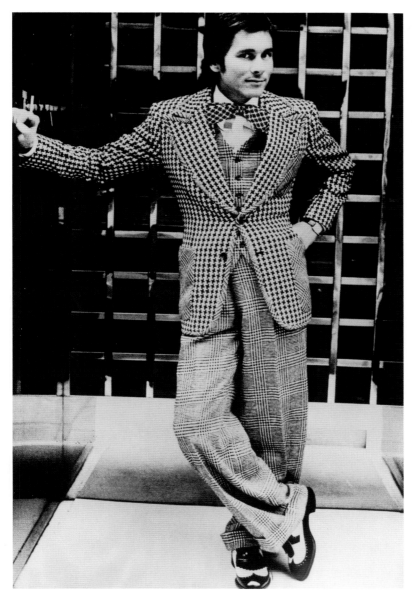

Checkmate Charlie, in a dizzying array of plaid and check.
1973 English tailor to the stars, Tommy Nutter, in London's Savile Row.

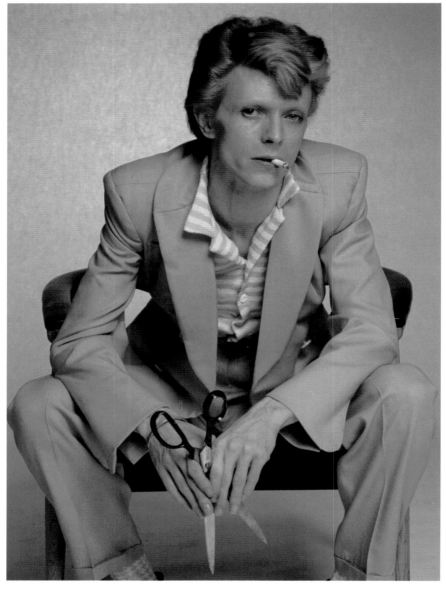

Yellow peril, a mustard draped jacket and trousers, with a matching striped shirt.
1974   English musician and actor, David Bowie with dyed red hair.

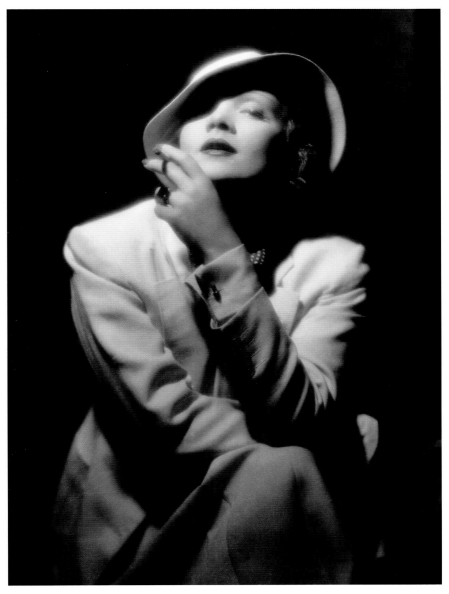

Mannish and marvellous, in a trouser suit, shirt with cuff links and a soft hat.
1934   German actress and singer, Marlene Dietrich, smoking a cigarette on set.

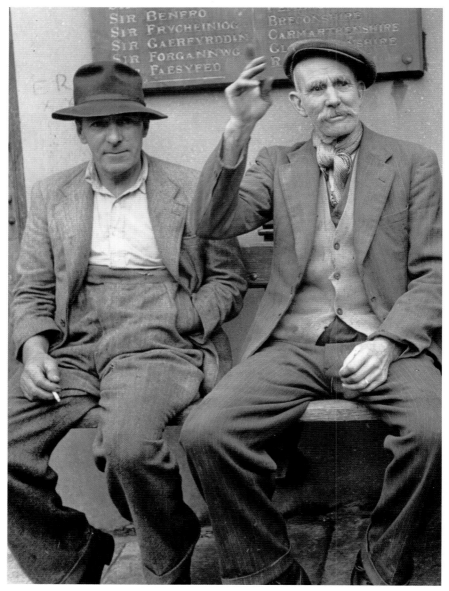

Conversation point, in country tweeds, high-waisted trousers, a cap or a hat.
1951 Elderly inhabitants sit below a memorial plaque, Conwy, Wales.

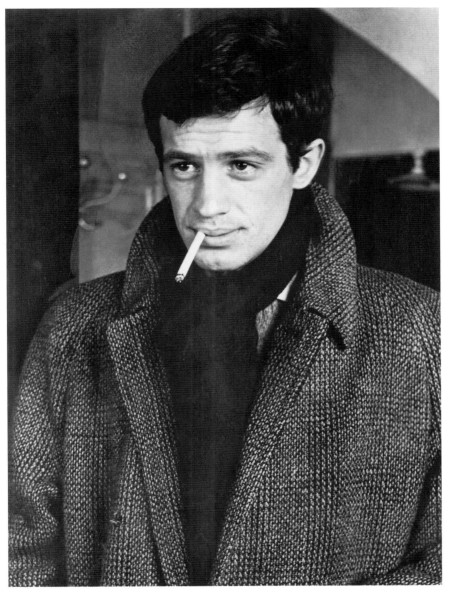

Black haired and brooding, in a tailored tweed coat over a suit, with a scarf.
1960 Frenchman Jean-Paul Belmondo, one of a new wave of actors.

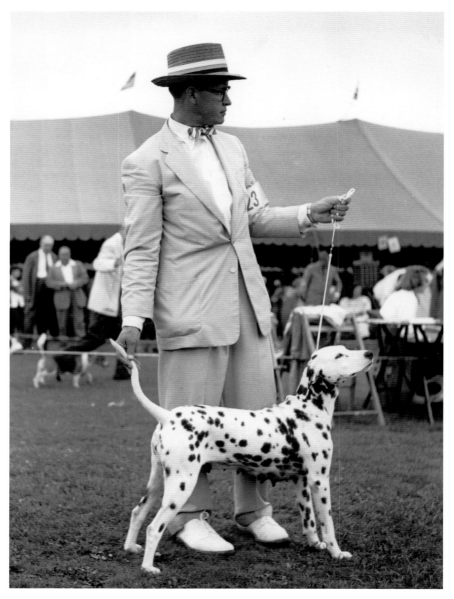

The dog days of summer, in a cream suit, bow tie, hat and white lace-ups.
1955   A Dalmatian competing at the Westchester Country Club, Rye, New York.

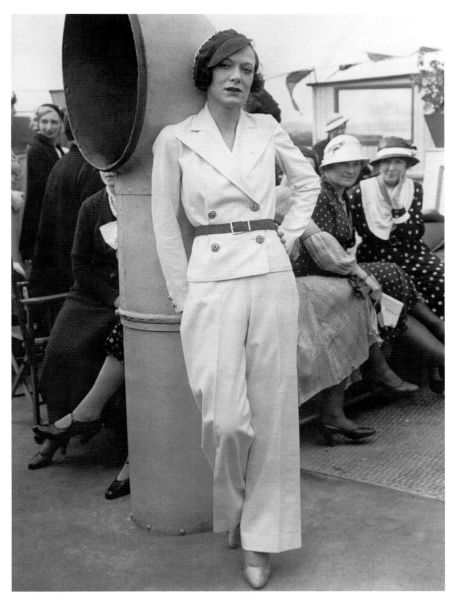

Modern miss, a trouser suit contrasts with the dresses and hats of the onlookers.
1932 A model on board a showboat in a Nicholl's of Regent Street fashion show.

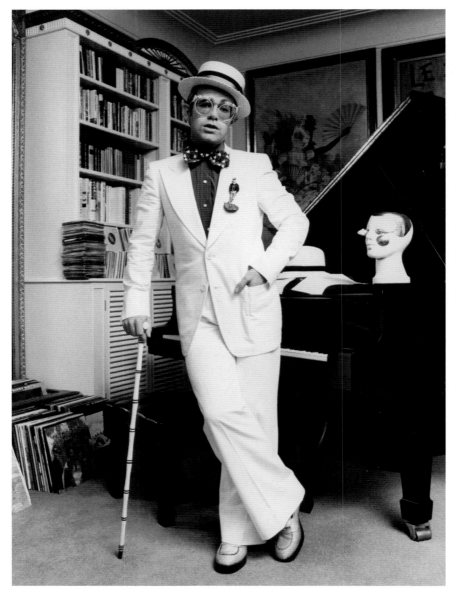

Piano man, in a perfect white suit, spotted bow tie, straw hat and stick.
1975   British singer, Elton John, at his house in Wentworth, England.

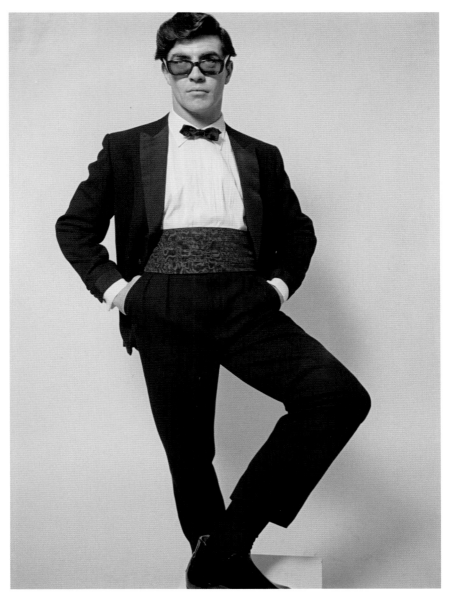

Dressed to impress, in a tight tuxedo, bow tie, cummerbund and shades.
1964   British actor, Alan Bates, promoting the film *Nothing But The Best*.

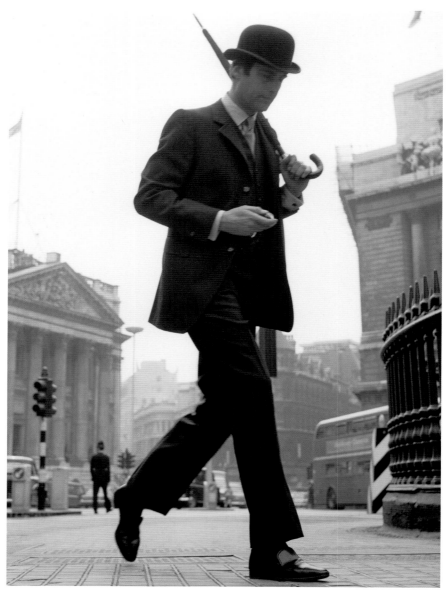

City slicker, in typical three-piece suit, bowler hat, umbrella and all.
1960 The model, Patrick Bashford, in a photograph for *Queen* magazine.

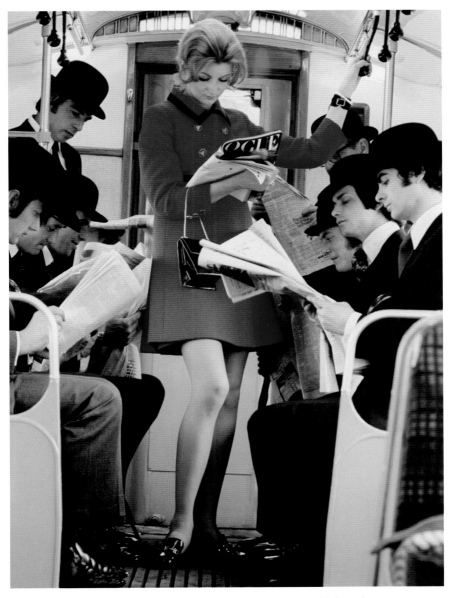

Little red riding coat, off to work in a double-breasted mini with brass buttons.
1966   A model on a London underground train reading *Vogue* magazine.

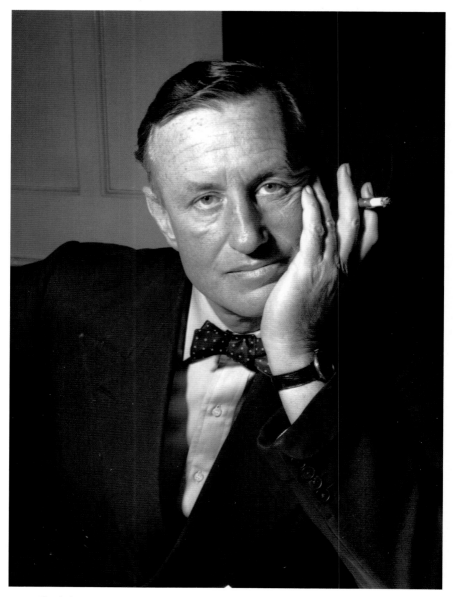

Cool character, suave and stylish in dark suit with a small bow tie
1958   Ian Fleming, British author and creator of the *James Bond* thrillers.

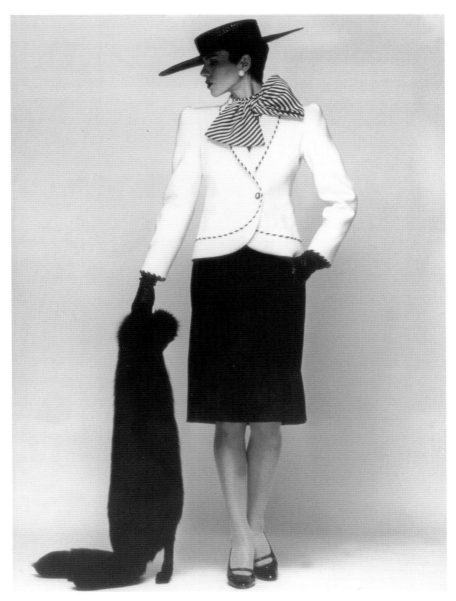

Power dressing, with square shoulders, a slim skirt and a black and white blouse.
1983 A suit from the Pierre Balmain Spring/Summer collection, Paris.

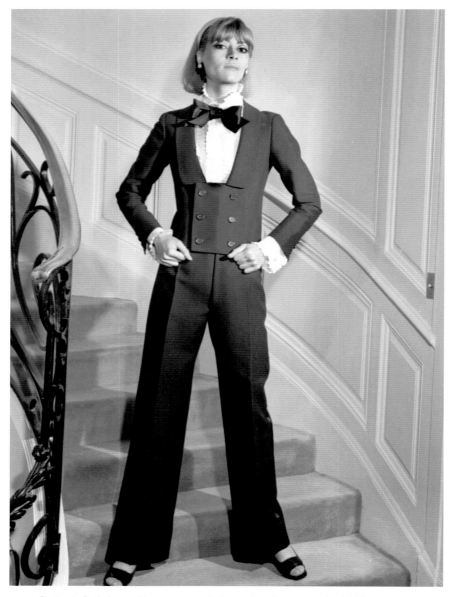

Posing in Paris, le smoking, a spencer jacket and perfect pants, classic YSL.
1967   A model in Yves Saint Laurent's Spring/Summer haute couture show.

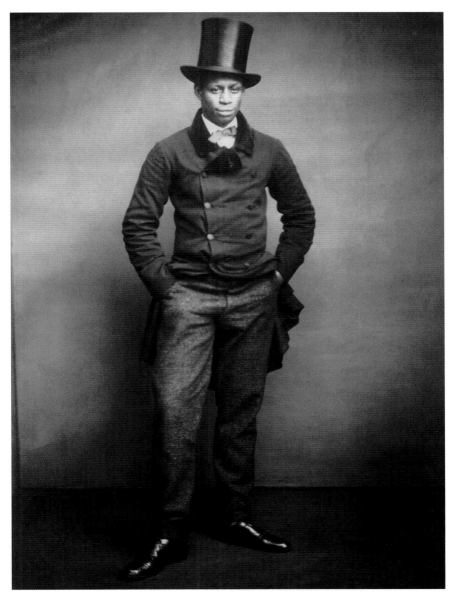

Dandified and dressed for best, in top hat and tails, and patent shoes.
1890 A young black man wearing a formal suit and stovepipe hat.

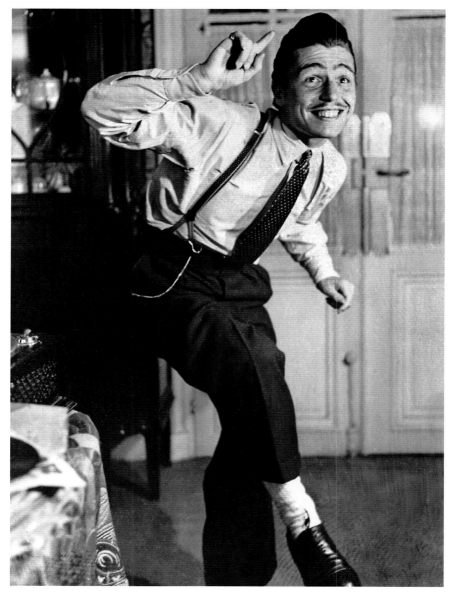

All that jazz, zoot suited and dancing, in the French fashion, to Zazou music.
1943   A young blood, with a quiff hairstyle, braces, and a collar and tie.

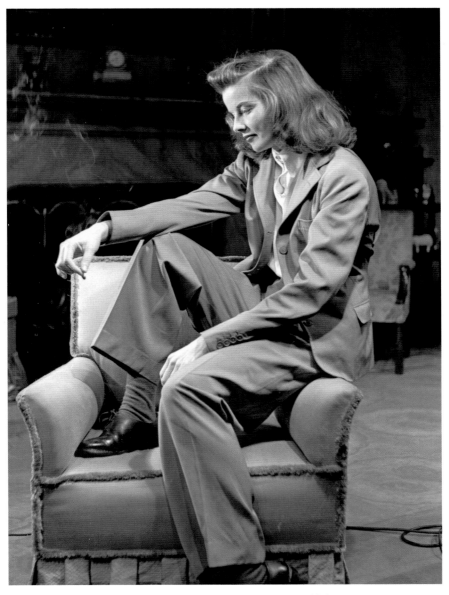

Stellar and smouldering, in a Spencer-Tracy suit, complete with brogues.
1938 American actress, Katharine Hepburn, sitting on the arm of chair smoking.

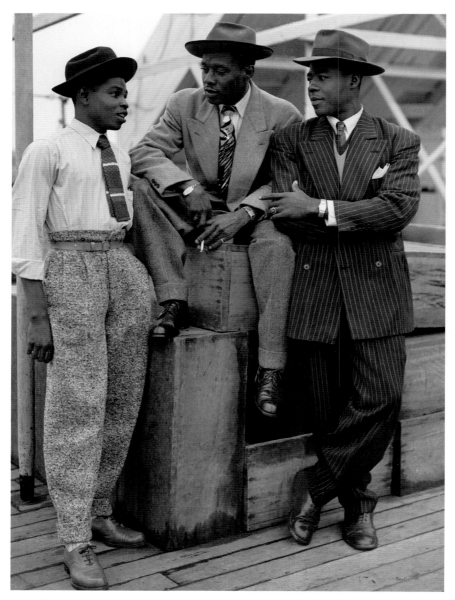

Shooting the breeze on the *Empire Windrush*, in zoot suits and trilby hats.
1948   Three Jamaican immigrants arriving at Tilbury Docks on an ex-troopship.

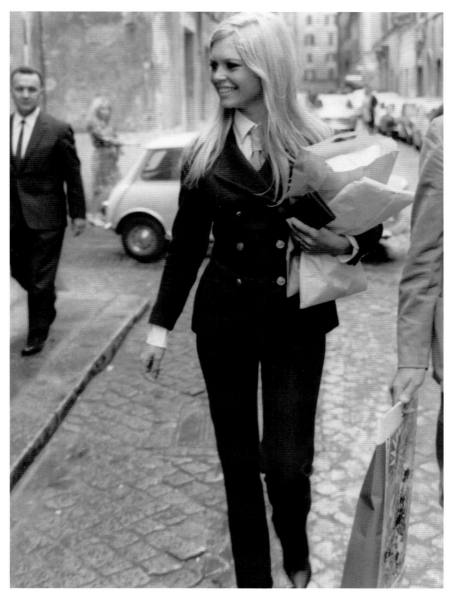

Feminine/masculine mix, a blonde bombshell in a severe suit, with collar and tie.
1967   French actress, Brigitte Bardot, shopping in the Via Margutta, Rome, Italy.

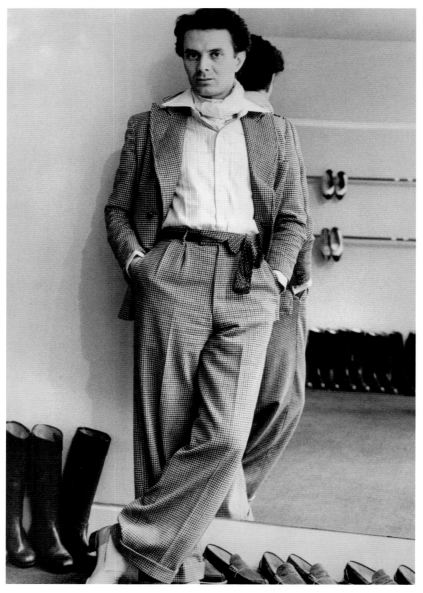

Savile Row style, a simple suit worn with a flamboyant pink scarf and shirt.
1974 Spanish shoe designer, Manolo Blahnik, dressed by Tommy Nutter, London.

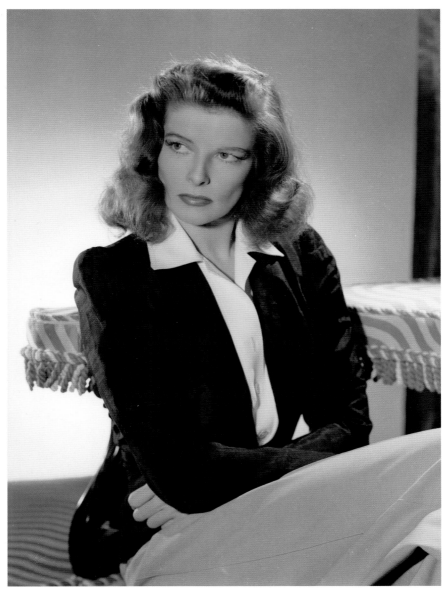

Screen siren, in classics, a black jacket, stone trousers and an open-necked shirt.
1941 American actress, Katharine Hepburn, had a propensity for men's clothes.

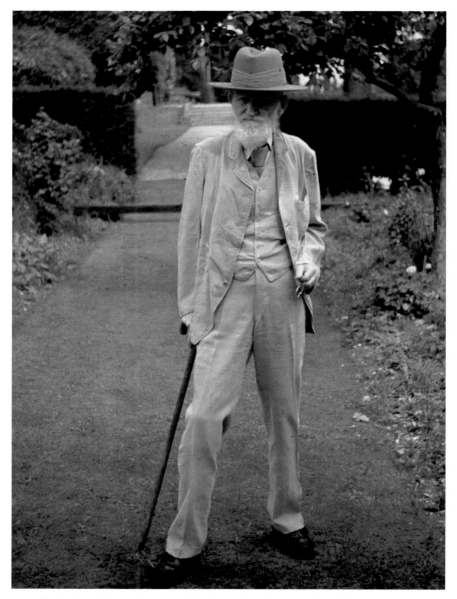

Pastoral poet, in a pale cream suit, with an elegant cane and camel hat.
1946   Irish playwright, George Bernard Shaw, at his home in Hertfordshire.

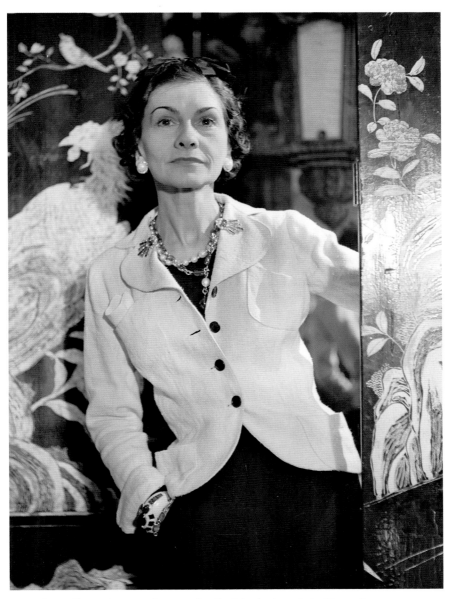

Couturière and creator, the masculine/feminine look, perfect with pearls.
1937   Coco Chanel, French fashion designer, in her fabulous apartment in Paris.

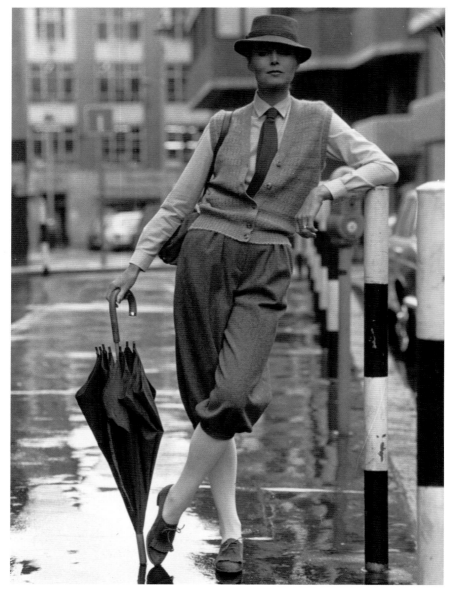

Knickerbocker glory, in breeches, brogues, a woollen waistcoat, collar and tie.
1980   A model in clothes from the Jaeger collection, near Carnaby Street, London.

315

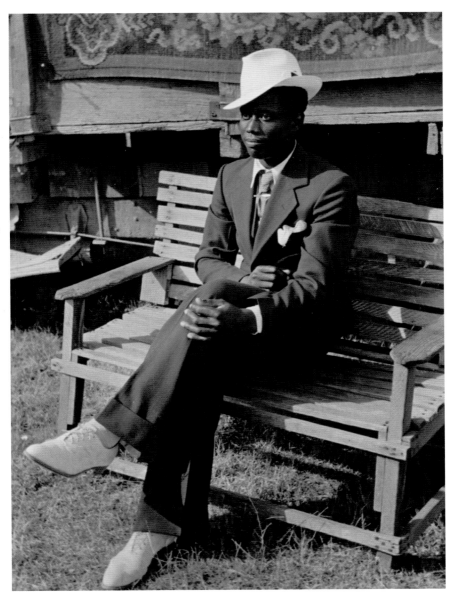

Summer in the city, dressed to impress in a white hat, shoes and handkerchief.
1930 A smart young man from Kansas City, Missouri, USA.

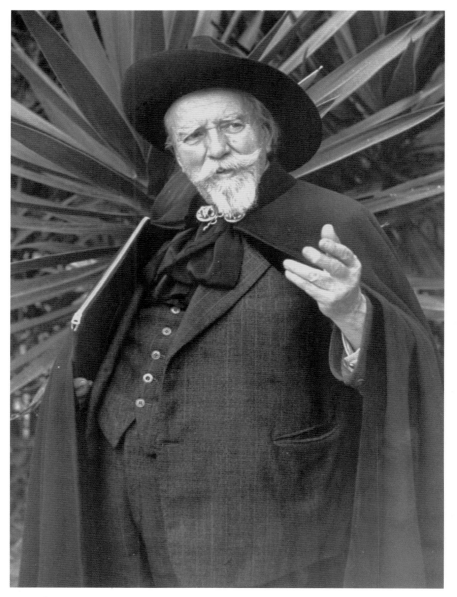

Caped crusader, elderly and elegant in a three-piece suit with a flamboyant bow.
1950 A portly gentleman in Mexico with a full white goatee beard and moustache.

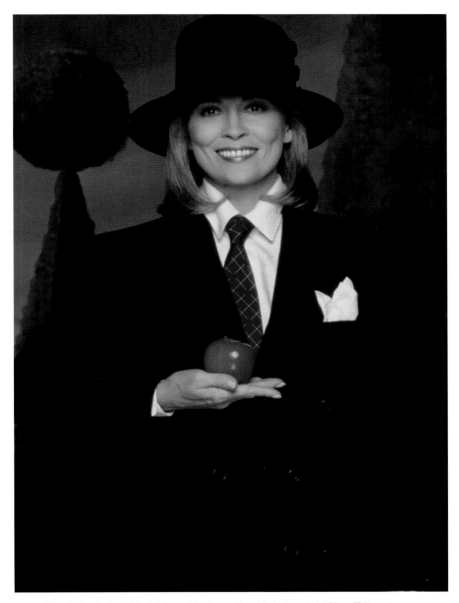

City slicker, in best black bib and tucker, with a big hat and a William Tell apple.
1987   American actress, Faye Dunaway, wearing a pinstripe suit, London.

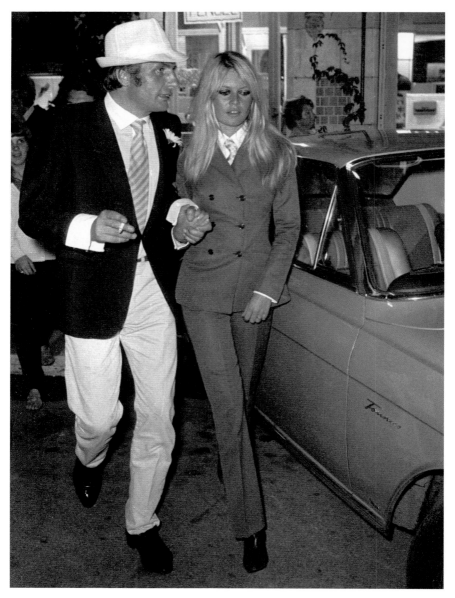

His and hers, suited and booted, matching outfits for a night out on the town.
1967   French actress, Brigitte Bardot, and her husband, Gunter Sachs, Deauville, France.

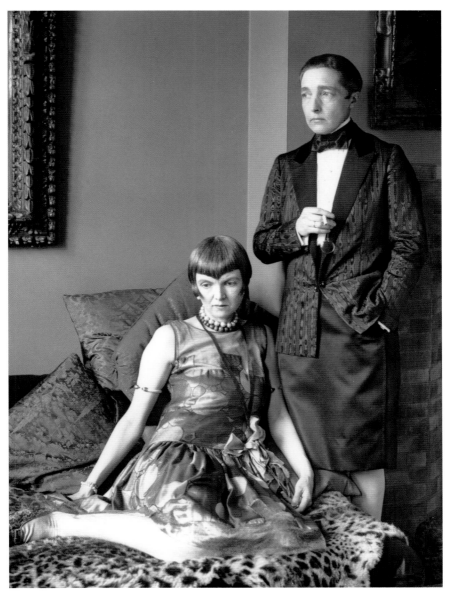

Hers and hers, an evening at home inspired by the novel *The Well Of Loneliness*.
1927 Writer, Marguerite Radclyffe Hall, and her friend Lady Una Trowbridge.

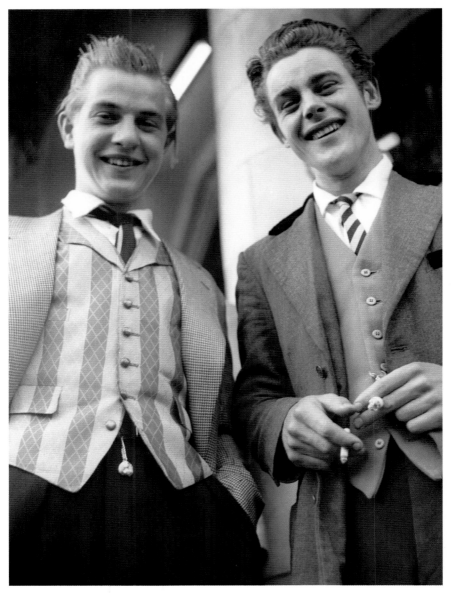

Dandy dressing, Brylcreemed quiffs, draped jackets and drainpipe trousers.
1955 Teddy boys, one with striped waistcoat and the other with a velvet collar.

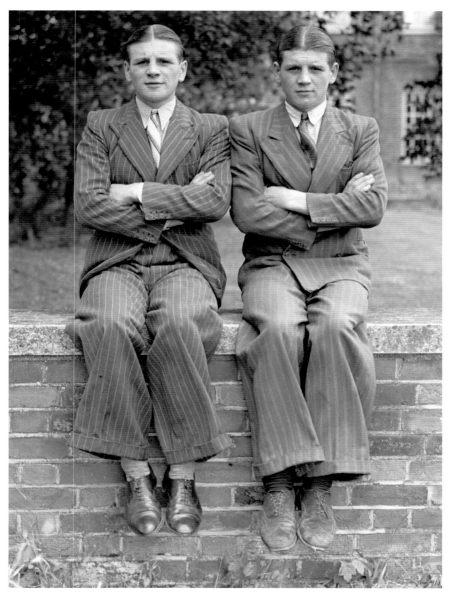

One for the price of two, single and double-breasted pin-striped suits with bags.
1938 Twins in pin-stripe suits sitting on a wall, their arms identically crossed.

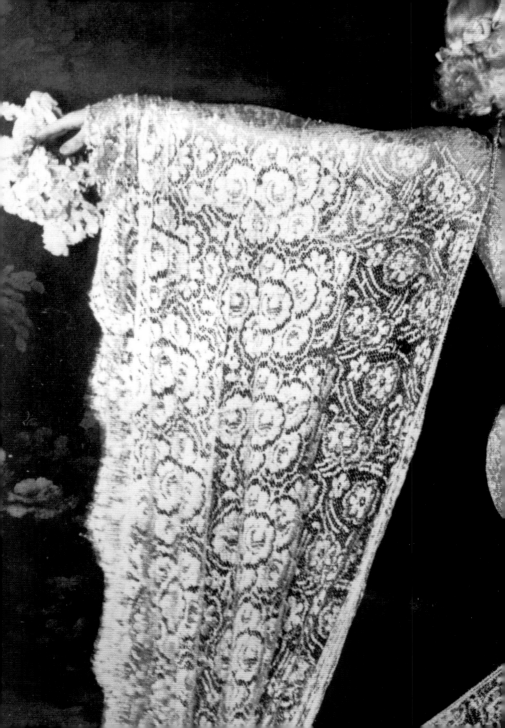

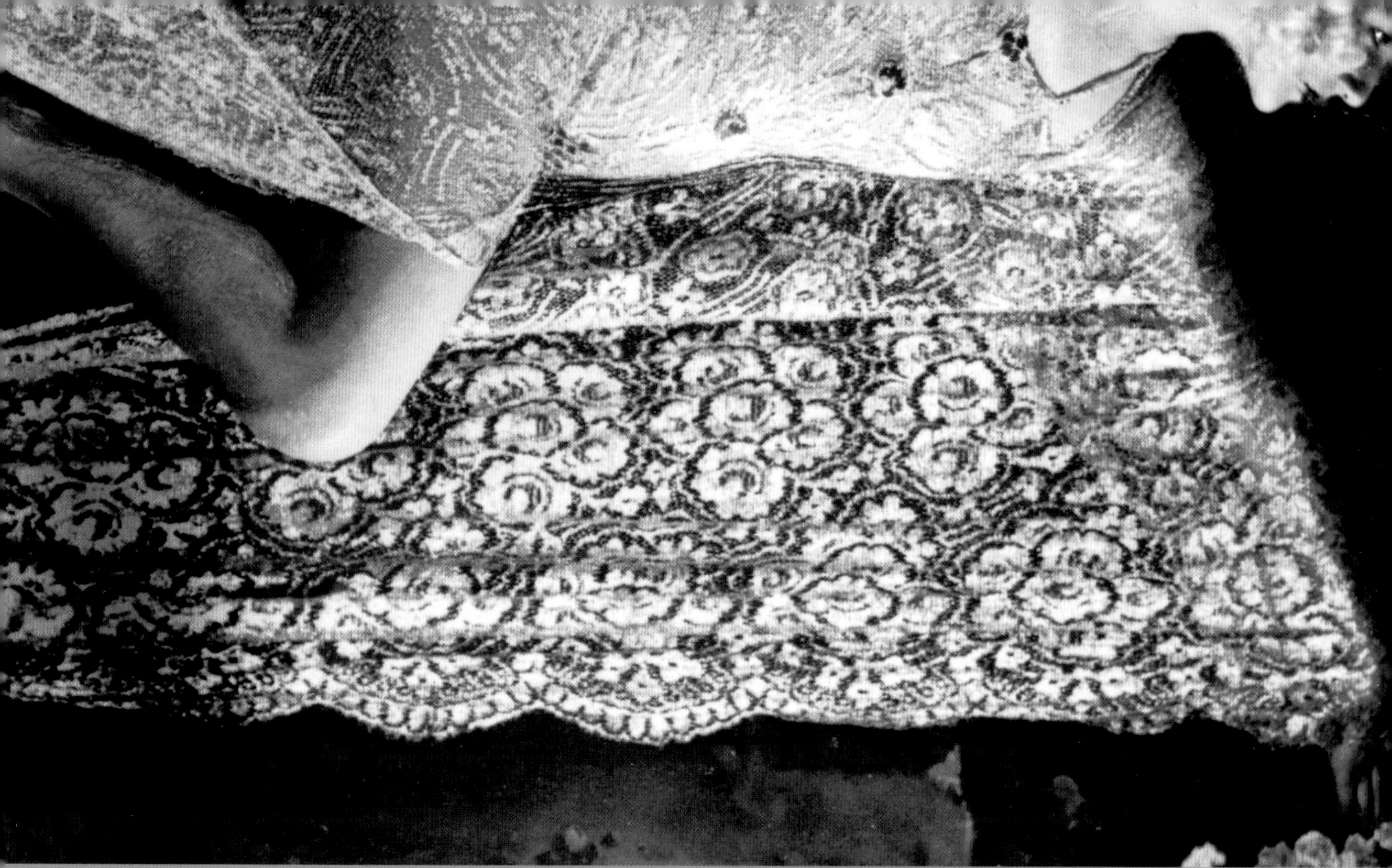

FRILLS AND FURBELOWS

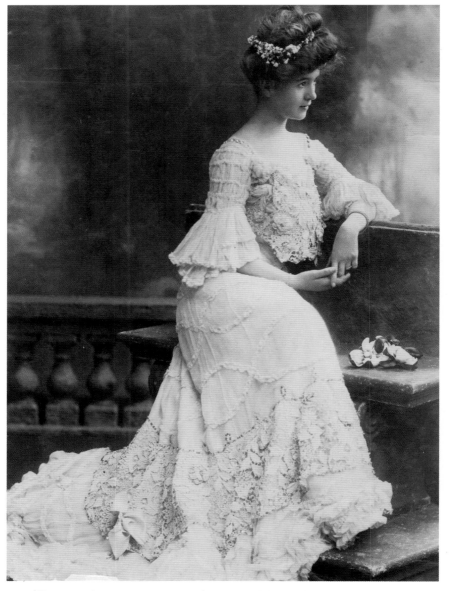

Silent star of stage and screen, a perfect portrait in ladylike looks.
1902 American actress, Carol McComas, in an extravagant white lace dress.

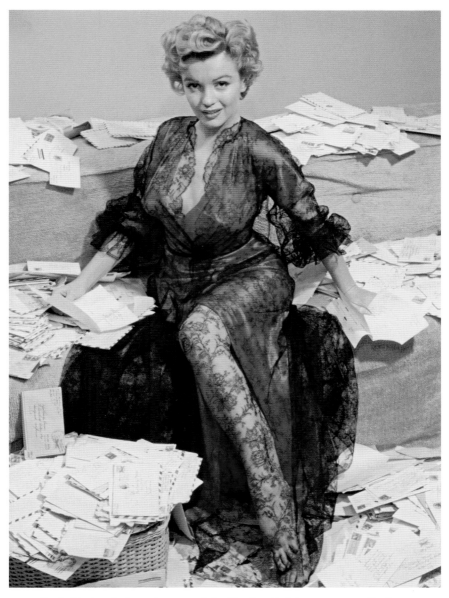

Too hot to handle, in a crimson negligé with a fine black lace gown over the top.
1952   American actress, Marilyn Monroe, after the release of *The Asphalt Jungle*.

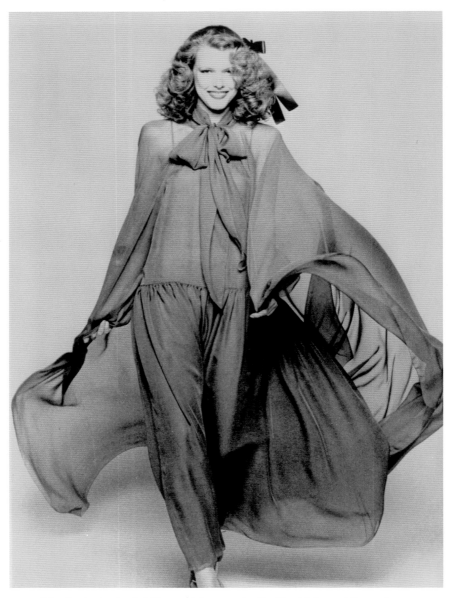

Billowing in clouds of chiffon, an all-in-one cat suit with a big bow at the neck.
1978   A model in a Chanel outfit from the Autumn/Winter collection, Paris.

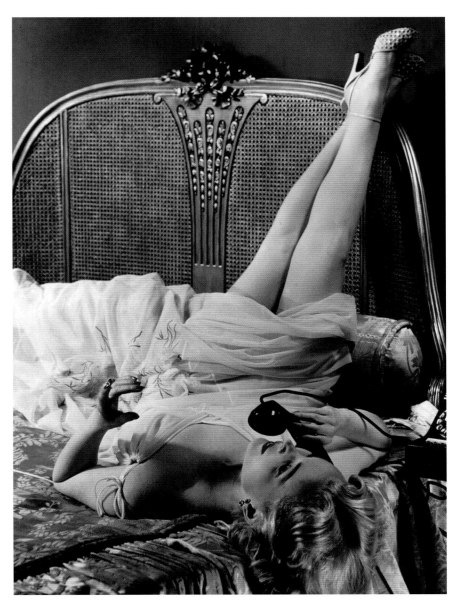

The end of an evening, lounging on a French bed in a beautiful chiffon gown.
1944 Hungarian-born American actress, Zsa Zsa Gabor, on the telephone.

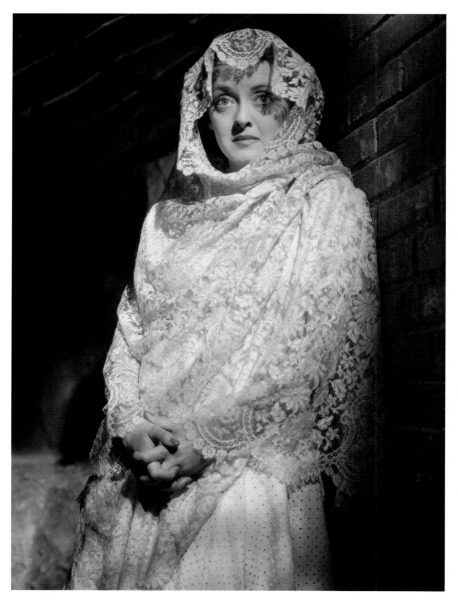

Murderess with intent, menacing in a virginal white lace mantilla and dress.
1940   American actress, Bette Davis, in William Wyler's film noir *The Letter.*

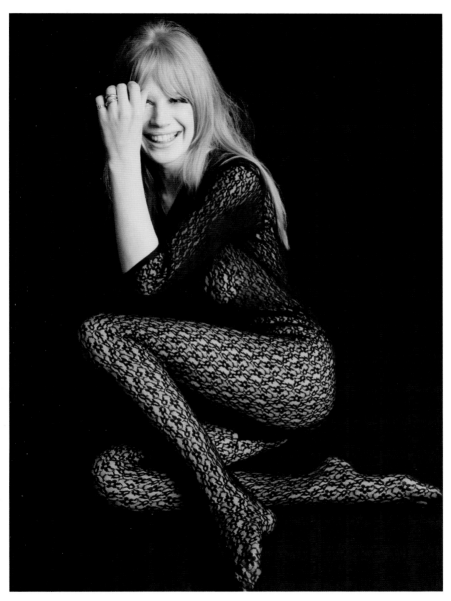

Rock and roll and lovely in lace, a black bodysuit is the perfect underpinning.
1966   English singer and actress, Marianne Faithfull, then Mick Jagger's girlfriend.

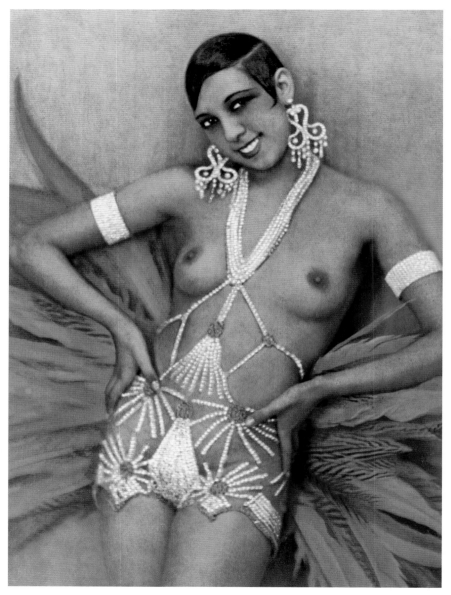

Bare all, cabaret chic in rhinestones, feathers, a smile and not much else.
1925   American singer and dancer, Josephine Baker, at the Folies Bergère, Paris.

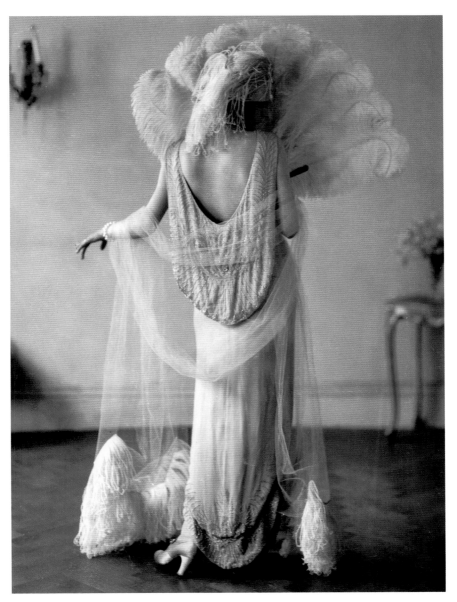

By appointment, a long chiffon evening gown trimmed with lace and feathers.
1924 A dress by British couturier, Norman Hartnell, designer to the Royals.

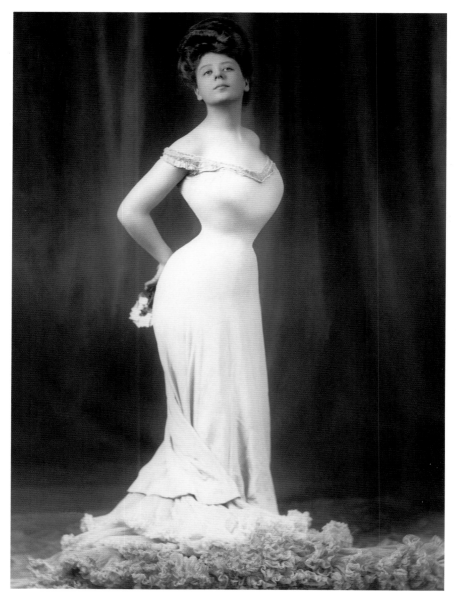

American beauty with curious curves, a fashion figure at the turn of the century.
1900 Danish-born actress, Camille Clifford, one of the *Gibson Girls*.

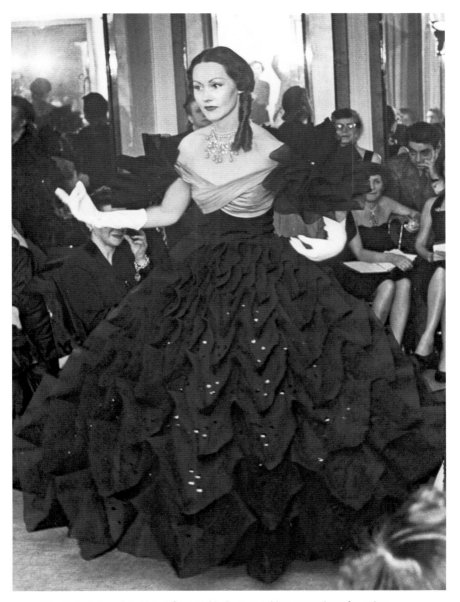

Terrific in tulle, a full-skirted, flounced ball gown, with a scattering of sequins.
1951 A French model in a black evening dress by Castillo at Lanvin, Paris.

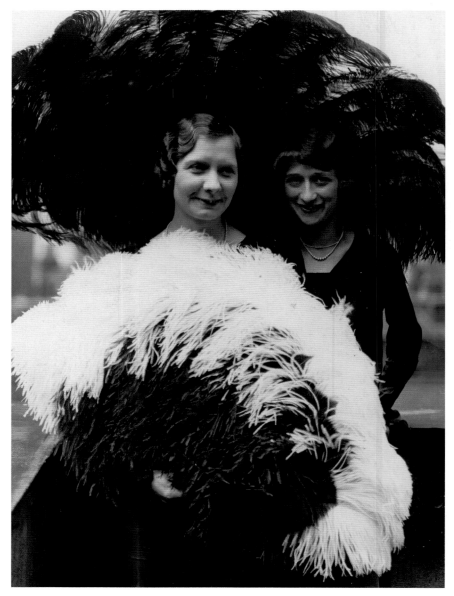

Fantastic feathers, the essential accessory for the flapper out on the town. 1925 Two ladies posing with ostrich fans and plain black evening dresses.

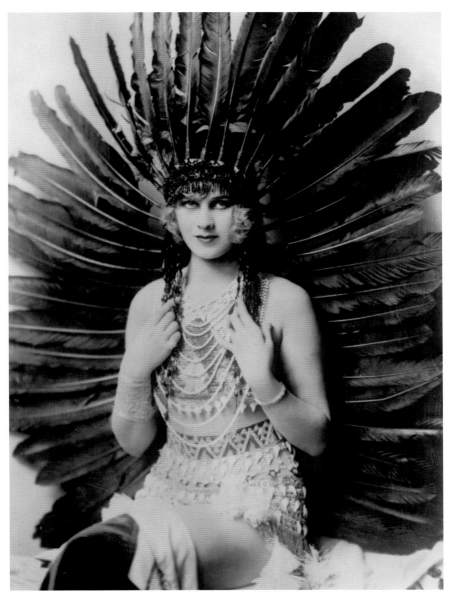

Great white chief, in cabaret costume inspired by American-Indian tribal dress.
1929 American dancer and singer, Hazel Forbes, of the Ziegfeld Follies, Paris.

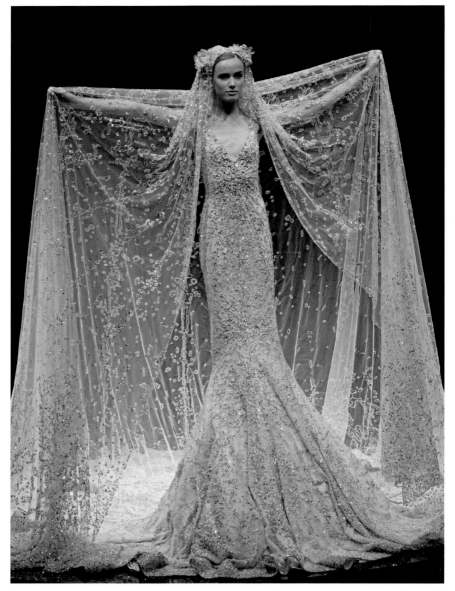

Wedding wonderland, lofty in fine white lace, with a red-carpet pizzazz.
2007   A creation by Lebanese designer, Elie Saab, for his couture show in Paris.

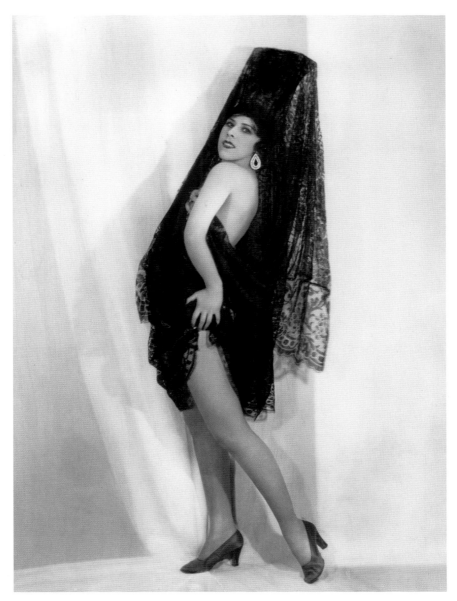

Wake Up And Dream in an enormous, black lace mantilla, and a lot of attitude.
1929 Russian-born American ballerina, Kyra Alanova, at the London Pavilion.

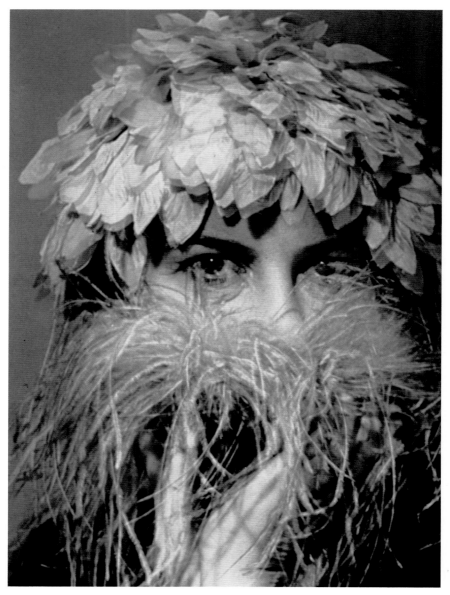

Camouflage chic, a hat made from leaves, and an elegant feather boa.
1966 American actress, Alice Pearce, in the play *Angel in the Wings*.

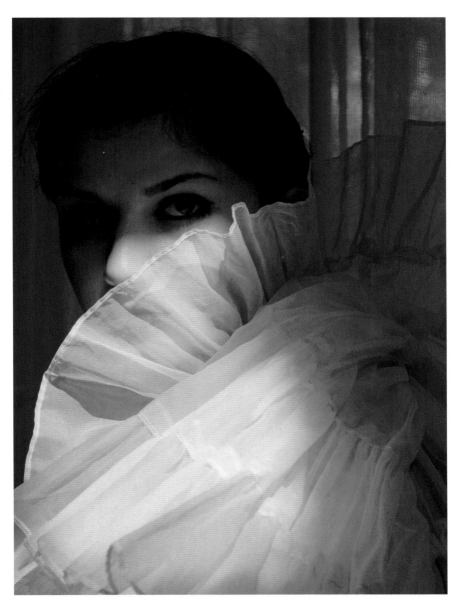

A frill too far, lending allure in a fan-shaped cloud of chiffon.
1960 A young woman wearing an organza ruffled top.

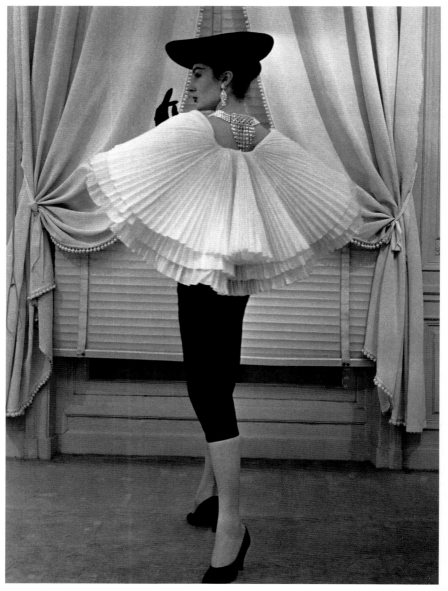

Matador inspired, a concertina pleated cape-blouse and a tight black pencil-skirt. 1956 A cocktail outfit designed by Parisian designer, Jacques Fath.

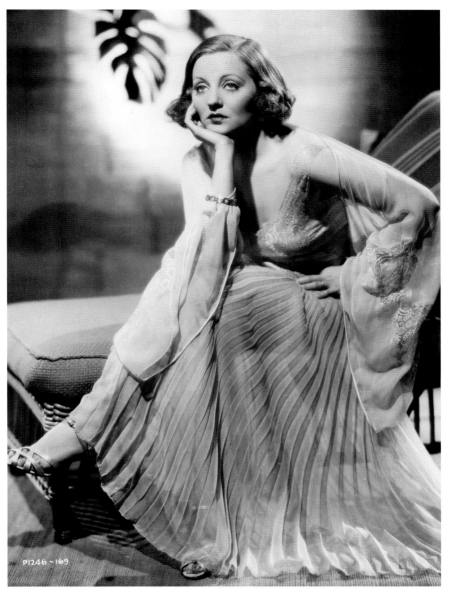

Pleated perfection, in a sunray-pleated chiffon dress with trumpet sleeves.
1932 American star, Tallulah Bankhead, daughter of a southern political family.

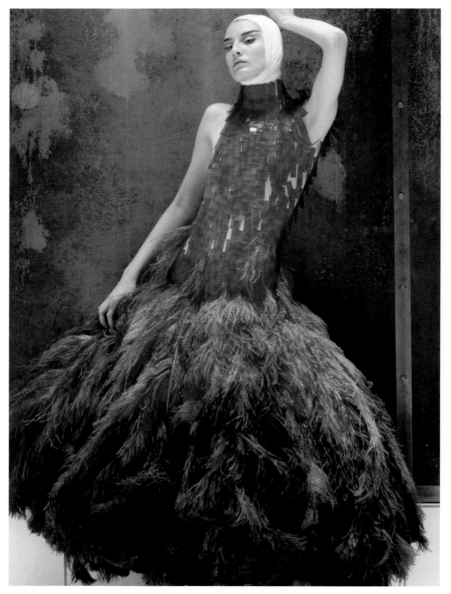

Fire bird, a fantasy dress in flame coloured feathers with a sequined bodice.
2000 A model in Alexander McQueen's Spring/Summer show in London.

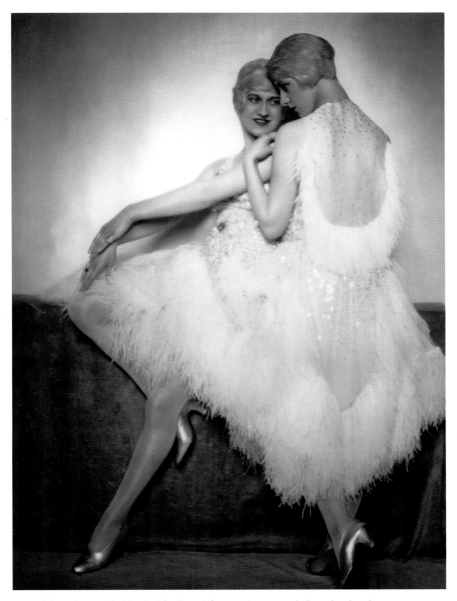

Mirror images, in identical feathered flapper dresses, and silver dancing shoes.
1925 The Rowe Sisters, the 'Greyhounds of Paris', dancers at the Casino de Paris.

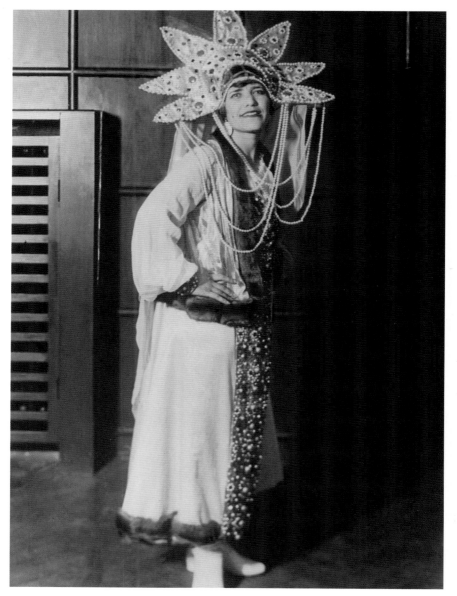

Russian romantic, a Tsarina head-dress dripping in pearls, and a fur-trimmed robe.
1935   Maria Rasputin, daughter of Russian mystic, the 'Mad Monk', on stage.

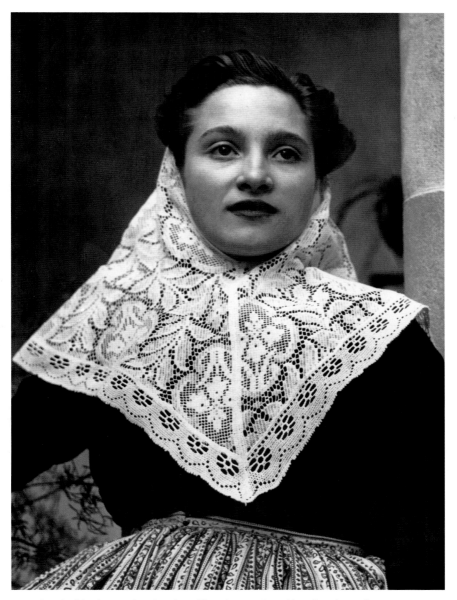

Land of the lace maker, showing off her fine crocheted handiwork at a fiesta.
1950 A woman wearing traditional costume with a lace headscarf, Majorca, Spain.

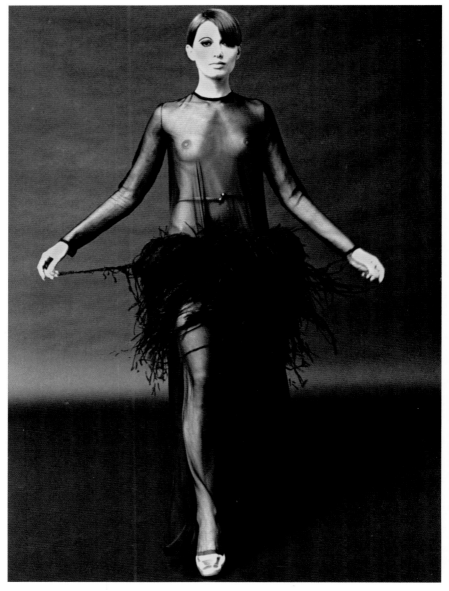

Sheer black magic, a black chiffon ankle-length gown with a feathered over-skirt.
1968   A model in a see-through dress by Yves Saint Laurent, shown in New York City.

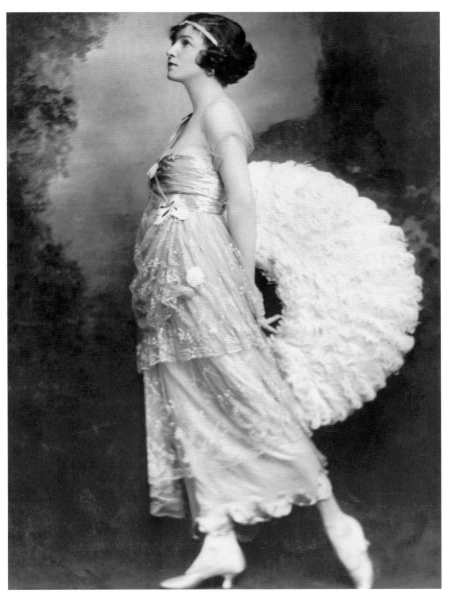

Fantail fantasies, a silk and lace strapless dress with a very large fan for effect.
1918 American ballroom dancer and actress, Irene Castle, New York City.

348

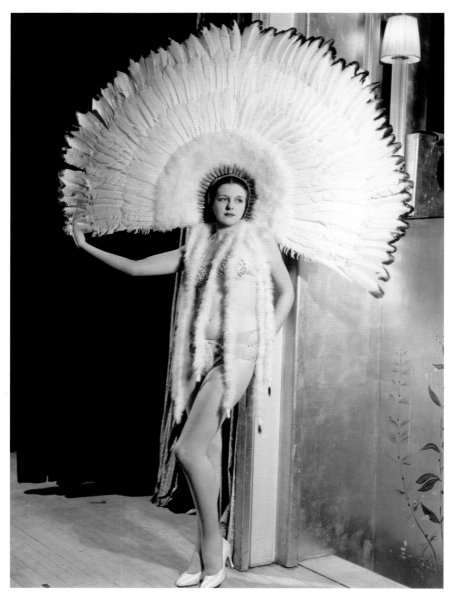

Top notch, in a vast feather head-dress, worn with a little bit of a sequined bikini.
1936 A performer in *Midnight Vanities* at the Grosvenor House, London.

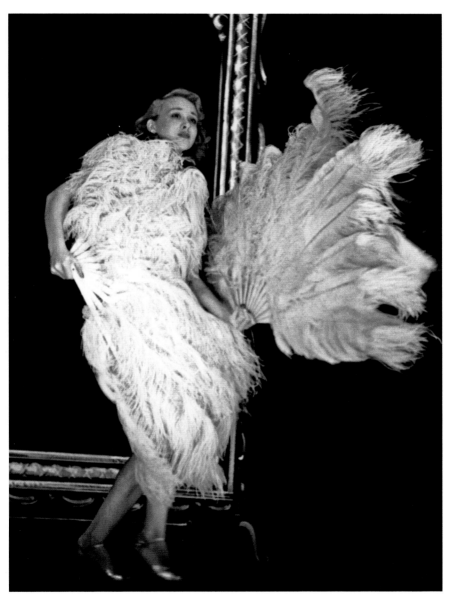

Fashionable with fans, ostrich feathers covering a multitude of sumptuous sins.
1953   A chorus girl in *Revue de Ville* at the Windmill Theatre, London.

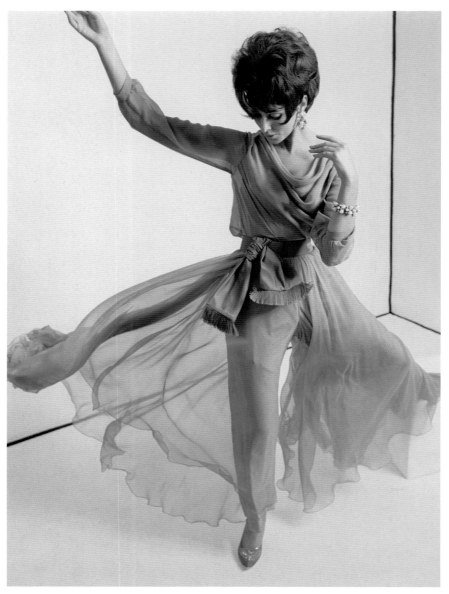

Wafting around, a chiffon tunic with a cowl neck over slim, silk trousers.
1963 A model poses in a gauzy outfit with a sash, in a photograph for *Vogue*.

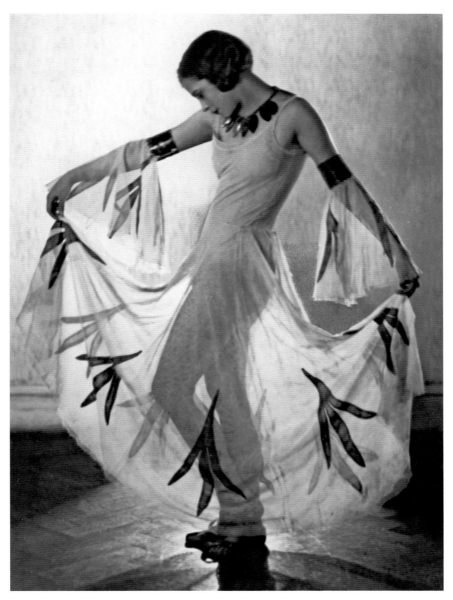

Diaphanous dressing, sheer white tulle with a leaf print, and slave bracelets.
1929 American singer/dancer, Bunty Pain, one of Cecil B. Cochran's chorus girls.

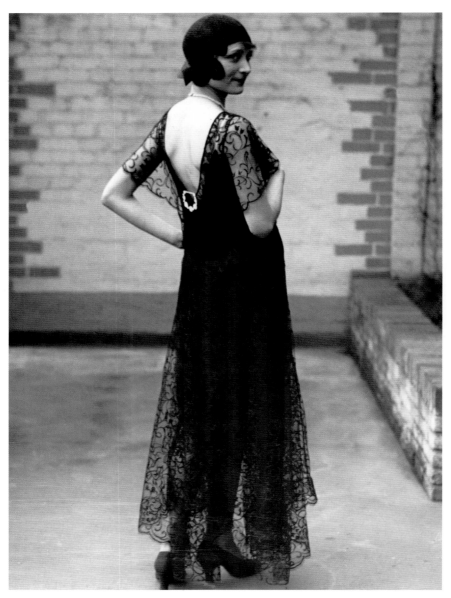

Backwards looks, a long evening dress with a diamanté brooch and a cloche hat. 1930   A fashionable creation from Paris, in black tulle with a cape of black lace.

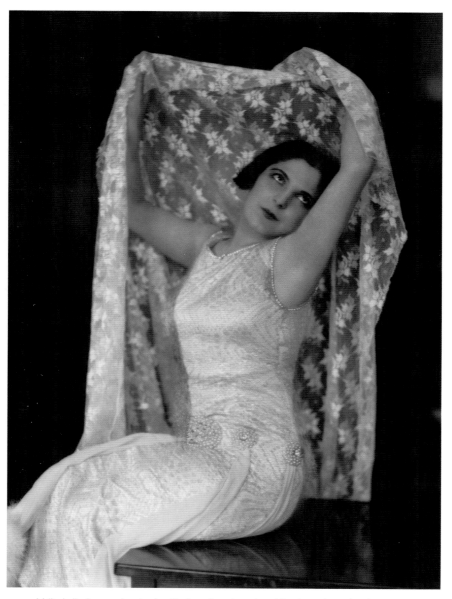

Veiled allusions, a simple sheath dress in pale satin, with a large lace shawl.
1925 Russian dancer and singer, Lola Krasavina, wearing a figured-silk gown.

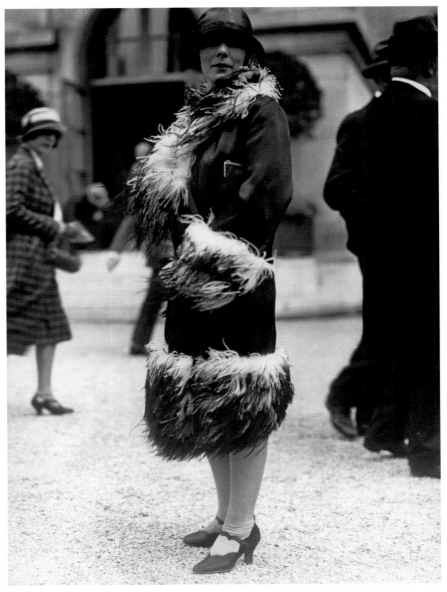

Feminine and fluffy, flapper style with a matching cloche hat and scalloped shoes.
1926 A lady in a black satin coat trimmed with ostrich feathers, by Betty of Paris.

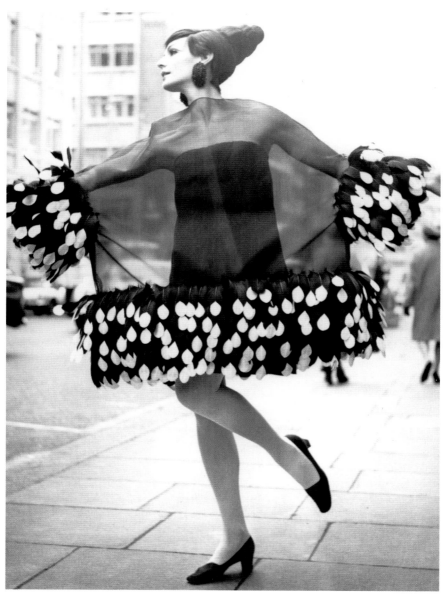

Short shift, a strapless dress with an organza pancho, trimmed with feathers.
1967 A model in a cocktail dress from the Christian Dior London collection.

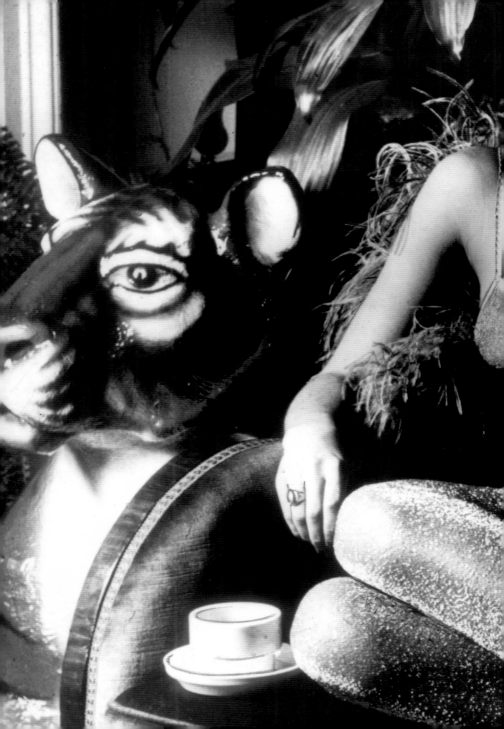

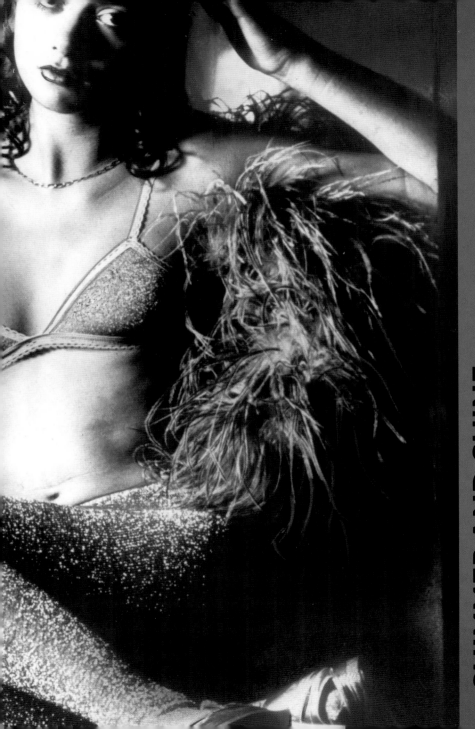

SHIMMER AND SHINE

358

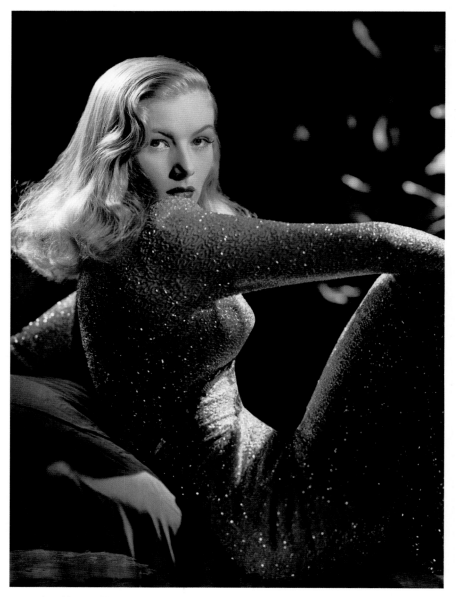

A golden goddess, in a glittering gown, bias-cut to cling to the body.
1941   American actress, Veronica Lake, as Sally Vaughn in *I Wanted Wings*.

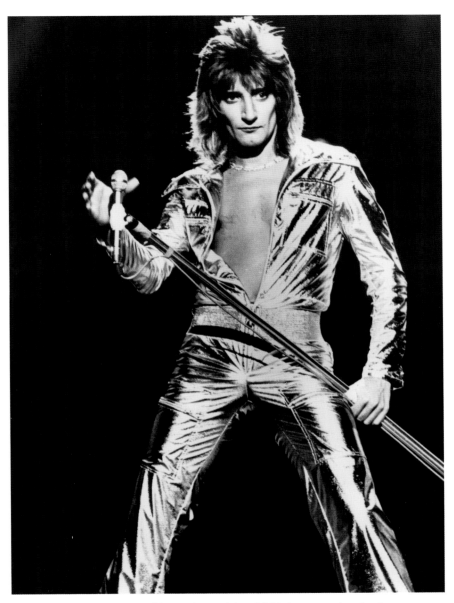

Spectacular in silver, an all-in-one jumpsuit in a foil fabric, very rock and roll.
1976   Scottish singer, Rod Stewart, on television in *A Night On The Town*.

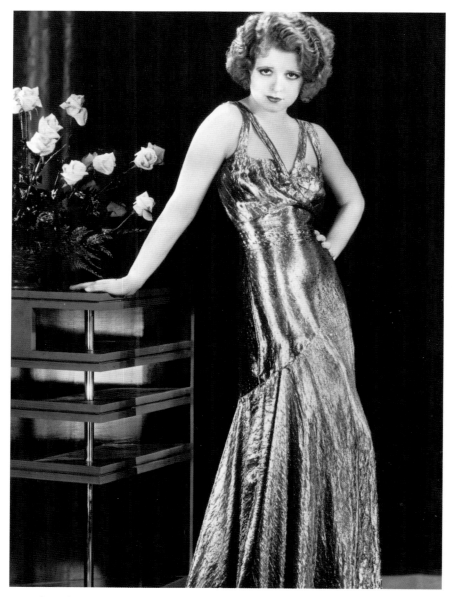

Sexy siren, shimmering in a figure-hugging, silver lamé dress with a fishtail skirt.
1931   American silent screen star and flapper, Clara Bow, in the film *No Limit.*

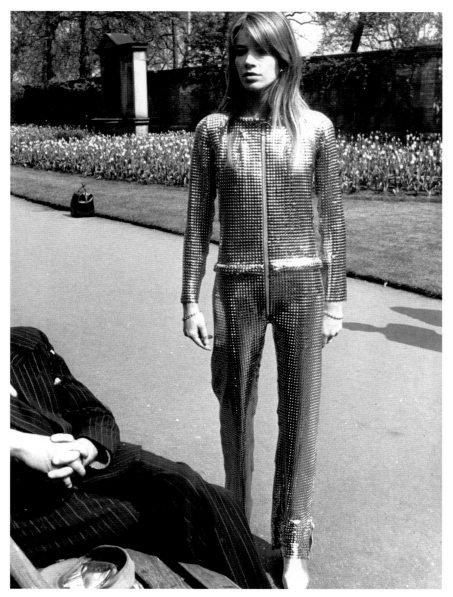

A chain-mail cat suit, reminiscent of Lancelot in *The Knights of the Round Table*.
1968   French singer, Françoise Hardy, at the Embankment Gardens, London.

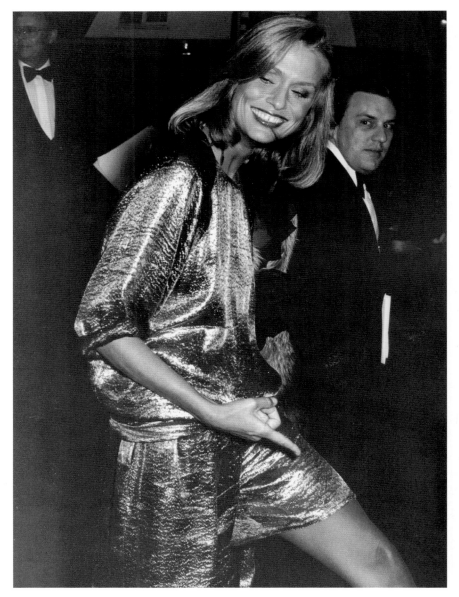

Glittering prizes, in a gold lamé mini dress and jacket, worn with a gorgeous grin.
1980   American model and actress, Lauren Hutton, at the 52nd Academy Awards.

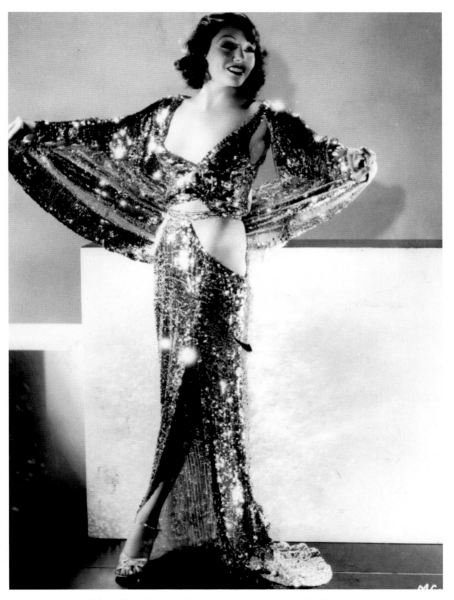

In the spotlight, with a plunging, silver lamé gown, scattered with sequins.
1931   Mexican dancer and actress, Lupe Vélez, wife of actor Johnny Weissmuller.

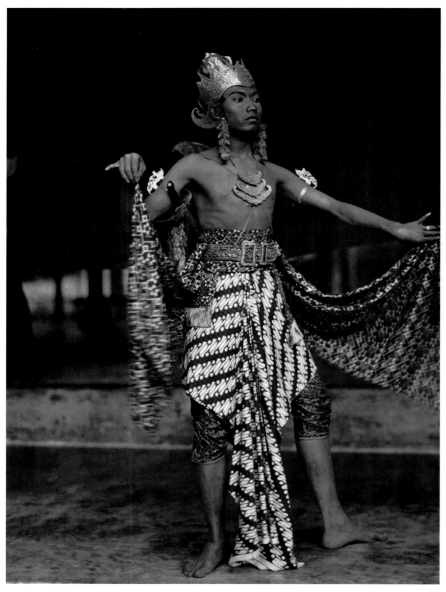

Woven wonders, a costume in batik and cloth of gold, with a silver head-dress.
1930   A Javanese dancer in traditional dress, jangling with jewellery.

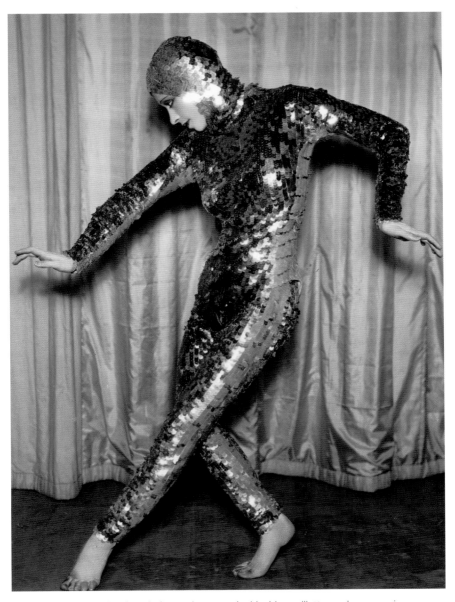

Snake shapes, in a hooded cat suit, covered with shiny paillettes or huge sequins.
1931   Eve, a contortionist, in *The Revue Show* appearing at the London Pavilion.

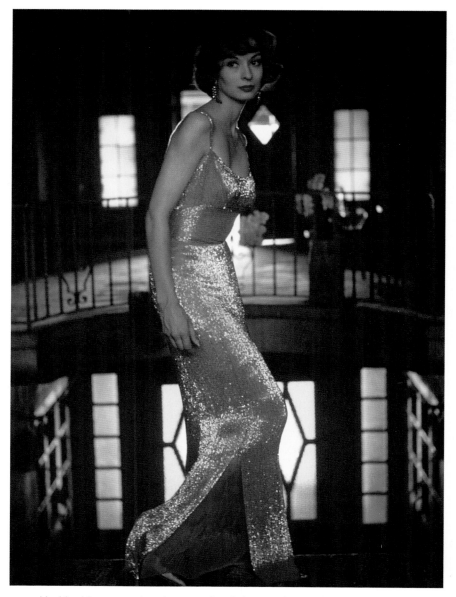

Liquid gold, gorgeous in a glamorous, beaded gown, glittering from head to toe.
1959 A model in a sheath dress by the American costume designer, Helen Rose.

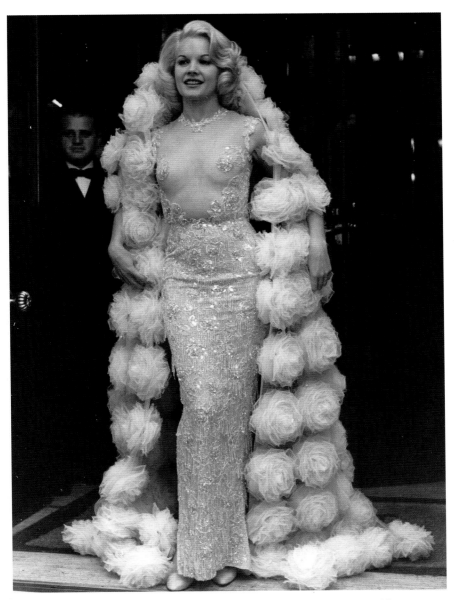

Sheer luxury, in an ankle-length, transparent gown, and swathed in acres of fur.
1964 American actress, Carroll Baker, in London, dressed by Balmain, Paris.

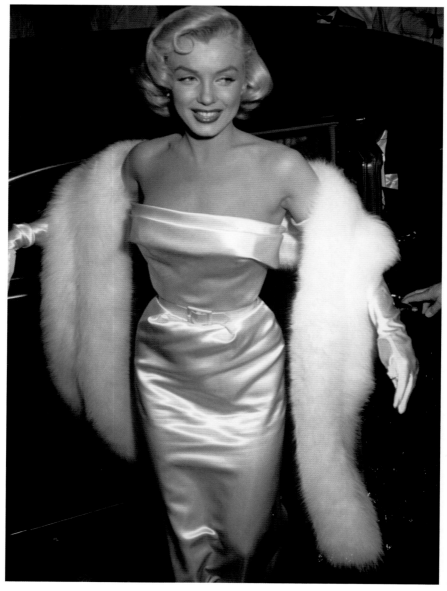

Starring in satin, a strapless dress, with a mink shawl and gloves, all in white.
1954 Marilyn Monroe at the opening of *There's No Business Like Show Business*.

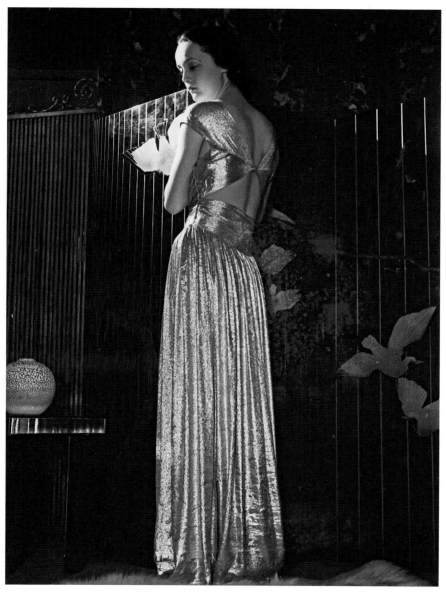

Night lights, a full-skirted, long dress with a bare back, excellent for exits.
1935 A model in an evening gown by French designer, Jeanne Lanvin, Paris.

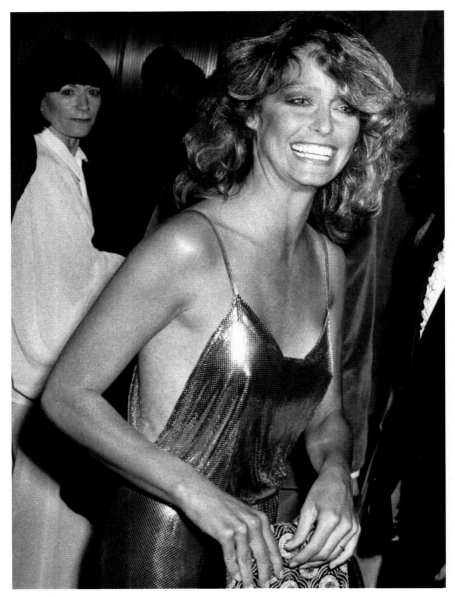

Charlie's angel, a very minimal chain-mail dress with shoe-string straps.
1978   American actress, Farrah Fawcett-Majors, at the 50th Academy Awards.

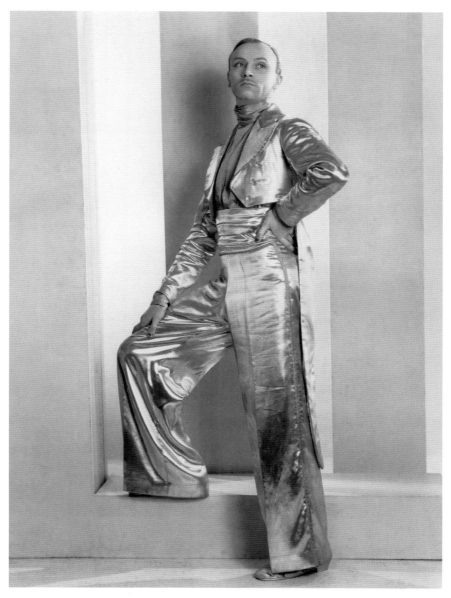

Dancing king, in a bum-freezer jacket and baggy trousers, lovely in Lurex.
1932   A man in a shiny suit with a cummerbund; his hair is styled by Antoine.

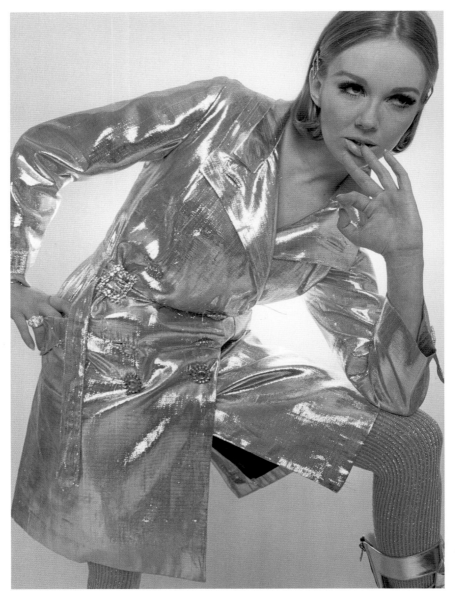

Pretty in PVC, a silver trench worn with matching boots and thick ribbed tights.
1965   A model wearing a belted coat in a photograph for *Queen* magazine.

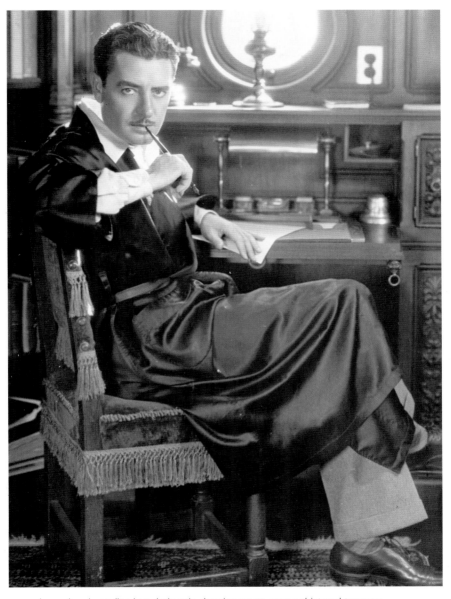

Lover boy, brooding in a dark satin dressing gown, over a shirt and trousers.
1930   American silent star, John Gilbert, ponders with a pen at his writing desk.

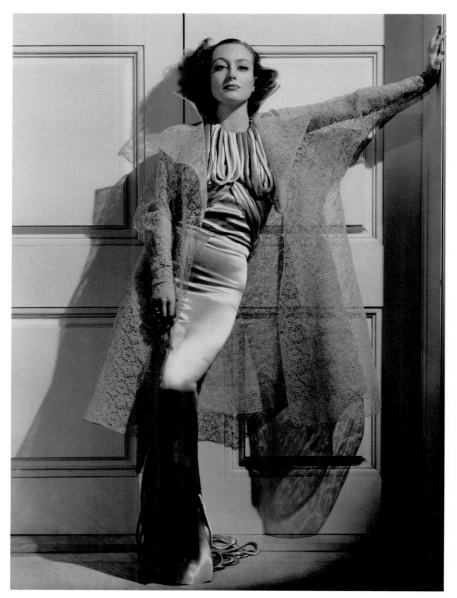

Glamorous in a gown, with a draped bodice and sheath shirt, with a lace coat.
1935 American actress, Joan Crawford, in costume for *Forsaking All Others*.

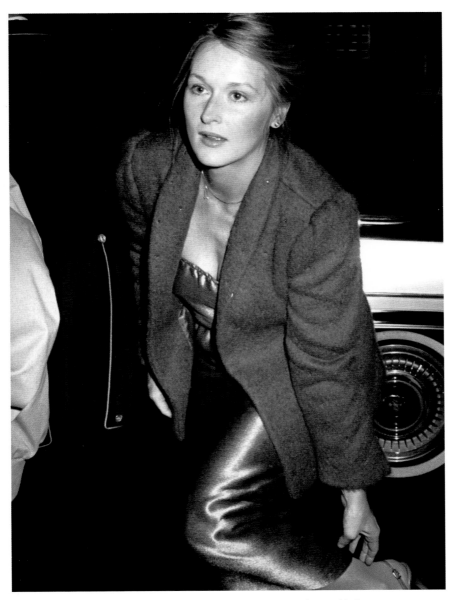

Man/woman mix, in a strapless satin dress under a tailored tweed jacket.
1979   American actress, Meryl Streep, at Woody Allen's New Year's Eve party.

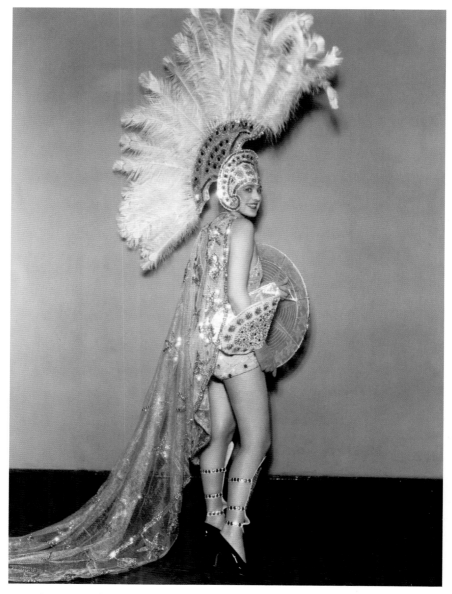

A gorgeous gladiator, with a huge feathered head-dress and a shield.
1930 A chorus girl in the musical *Evergreen* at the Adelphi Theatre, London.

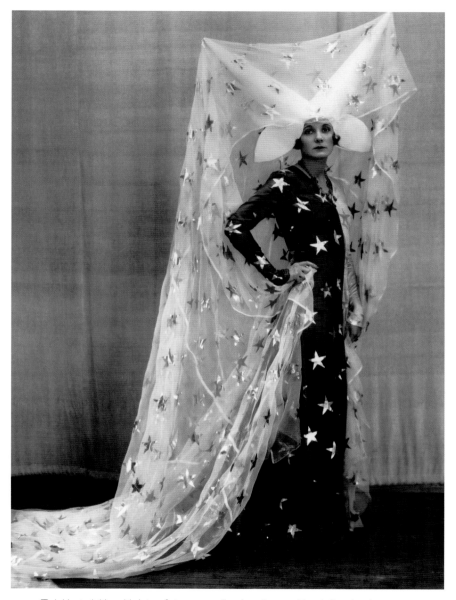

Twinkle, twinkle with lots of stars, a medieval costume with a tulle wimple.
1929 Lady Castlerosse dressed for the Galaxy Ball, at London's Park Lane Hotel.

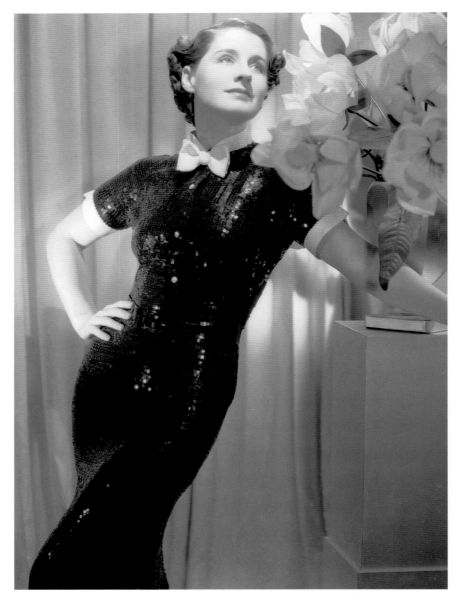

Black magic, a tight sheath dress with a little white bow tie, dressed for night.
1934   Canadian actress, Norma Shearer, wearing a shimmering sequined gown.

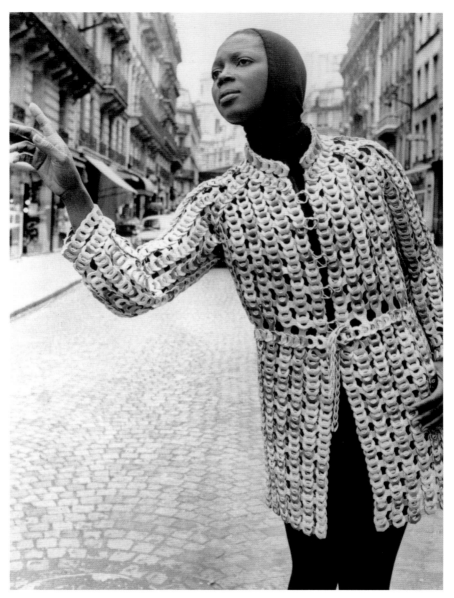

Chain-mail reaction, a woven leather coat, worn over a black hooded bodysuit.
1973   An outfit by Paco Rabanne for his Autumn/Winter collections held in Paris.

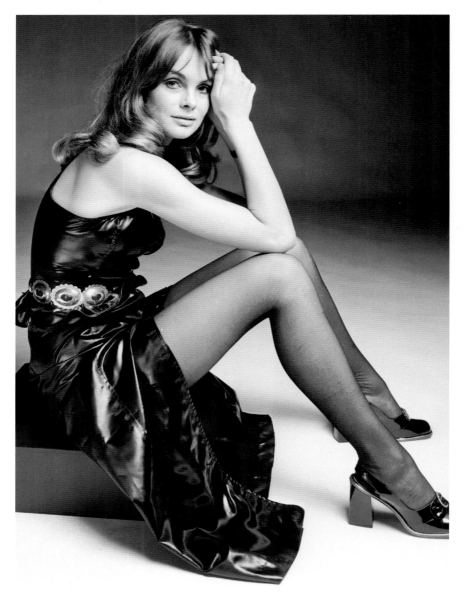

Shine on, in a black dress slashed to the thigh with a Mexican silver belt.
1973   British model, Jean Shrimpton, in a PVC dress and matching shoes.

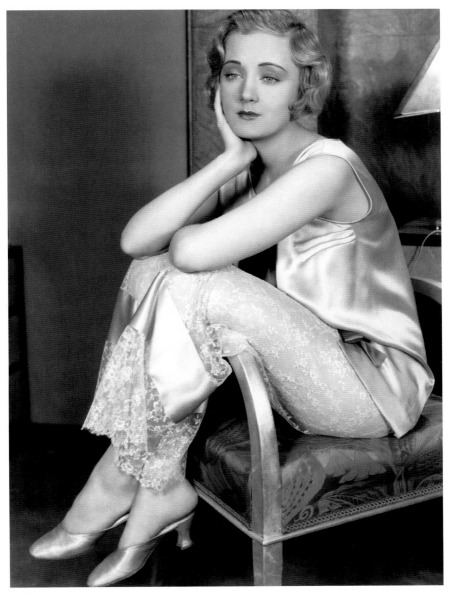

Silent night, in a satin top over lace and satin pyjamas, with little slippers.
1930   American actress, Josephine Dunn, in the film *Safety In Numbers*.

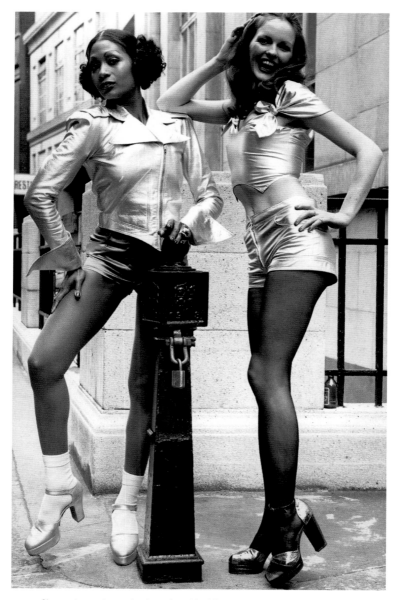

Short shorts, in synthetic satin with tight tops and platform, ankle-strap shoes.
1972 Students at the Kingston Polytechnic School of Fashion show in London.

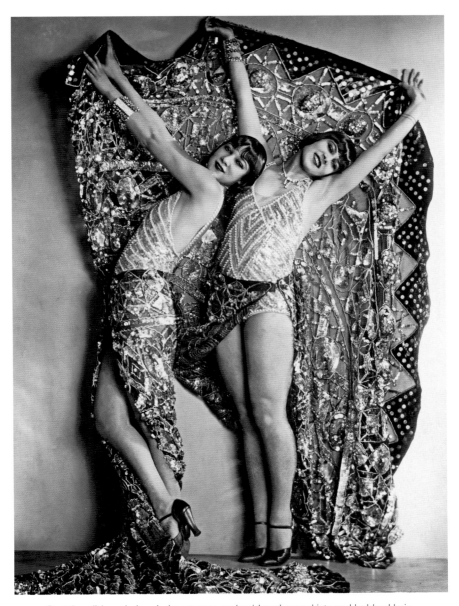

Curtain call, bare in beaded costumes, embroidered over-skirts and bobbed hair.
1929 Chorus girls in a revue at the Stadttheater, Vienna, Austria.

394

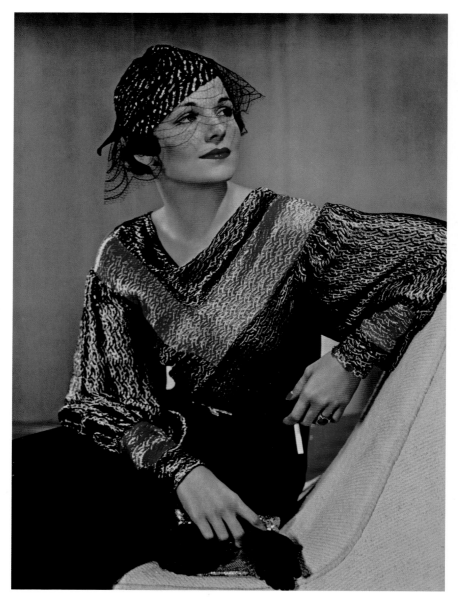

Cigarette break, a patterned silk blouse with batwing sleeves, and a pencil skirt.
1936 A woman in an advertising campaign for *Lucky Strike*.

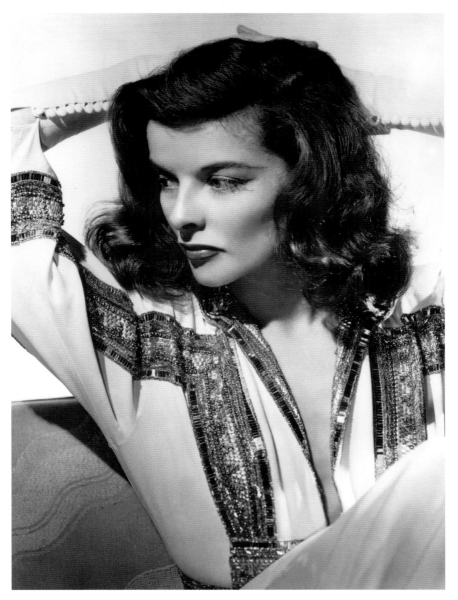

A Grecian goddess, a peasant shirt with bands of bright embroidery.
1935 American actress, Katharine Hepburn, with her arms behind her head.

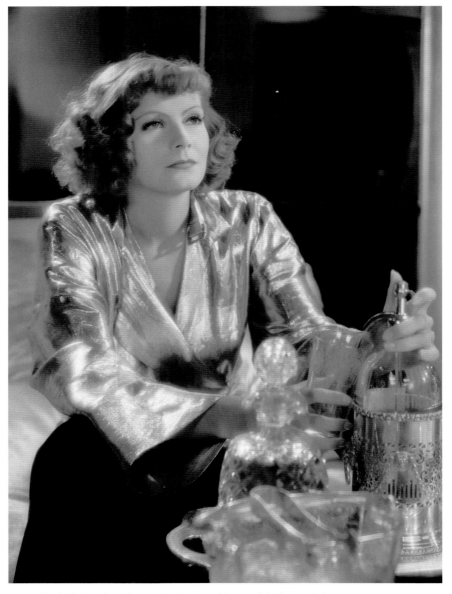

Cocktail time, in a silver wrap blouse, with a trayful of crystal decanters.
1931   Swedish-born actress, Greta Garbo, in a scene from *The Rise of Helga*.

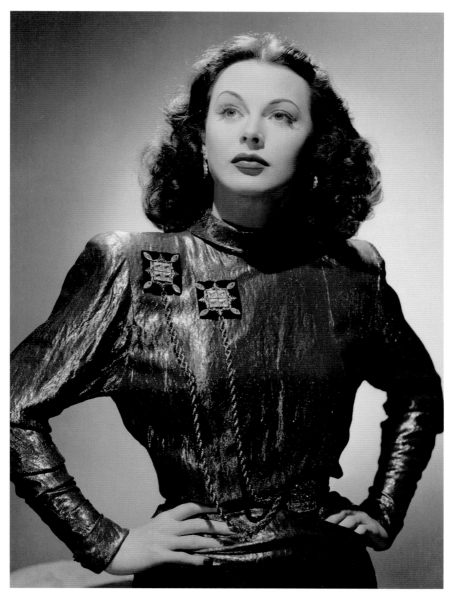

Black magic, in a dark polo-neck blouse with square shoulders, and a gold chain. 1944 Austrian-born actress, Hedy Lamarr, as Irene in *The Conspirators*.

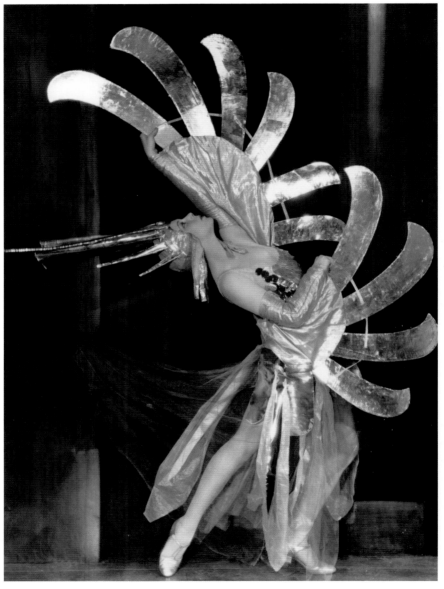

High profile, dancing in a curious costume with fin sleeves and a silver crown.
1929 Austrian-born dancer, Tilly Losch, Countess of Carnarvon, in performance.

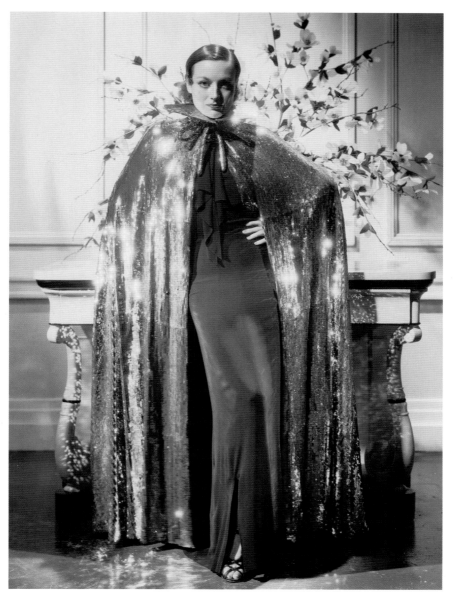

Caped crusader, in an ankle-length, collared cape over a dark sheath dress.
1934   American actress, Joan Crawford, in costume for the film *Sadie McKee*.

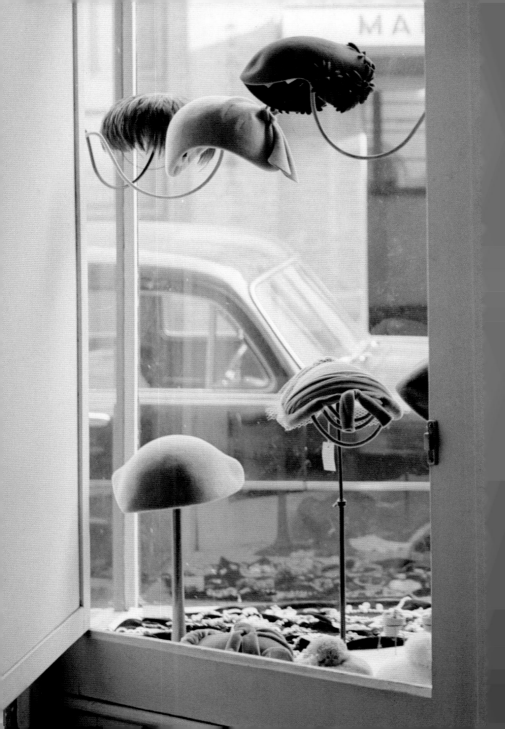

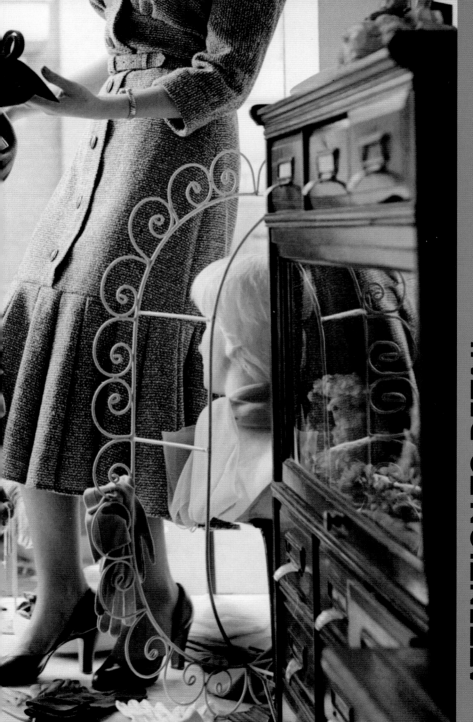

ATTENTION TO DETAIL

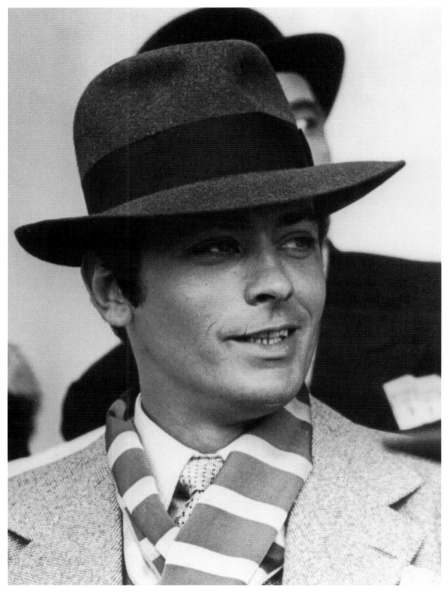

Gangster geek, in a fine fedora, a classic coat and a striped scarf.
1969   French actor, Alain Delon, on the set of *Borsalino*, Marseilles, France.

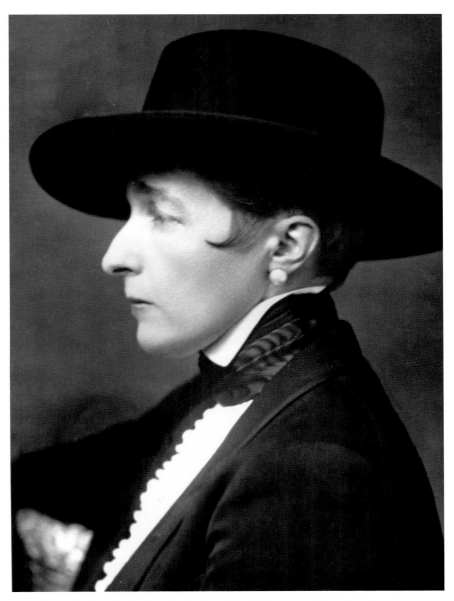

A profile of lesbian looks, a black trilby, a frilled shirt worn with pearl earrings.
1928 British novelist, Marguerite Radclyffe Hall, author of *The Well of Loneliness*.

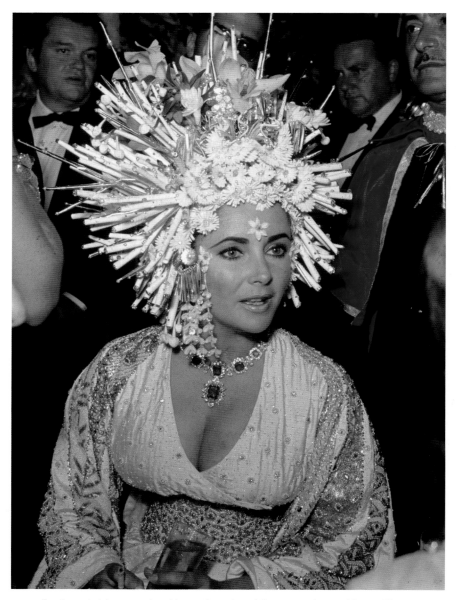

Exotic and elaborate, a headdress of pearls and flowers, and a sapphire necklace. 1967 Movie star, Elizabeth Taylor, decked out for a social function.

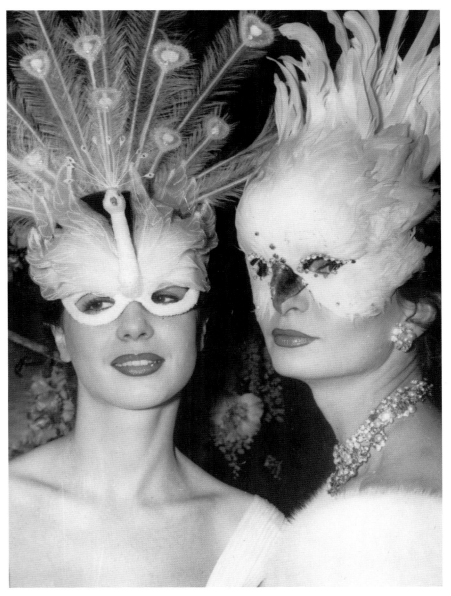

Birds of paradise, carnival masks with peacock and cockerel feathers.
1956   Parisian ladies bedecked by the French beauty specialist, Fernand Aubry.

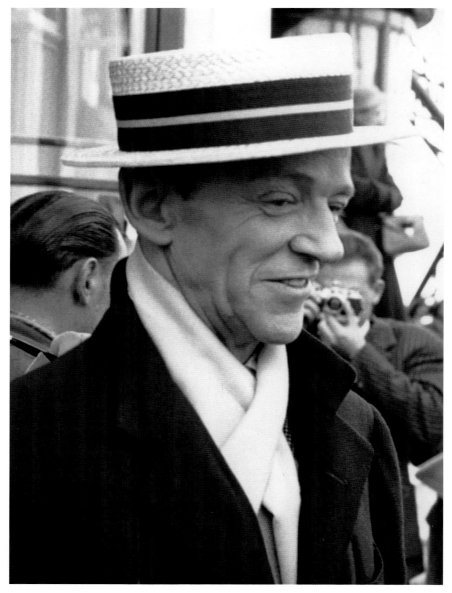

Tripping the light fantastic, in a boater, classy coat and a white scarf.
1956 American actor, Fred Astaire, in Paris filming the musical *Funny Face*.

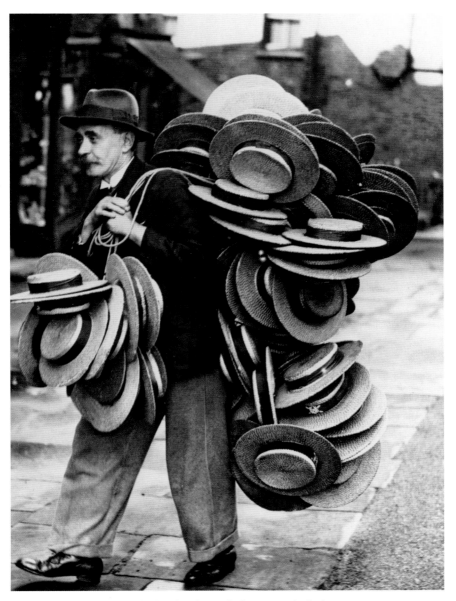

Boys will be boys, bashed-up hats in need of some tender loving care.
1930 A man with a bundle of boaters due for renovation, Harrow School, England.

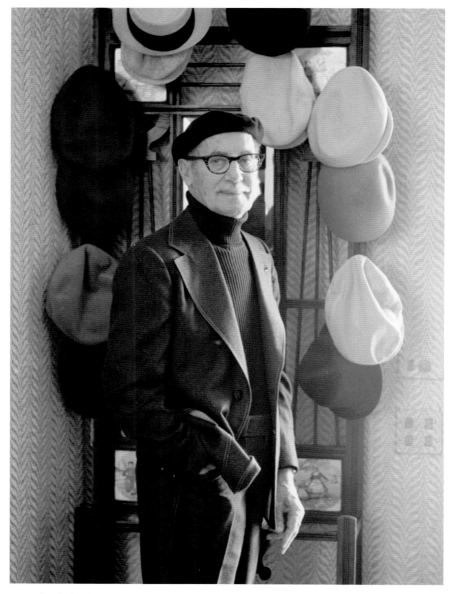

Spoilt for choice, what shall I wear, a beret, a cap, a rain hat or a trilby?
1970   Comic actor, Groucho Marx, at his home in Beverly Hills, California, USA.

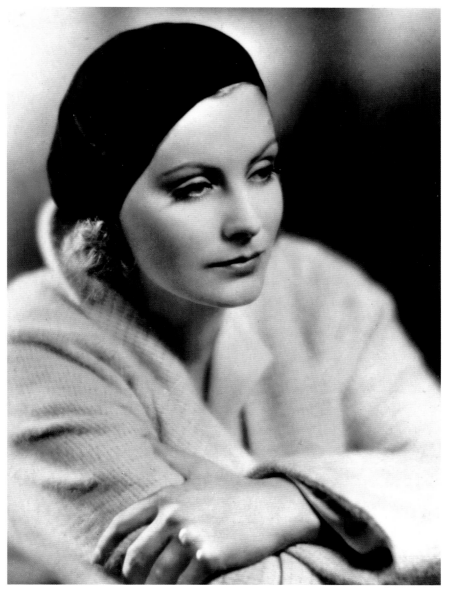

Mata Hari, mysterious in a black beret and a white mohair coat.
1930 Swedish-born actress, Greta Garbo, went from silent to spoken roles.

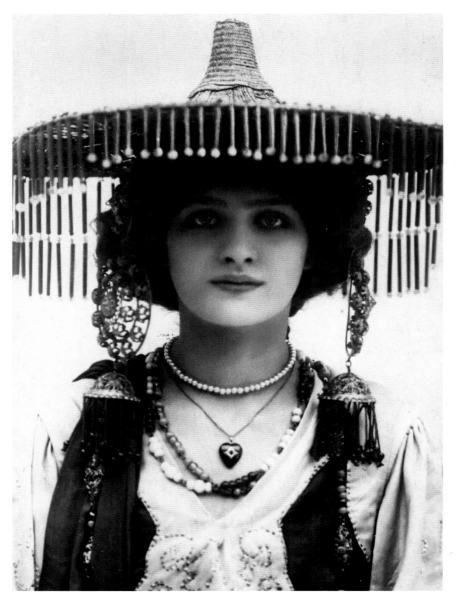

Passion in a pagoda, with a bamboo coolie hat, waistcoat and strings of beads.
1901   Actress, Lily Elsie, from the hit musical *Chinese Honeymoon* in London.

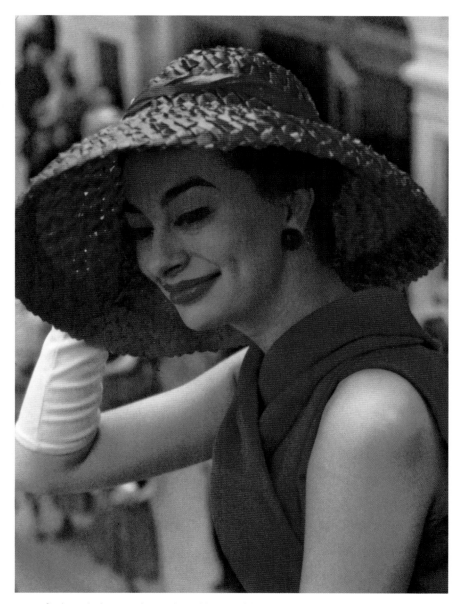

Soviet style, in a coral straw hat with a matching wrap dress and ladylike gloves.
1959 A Christian Dior model from France at the GUM department store, Moscow.

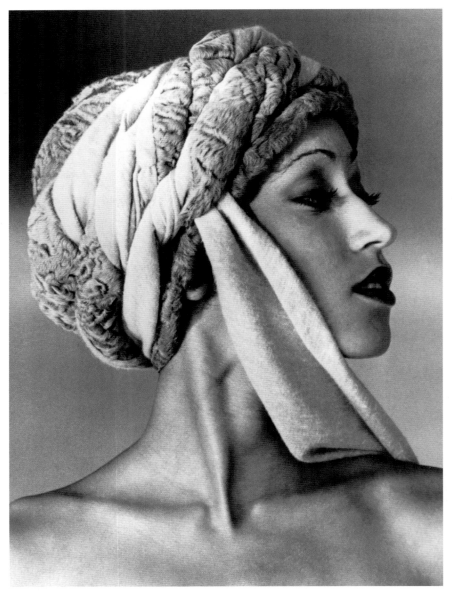

Wrapped and rolled, twisted fabric headgear, inspired by *Lawrence of Arabia*.
1975 A turban made from astrakhan and jersey by French milliner, Jean Barthet.

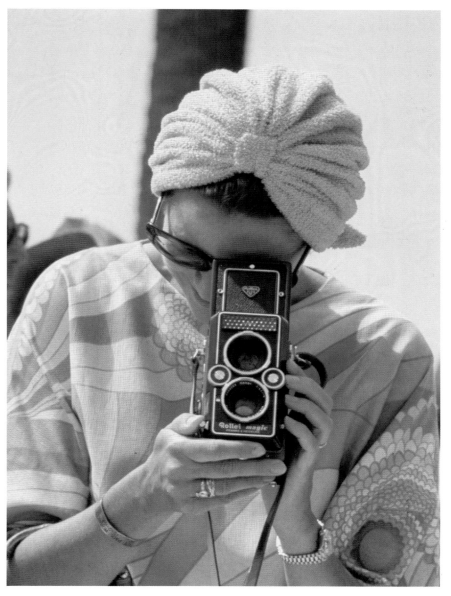

Royal and relaxed, in a peach towelling turban and a Pucci print dress.
1972   Princess Grace of Monaco at the Palm Beach Club, Monte Carlo.

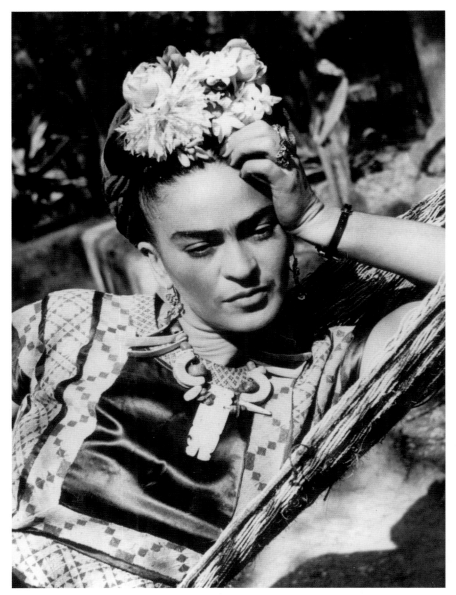

Portrait painter, in a bright print dress, an ethnic bone necklace and a turban.
1950 Mexican artist, Frieda Kahlo, wearing a folk costume and flowers in her hair.

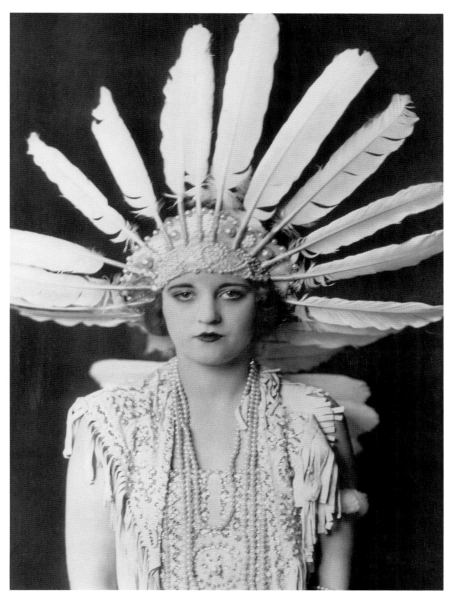

Sioux chic, in pearls and feathers, with a fringed, embroidered costume.
1925 American actress, Tallulah Bankhead, wearing a huge headdress and beads.

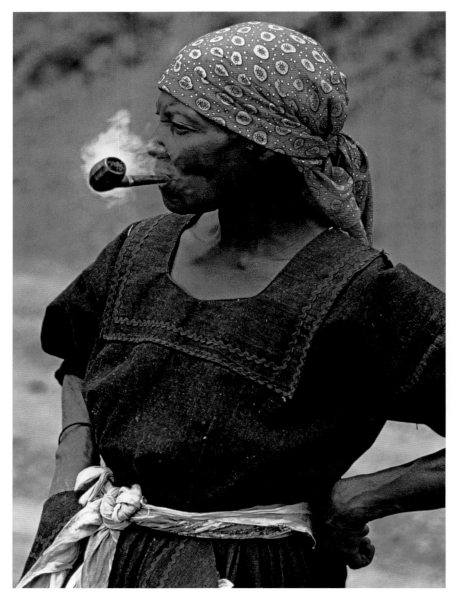

Hip in Haiti, a denim dress with rickrack trim and an orange print scarf.
1961   Hand on hip, an old woman takes a long drag on her smoky pipe, Haiti.

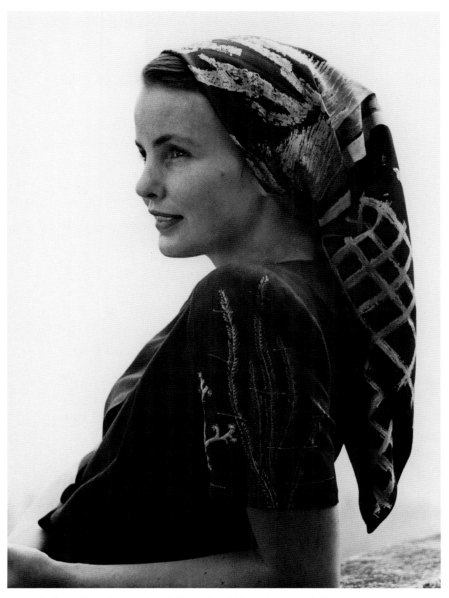

Perfect prints, a large, printed silk scarf, stylishly tied peasant fashion.
1947   A headscarf by Aschers, London, specializing in fabrics designed by artists.

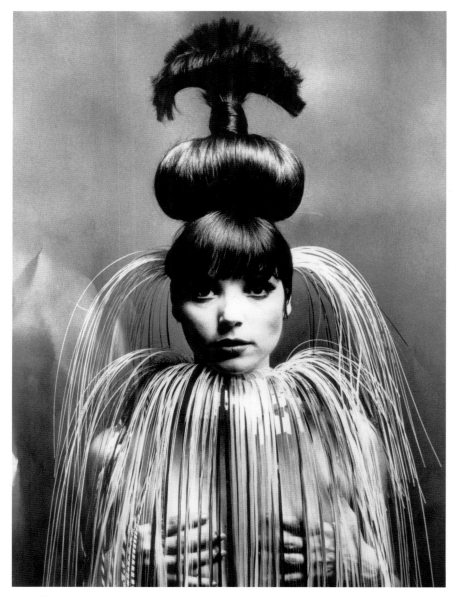

Fountain of fashion, a large bun spouting blond tresses, and a matching necklace.
1966 Italian model and actress, Elsa Martinelli, with her hair in a giant topknot.

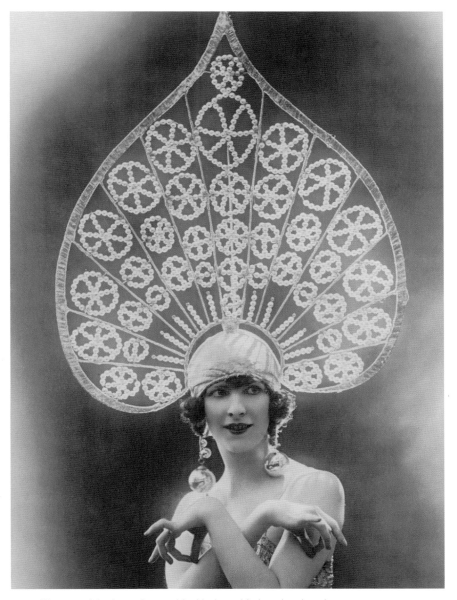

The ace of shades, a chorus girl with that added card up her sleeve.
1925 A dancer in a large pearl-encrusted headdress in the shape of a spade.

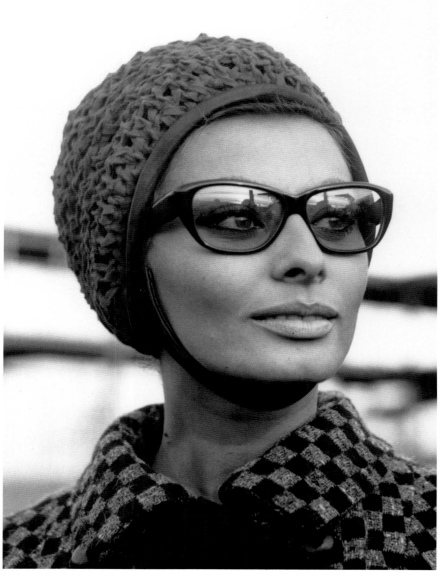

Starring in spectacles, with a crocheted helmet and a checkerboard coat.
1965   Italian film actress, Sophia Loren, at London Airport.

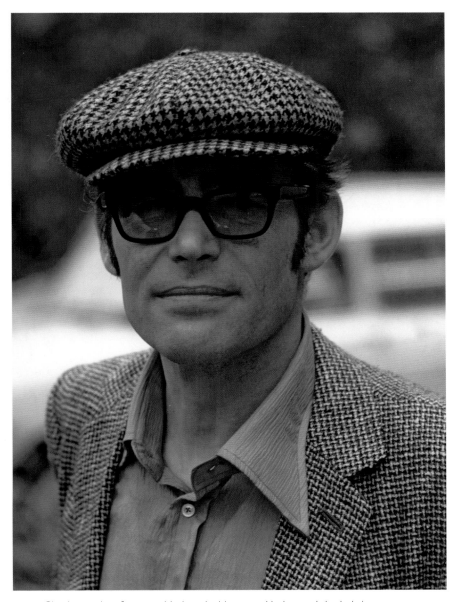

Checkmate, in a flat cap, a black and white tweed jacket, and shaded glasses.
1967 Irish actor, Peter O'Toole, in Bermuda.

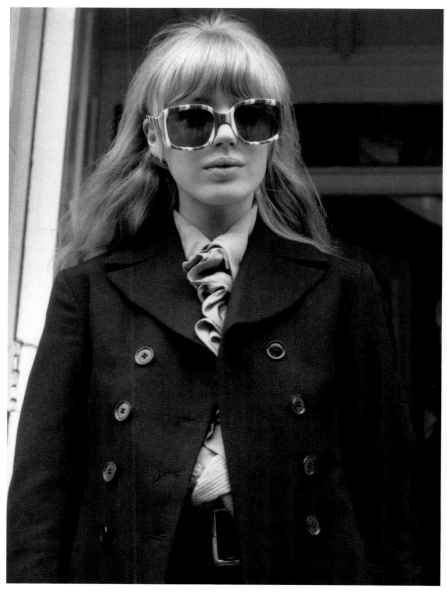

Pop princess, in big goggle glasses, a reefer jacket and a frilly shirt.
1967 Actress and singer, Marianne Faithfull, outside Chichester Court, England.

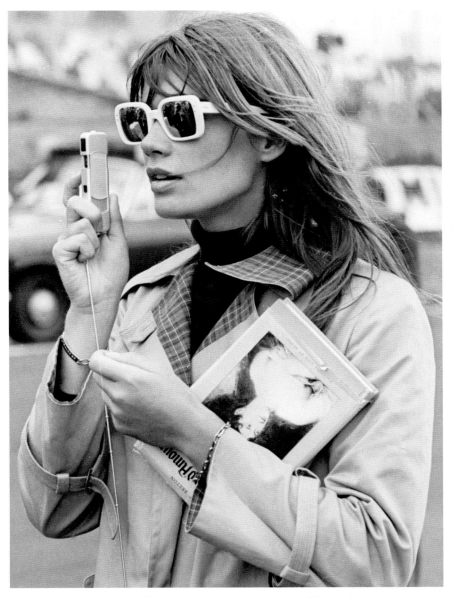

Make tracks, in a reversible trench coat and large, square white sunglasses.
1966   French actress, Françoise Hardy, in *Grand Prix*, Brands Hatch, England.

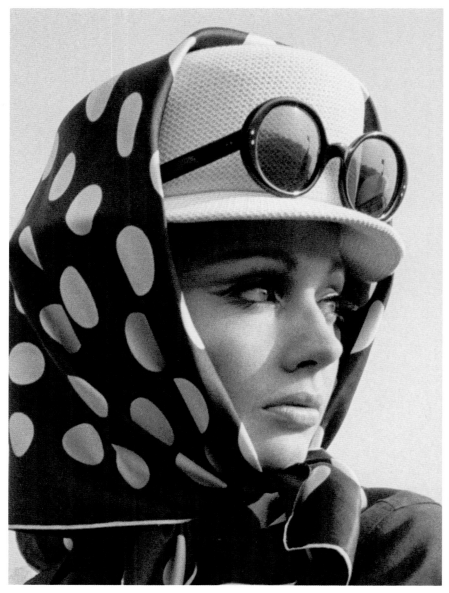

Sporty in spots, dressed for a drive in a bowler hat, scarf and round sunglasses.
1965   A young woman with her chauffeur in an E-Type Jaguar sports car (stage left).

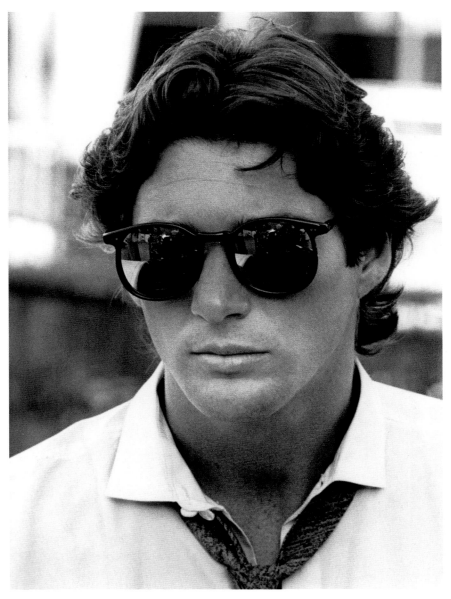

Just a gigolo, cool looks in a white shirt, loosened tie, a star in shades.
1979   American actor, Richard Gere, at the Hollywood Foreign Press Club, USA.

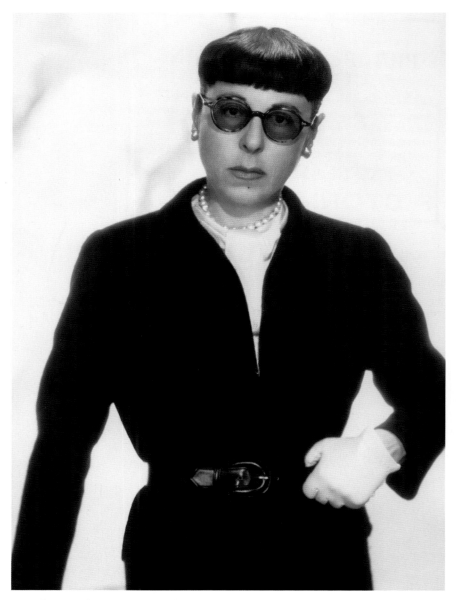

Strong style, a severe, square haircut, round glasses, pearls and white gloves.
1955 American costume designer, Edith Head, wardrobe mistress at Paramount.

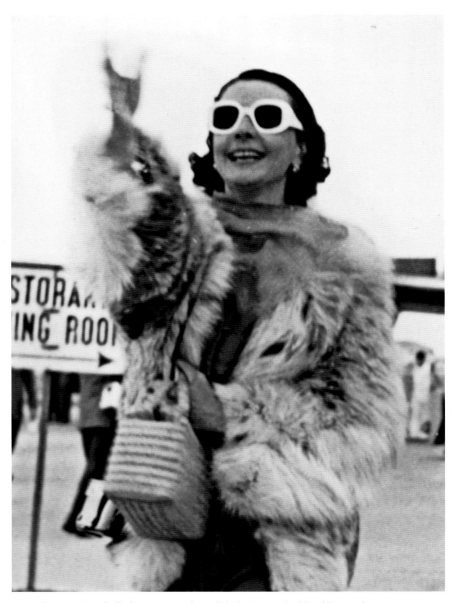

Star quality, a fluffy fur coat, carrying a little basket, and with white sunglasses.
1953   British actress, Vivien Leigh, arriving at Rome airport.

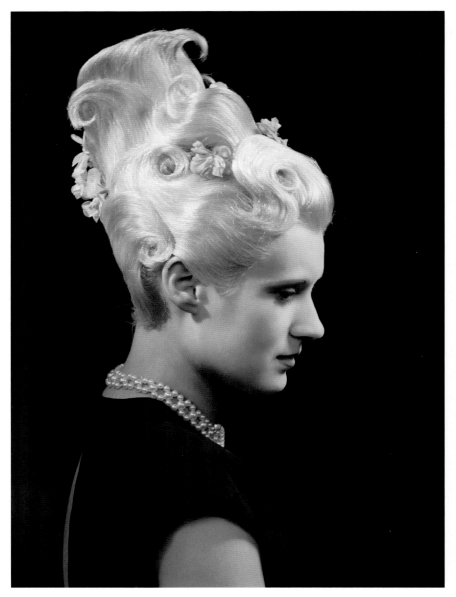

Curious curls, Empire-inspired coiffure in platinum blonde decorated with flowers.
1950   Socialite, Beryl Hardesty, wearing a magnificent creation of lacquered hair.

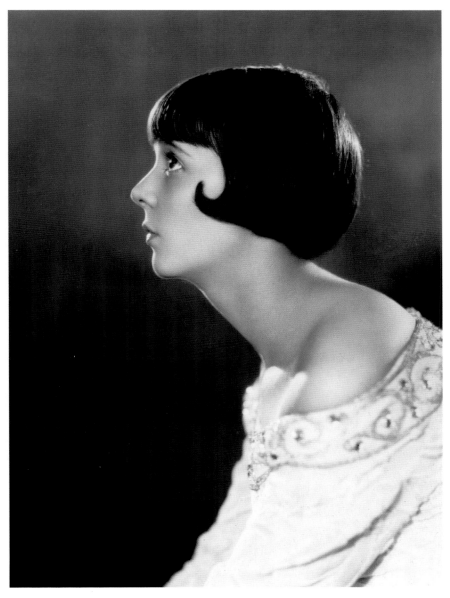

Perfect profile, a fine black bob, with a square fringe and kiss curls.
1926   British actress, Jessie Matthews, at the Prince of Wales Theatre, London.

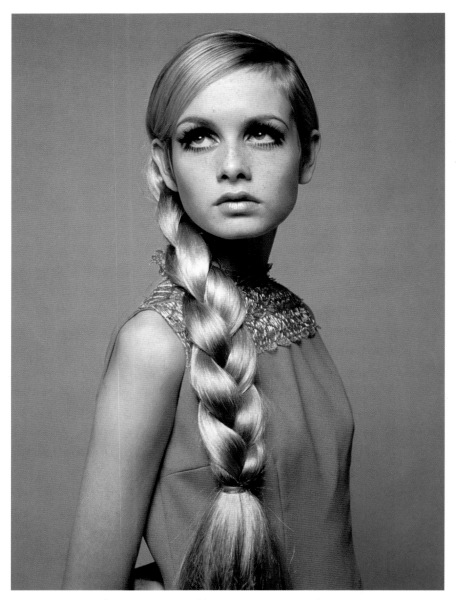

Plaited to perfection, a blond, pigtail hairpiece attached to a short, sharp haircut.
1966 British model, Twiggy, in a coral pink dress, edged with gold embroidery.

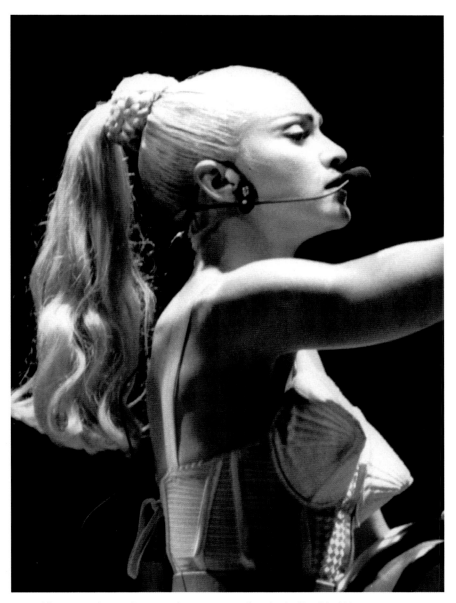

Like an angel, sexy chanteuse in costume, performing in *Blond Ambition.*
1990   American singer, Madonna, in a Jean-Paul Gaultier bullet-bra corset.

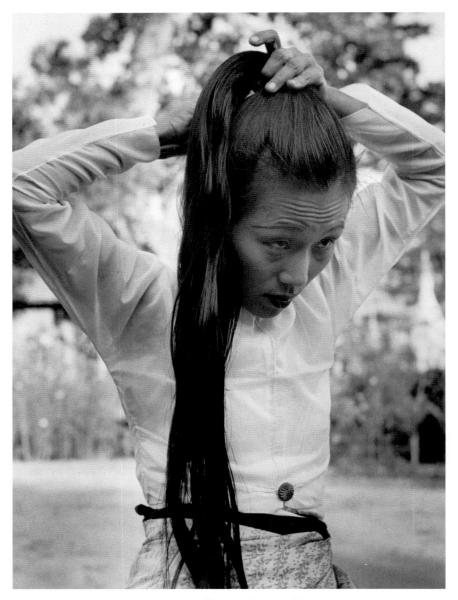

Long and lean, tying a bun on top of her head, in a traditional sarong kebaya.
1949   A young Burmese girl styling her hair, using coconut oil.

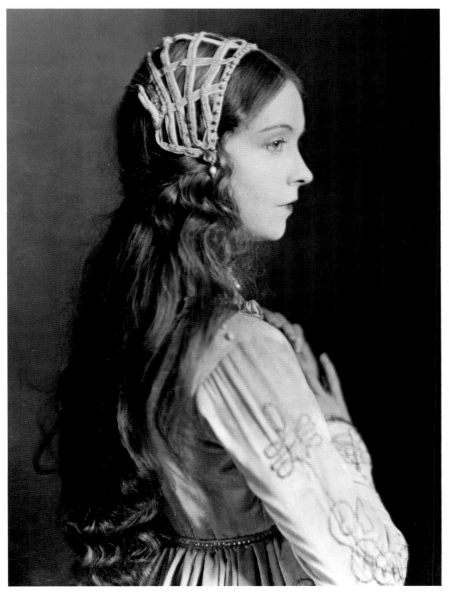

Costume drama, in a medieval, crewel-embroidered costume with a pearl cap. 1915 American actress, Lillian Gish, wears a high-waisted dress and a skullcap.

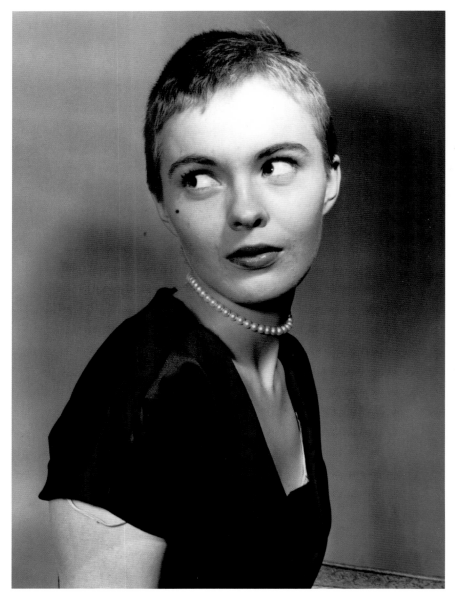

Gamine and gorgeous, with short feather-cut hair, pearls and a little black dress. 1957 American actress, Jean Seberg, at the time of her film debut in *Saint Joan*.

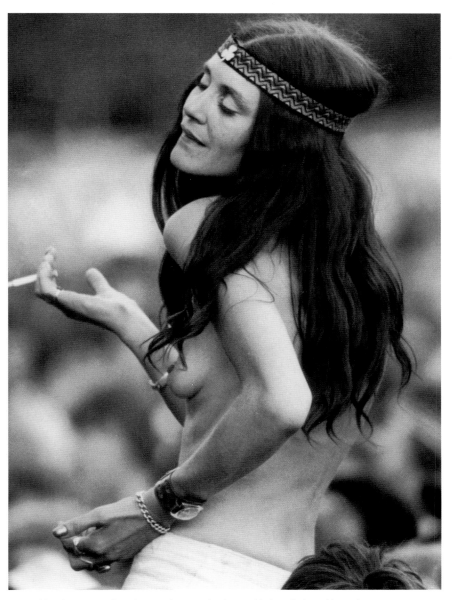

Hanging out and getting on down, quite bare with long hair and bracelets.
1979   A hippy enjoying the atmosphere at Knebworth Rock Festival, England.

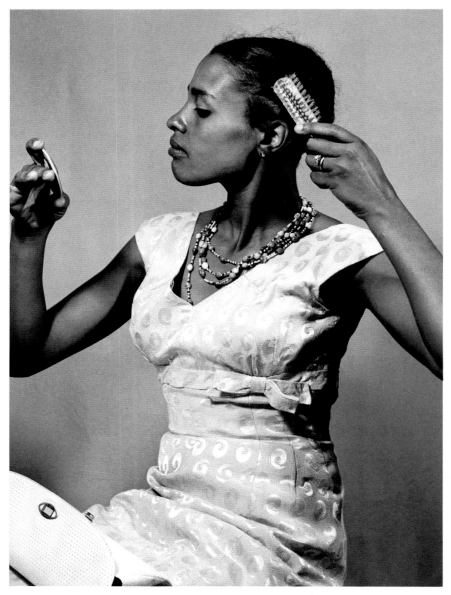

Black beauty, in a V-neck, printed frock with a high waist, and cropped hair.
1955 *Drum* magazine cover girl, Priscilla Mtimkulu, brushing her hair.

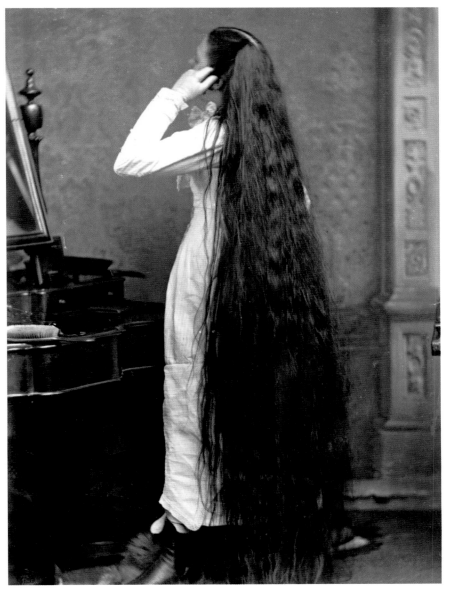

Rapunzel, Rapunzel, with her very long hair touching the ground.
1890 Miss Milo in front of a dressing table, preparing for bed in her white nightie.

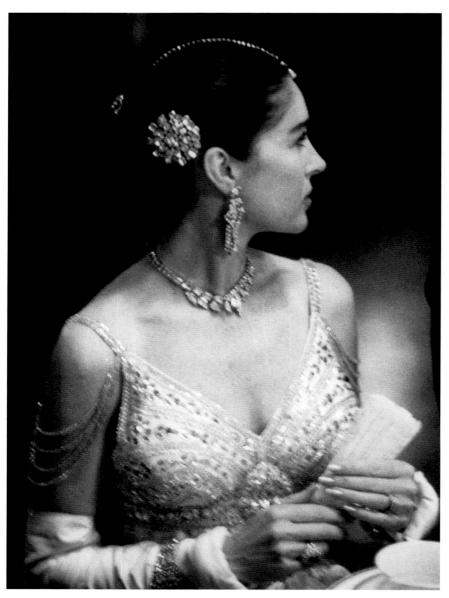

Bejewelled and bewitching, in a beaded dress with hair clips and long earrings.
1956   A guest at a New Year's Eve party in Hollywood, Los Angeles, USA.

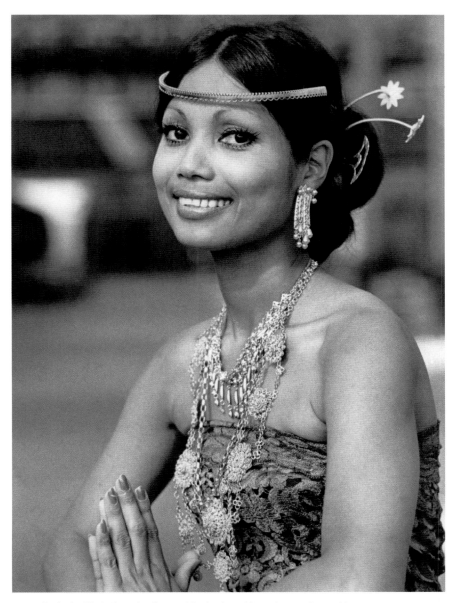

Bedecked in Indonesian finery, dripping in gold earrings and a necklace.
1972 Asian glamour, Patsy Pany, wearing a batik sarong and loads of jewellery.

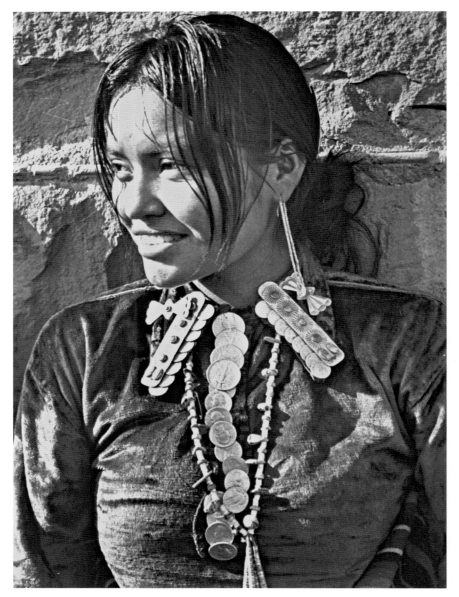

Silver mine, handcrafted collar caps and necklace of coins strung like a tie.
1948   A beautiful young Navajo Indian woman standing outside a reservation.

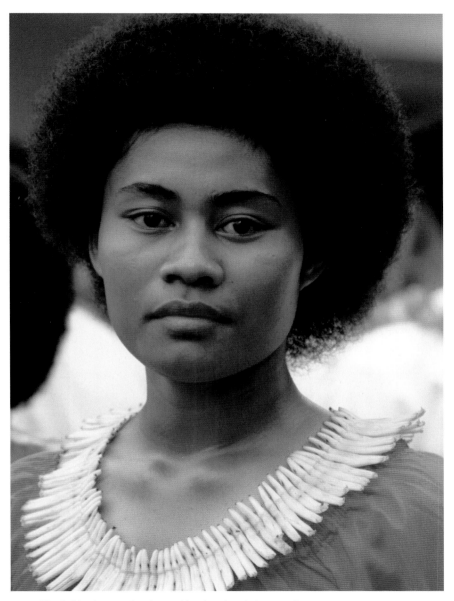

Tooth fairy, in a scarlet dress with a handmade bone collar.
1982   A young girl wearing a whale-tooth necklace in Fiji, South Pacific.

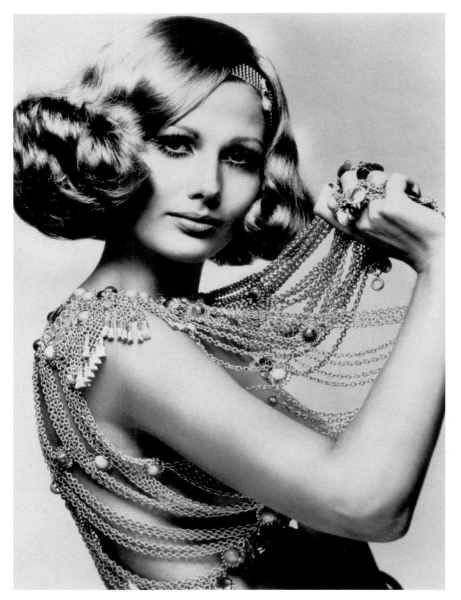

Charm in chains, dare to be bare in this Seventies metal-decorated "blouse".
1975   A young woman modelling a beaded jewellery top.

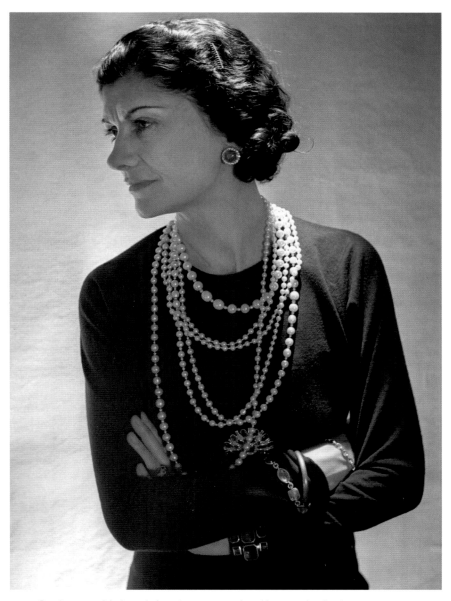

Pearly queen, Madame in her signature pearl necklaces and a simple sweater.
1936   Coco Chanel, French couturière, Paris, in bangles and beads.

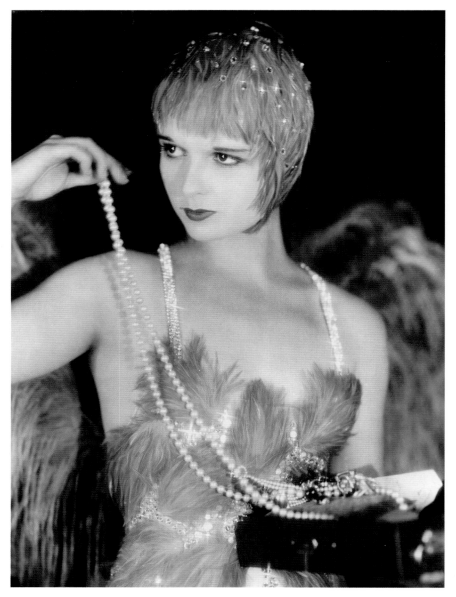

Blackmailing beauty, in a feathered wig and dress, with diamanté and pearls.
1929 American actress, Louise Brooks, in costume for *The Canary Murder Case*.

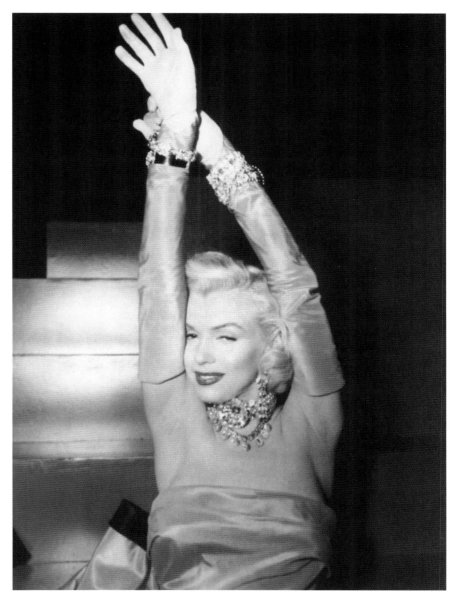

Terrific in terracotta, a satin and silk strapless dress, with diamonds galore.
1953 American actress, Marilyn Monroe, in *Gentlemen Prefer Blondes*.

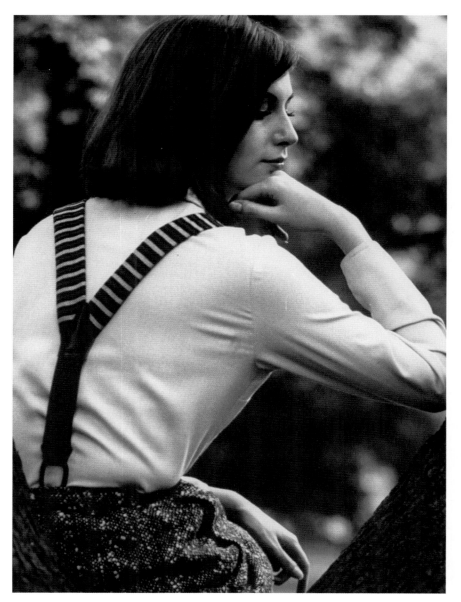

Keep up with the trends, in a white shirt and tweed bags held up high.
1962 Young college girl wearing striped braces with mannish trousers.

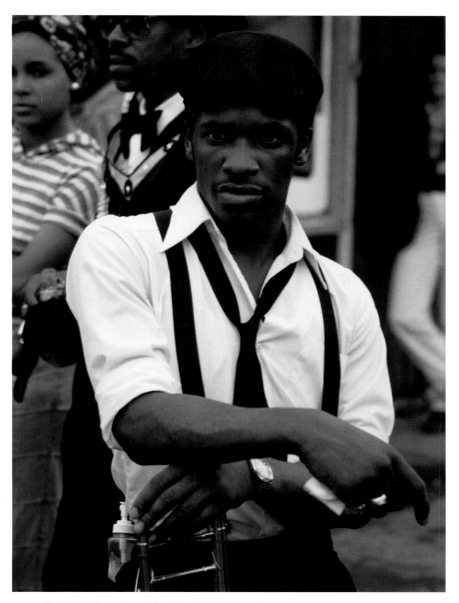

Cool dude, in a crisp white shirt, a black tie and braces.
1960   A spectator at a jazz festival, probably in the Southern States of America.

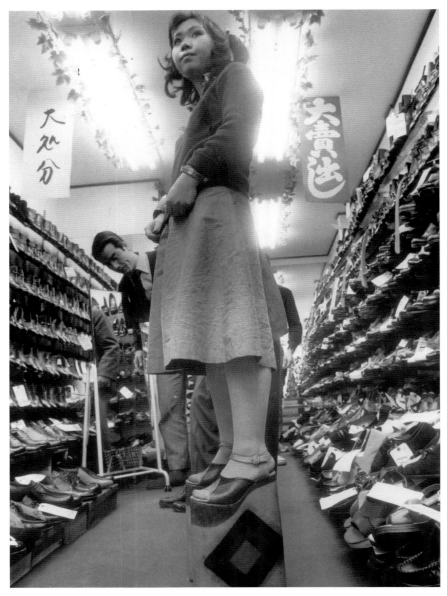

Sky high, perilous platforms in cowhide give a lofty view over the shop.
1973 Wooden-soled shoes, 51 cm high and each weighing 4 kg. Tokyo, Japan.

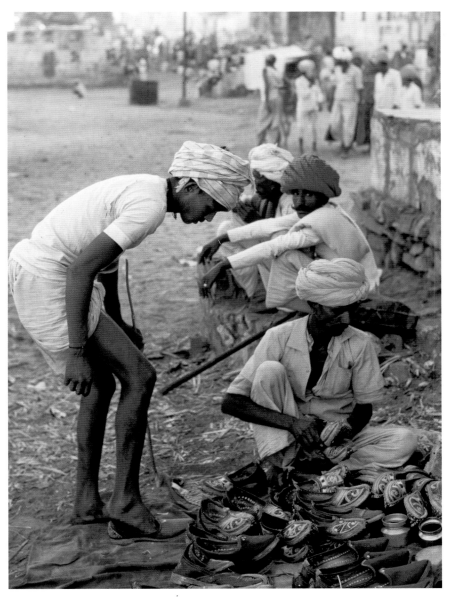

Street style, handmade embroidered shoes from a hawker, if the shoe fits buy it.
1972 A man tries on slippers at a street stall in India.

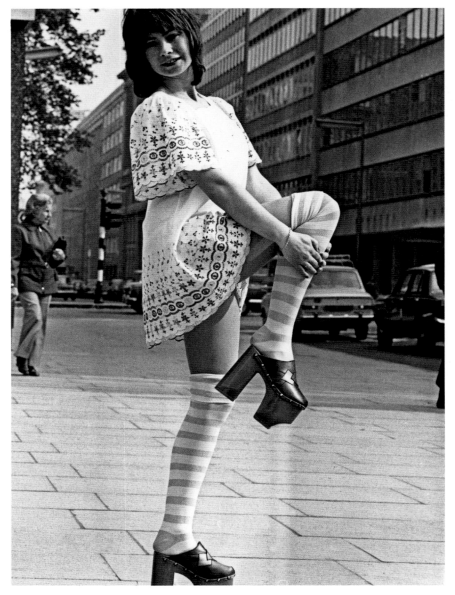

London in lace, a white, broderie anglaise mini, with striped socks and silly shoes.
1972 Model, Sue Coddington, with eight-inch-high heels on her platform shoes.

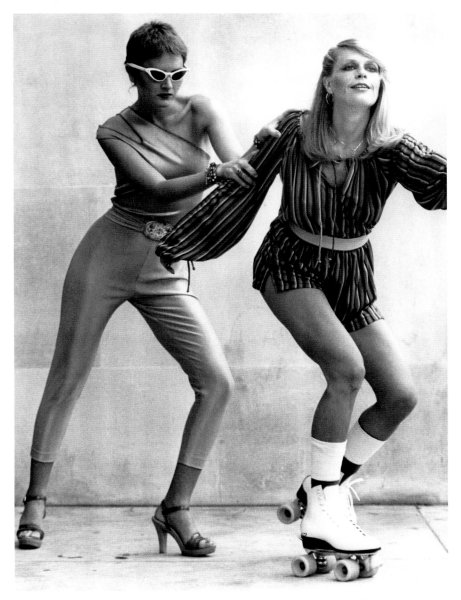

Roller blades, in striped shorts or one-shouldered Lycra cat suit, very Seventies.
1978   Denise Crosby, granddaughter of Bing Crosby, and Cathy Moore in London.

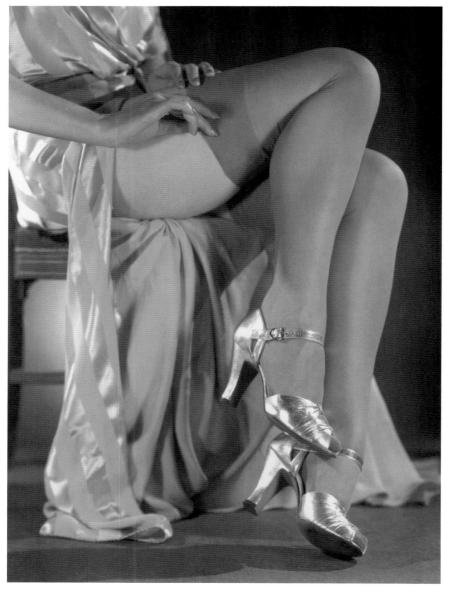

Lingerie loveliness, nylons were a girl's delight in the war, shiny and stretchy.
1940   A woman pulling on stockings, in a silk dressing gown and metallic sandals.

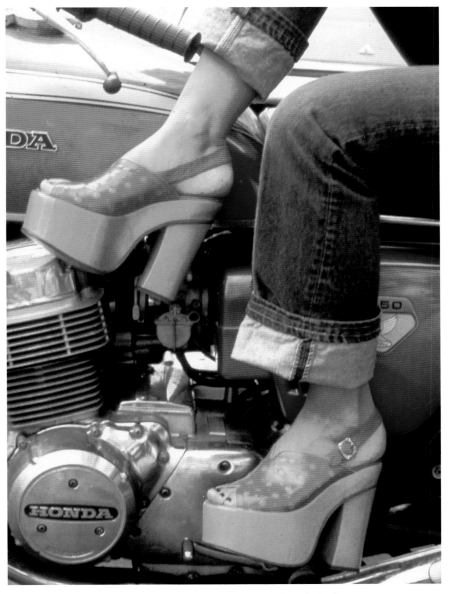

Dangerous driving, whacky footgear worn with turned-up denim jeans.
1970 Women's platform shoes with tangerine leather soles and red floral tops.

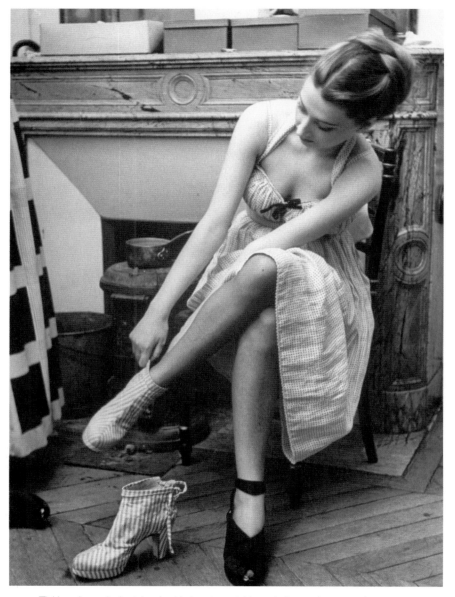

Ticking along nicely, striped ankle boots, matching a halter-neck cotton dress.
1951 A model changing her shoes for Pierre Balmain's fashion show, Paris.

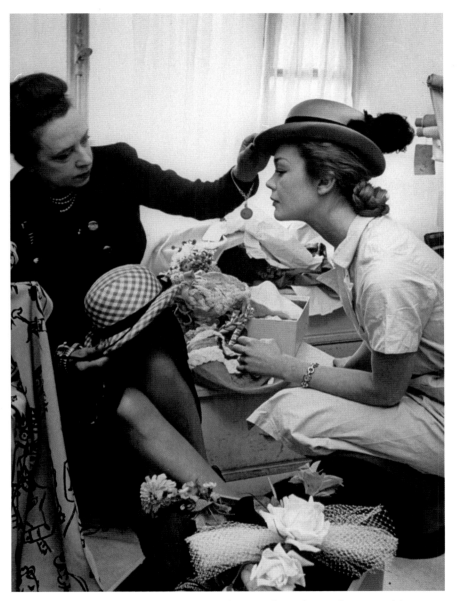

Hot stuff, contender for Chanel's crown, Schiaparelli was famous for strong pink.
1951 Italian designer, Elsa Schiaparelli, trying out hats on a model's head.

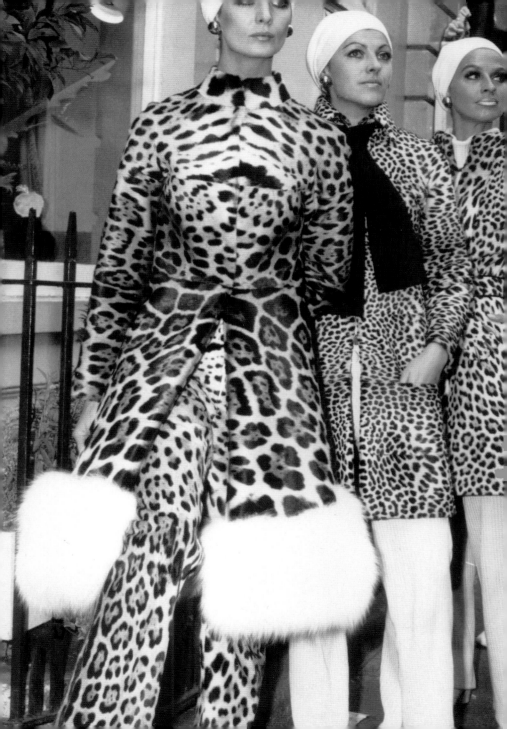

ANIMAL MAGIC

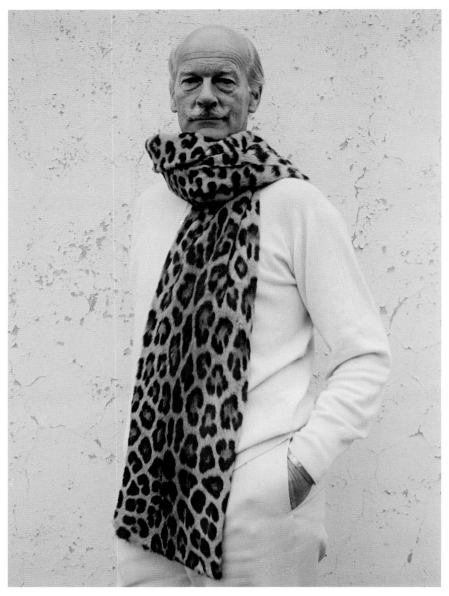

Portrait of a paparazzo, elegant if elderly, a white, moustache, sweater and jeans.
1970 English fashion photographer, Norman Parkinson, in a leopard-print scarf.

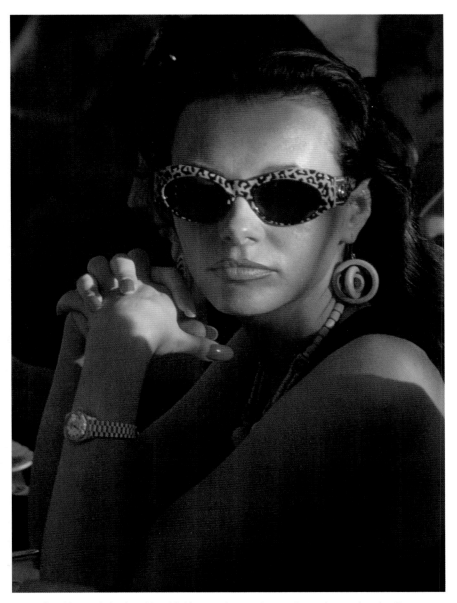

Sunshine and shades, chic with big wooden earrings and very long, painted nails.
1994   A young woman in leopard-print sunglasses, Yalta, Crimea, Ukraine.

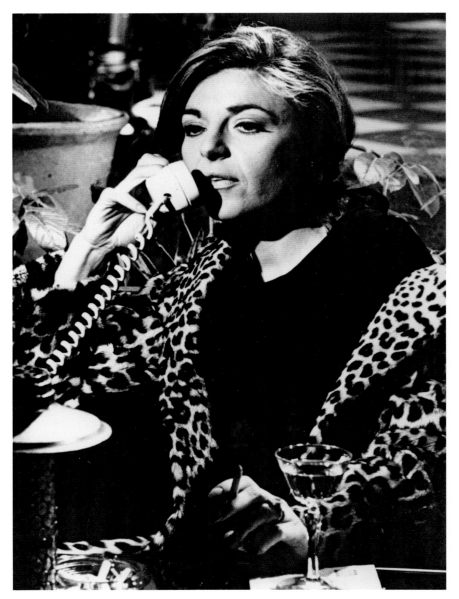

Femme fatale, too hot to handle, in a fur coat, with a cigarette and a cocktail.
1967   American actress, Anne Bancroft, as Mrs. Robinson in *The Graduate*, USA.

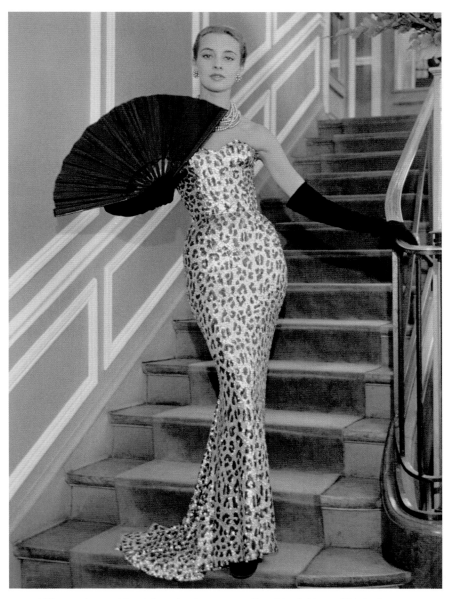

Lithe as a leopard, lovely in a strapless gown with a fishtail skirt and black gloves.
1953 A model in a Christian Dior dress from his Autumn/Winter collection in Paris.

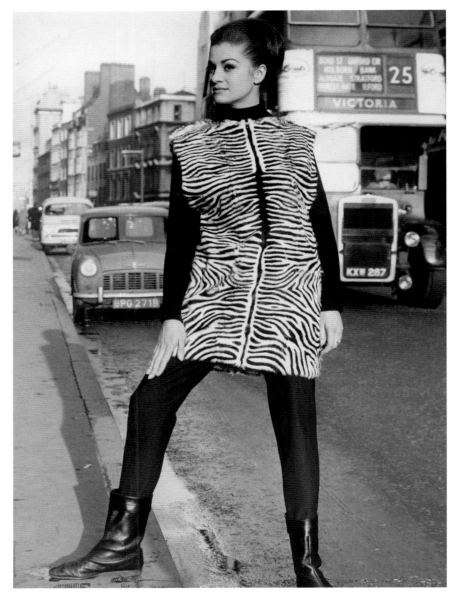

Seriously Sixties, in black and white, with a black polo neck, leggings and boots.
1965   A model in a zebra tabard by furrier, Calman Links, Bond Street, London.

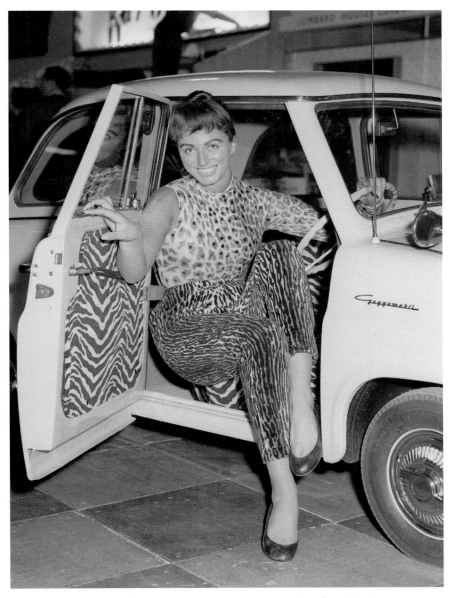

Mix and match, zebra stripes and leopard spots, to go with your car interior.
1956   Model, Jackie Collins, in an outfit by *Car Robes* at the Motor Show, London.

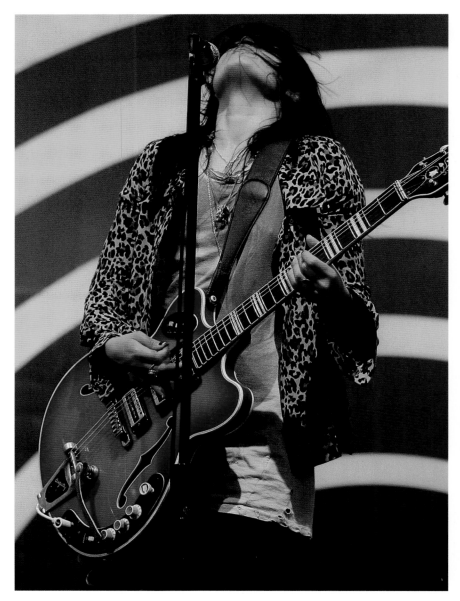

Post-punk pop, concert chic in an animal-print jacket, ragged T-shirt and jeans.
2009   American singer, Alison Mosshart, of *The Kills* in Melbourne, Australia.

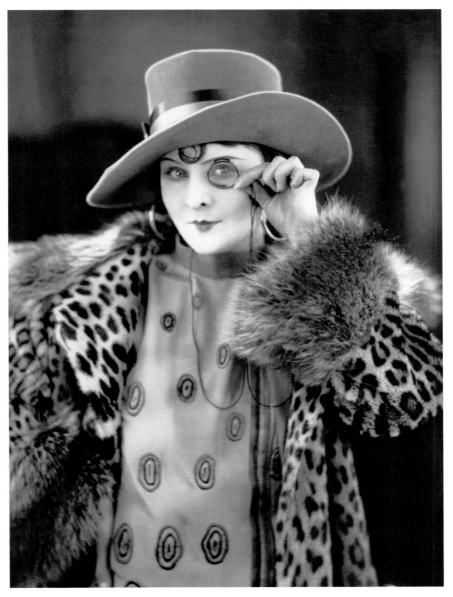

Keep an eye on it, a leopard-skin coat with luscious fox collar and cuffs.
1925   A flapper in a fine fedora hat, sporting a monocle and a kiss curl.

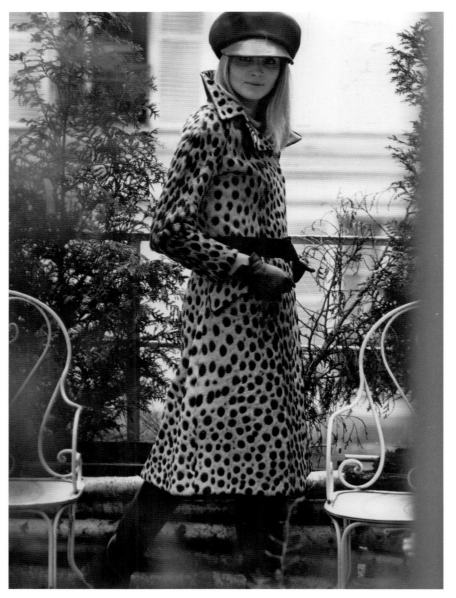

Superbly Sixties, city chic in a slim coat with a black belt, boots and gloves.
1967 A model wearing a spotted fur and a leather chauffeur's cap.

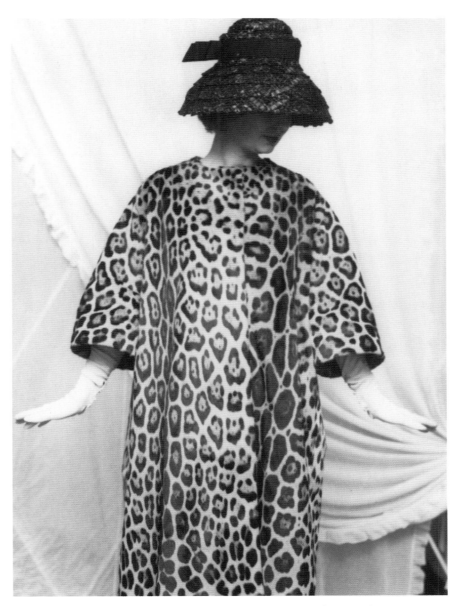

A singular silhouette, an A-line coat worn with a black straw, flowerpot hat.
1960 A coat of jaguar fur, Lanvin, Paris, at Debenhams and Freebodys in London.

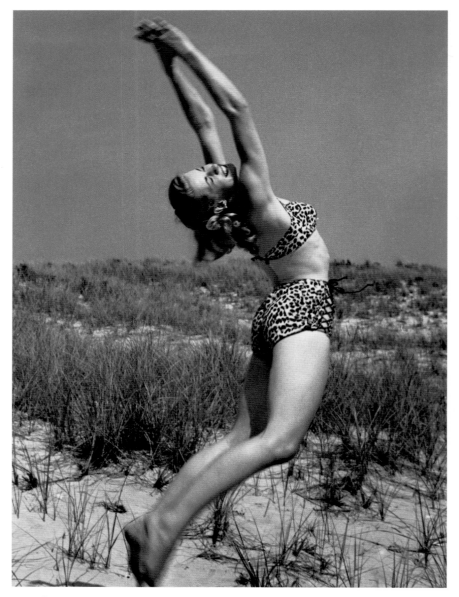

Beach babe, athletic and sun-kissed in a terrific two-piece.
1955   A model, in a leopard-print bikini, frolics in the dunes at the seaside.

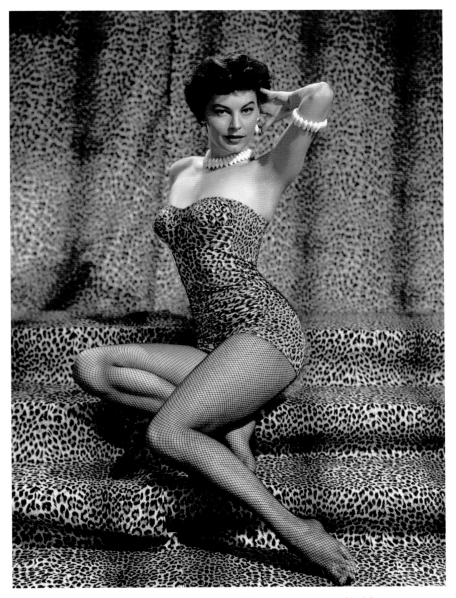

Cat woman, curvaceous in a strapless one-piece costume worn with tights.
1952 American actress, Ava Gardner, on steps draped in leopard print fabric.

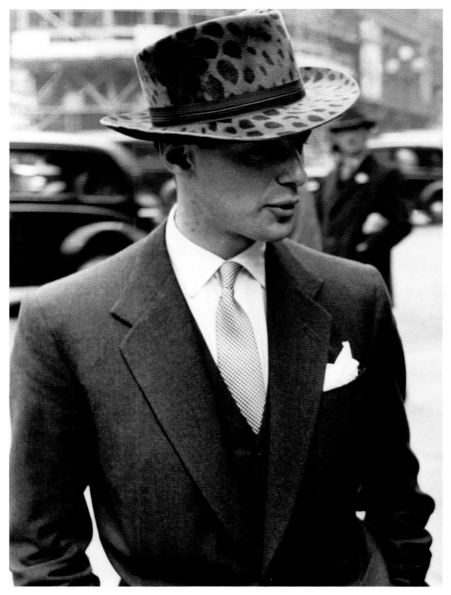

Dandy dude, city cool in a three-piece suit, complete with a pocket-handkerchief.
1956   A man wearing a velour leopard–print, flat-crowned hat.

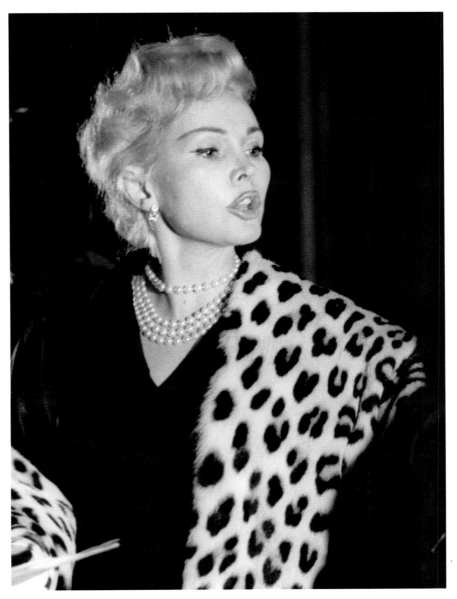

Show business, in an animal fur shawl with strings of perfect pearls and earrings.
1956   Hungarian-born American actress, Zsa Zsa Gabor, at the London Palladium.

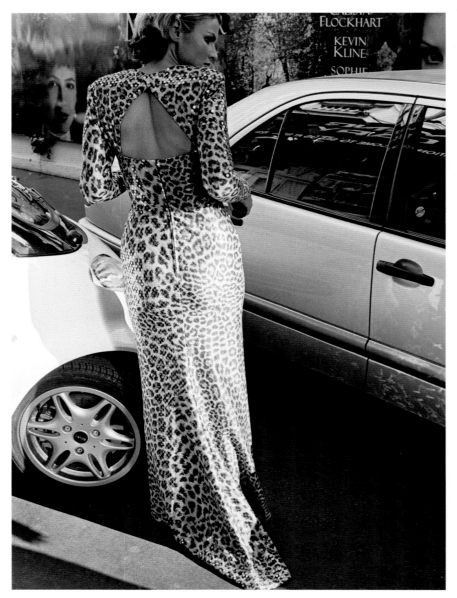

Exit stage left, in a divine ankle-length gown with a cutout back and long sleeves.
1998   A woman at the Hotel Carlton during Cannes Film Festival, France.

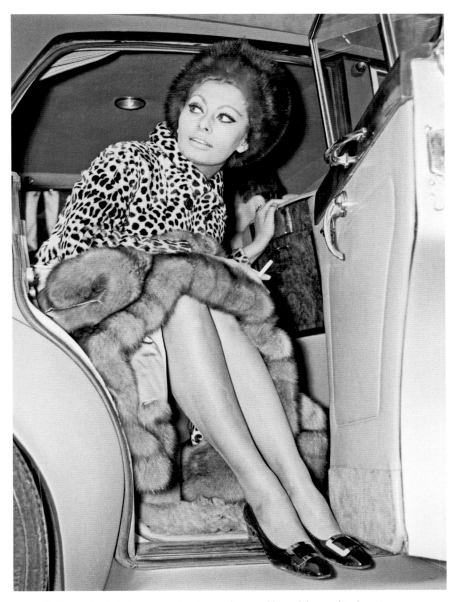

Perfect poise, ladylike as ever, in a leopard coat with a mink over her knees.
1966 Italian actress, Sophia Loren, gets into a car at London Airport.

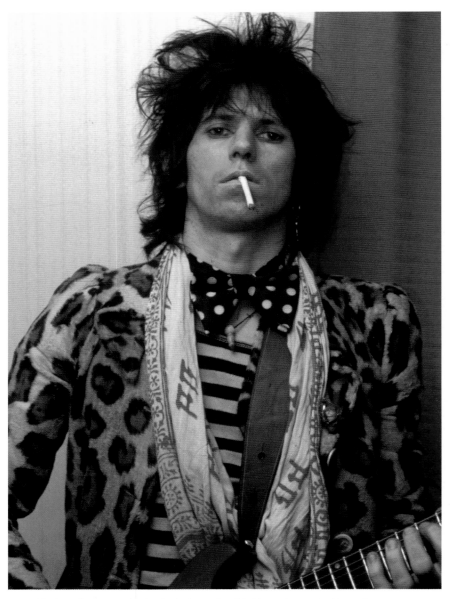

Rock on by, in an animal-print jacket, striped T-shirt and a spotted bow tie.
1974   British rhythm guitarist, Keith Richards, of *The Rolling Stones*.

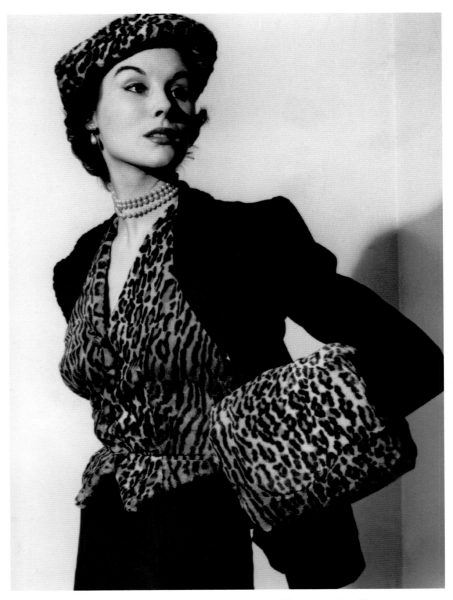

Posing in print, a leopard-print waistcoat, with a matching cap and muff.
1951 A model in London showing accessories made from a fake-fur fabric.

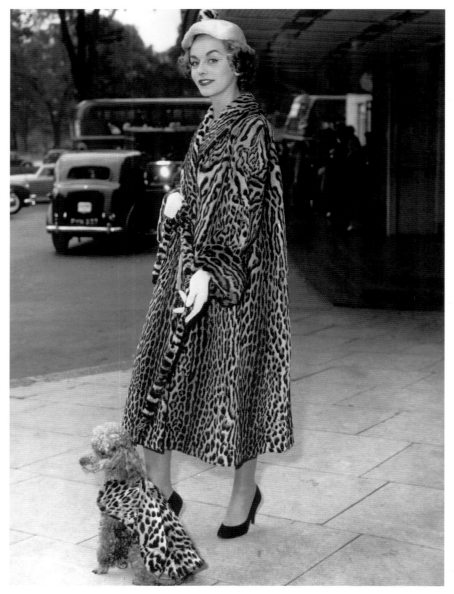

Hers and hers, a luxurious, long fur coat, worn with a white hat and gloves.
1945   A woman with her poodle in town, wearing matching leopard fur wraps.

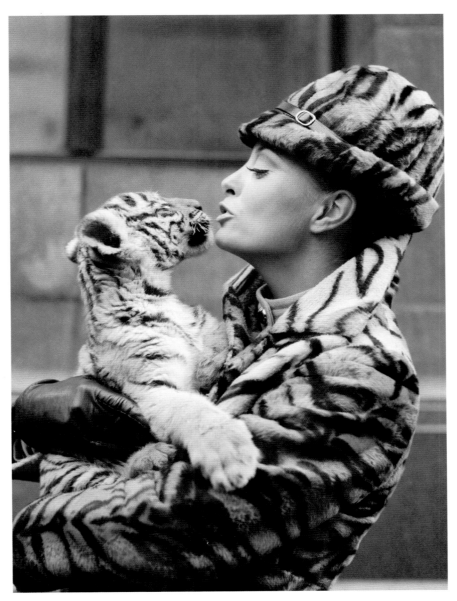

Faux-fur fashion, a coat and matching hat in fake fur, with a real baby tiger.
1971 A stewardess, in the uniform of National Airlines, with a Bengal tiger cub.

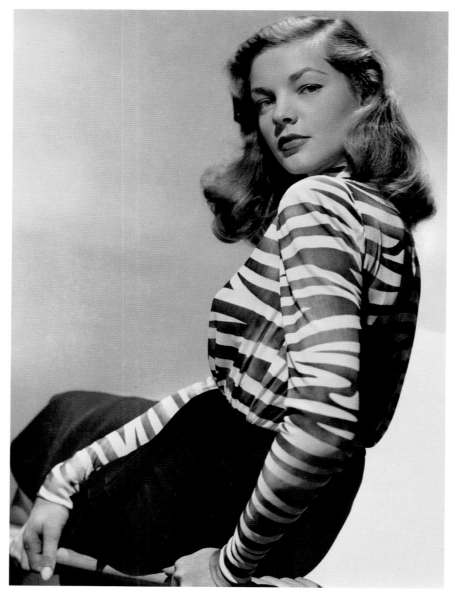

The perfect pin-up, a smouldering star in a striped top with a prim black skirt.
1944   American film actress, Lauren Bacall, wearing a zebra-print blouse.

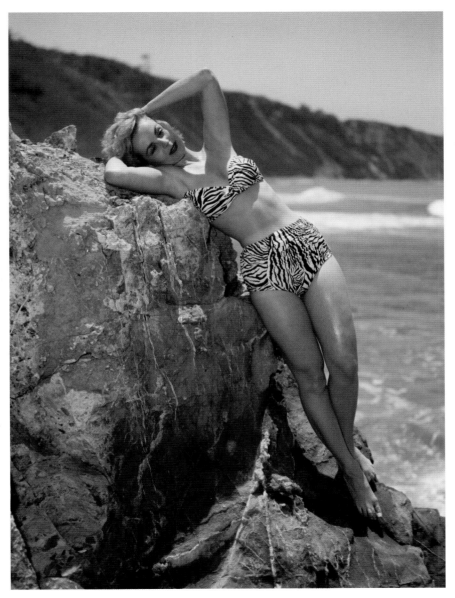

Sun kissed, in a bandeaux bra and big briefs, very me-Jane-you-Tarzan.
1955 A woman leans on a rock wearing a zebra-print bikini.

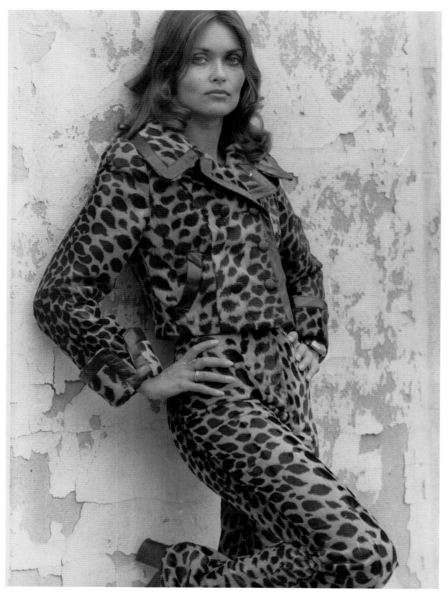

Head to toe, wearing a leopard-skin trouser suit with matching boots.
1972   British actress, Alexandra Bastedo, before starting her animal sanctuary.

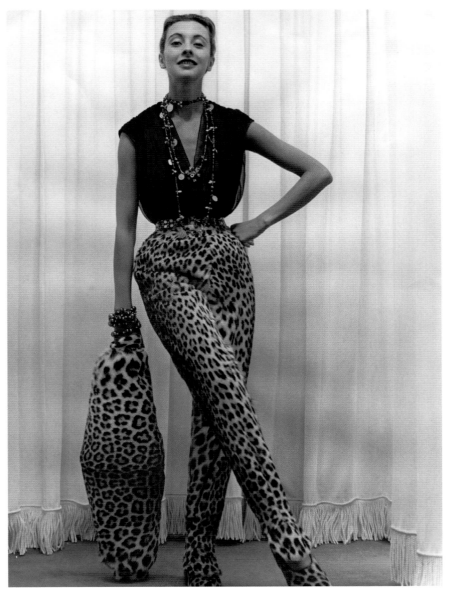

Wasp waisted, a pair of slim slacks, a V-neck top and a matching muff.
1951 A leopard-print outfit by Parisian designer, Pierre Balmain.

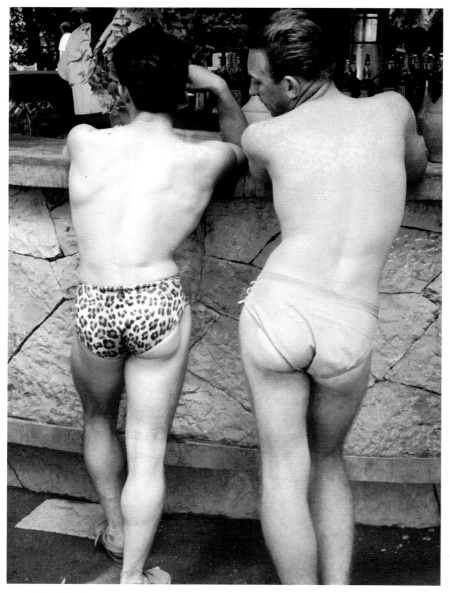

Cheeky chaps, in very small bathing trunks, plain and patterned.
1954 Holidaymakers standing at the bar of a holiday camp on Corfu, Greece.

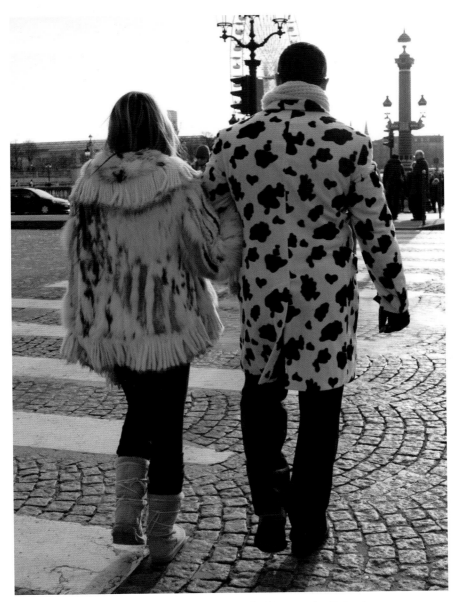

Walk on by, chilly in the city, rug up in a cosy fur, fake or real, with boots.
2007   Pedestrians in winter coats at the Place de la Concorde, Paris, France.

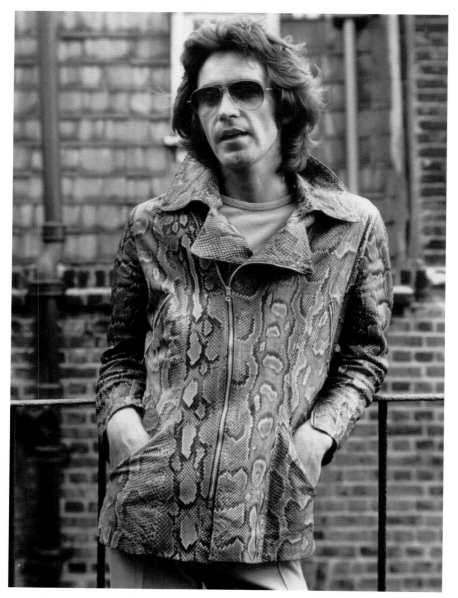

Zip up, in python with T-shirt and jeans and aviator sunglasses, too hip to live. 1970 English fashion designer, Ossie Clark, in a snakeskin bomber jacket.

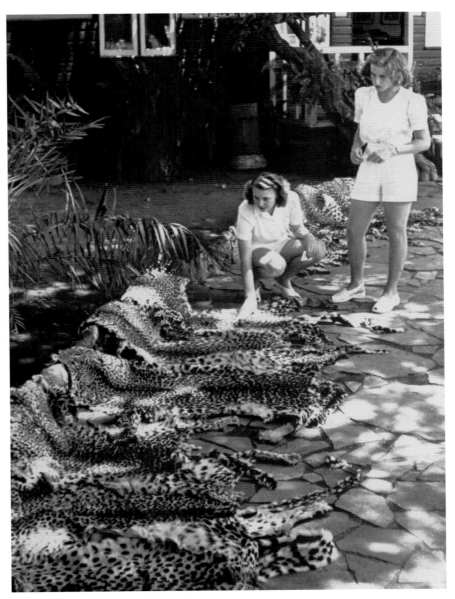

Shopping in shorts, looking through hundreds of pelts, unthinkable today.
1947 Women inspecting leopard skins in Africa. Which will make the best coat?

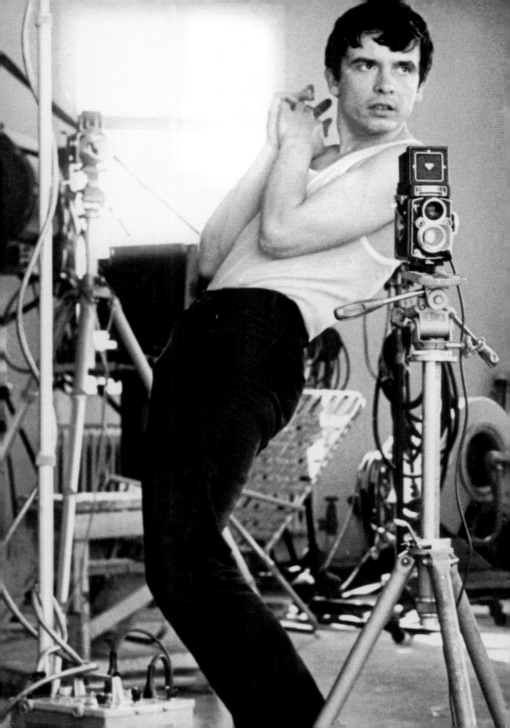

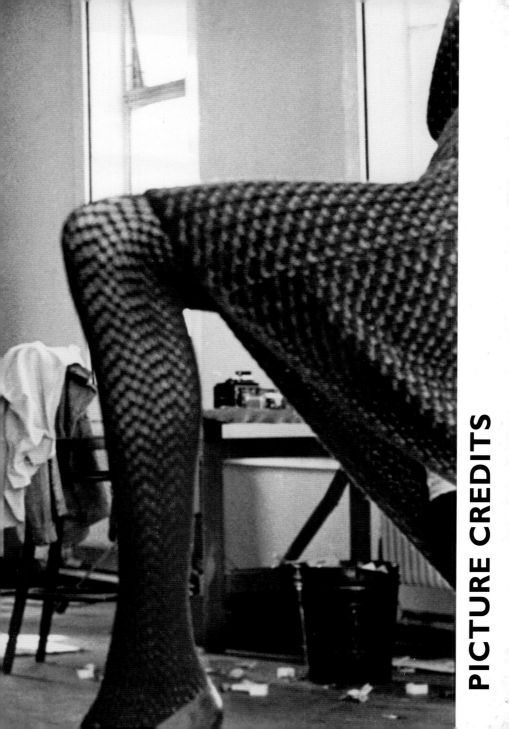

PICTURE CREDITS

Lumberjack look, bright plaid shirts or heavy knits, decorated with moose.
1949   College students in a biology lecture, Williamstown, Massachusetts, USA.

Customized clothes, just as on-trend in the early Seventies as is today.
1972   A woman wearing cut-off jeans and a halter-neck top in St. Tropez, France.

Pretty and punk, spots and stripes in graphic black and white with Mohawk hats.
2007   Models in hats by milliner, Philip Somerville, for his Autumn/Winter collection.

Baubles and beads, spice-coloured clothes would all be collector's items today.
1910   Tibetan women wearing traditional striped aprons, and abundant jewellery.

Summer style, racing-back swimsuits and a smart dress with a sailor collar.
1934   Three friends looking out to sea while relaxing on a beach.

Curvaceous in crimson, long black gloves, with a fine white fox stole for a pillow.
1955   American actress, Marilyn Monroe, wearing a red brocade evening gown.

A helmet like a halo, crocheted in pristine white, fastened under the chin.
1966   Model, Twiggy, wearing a quirky white bonnet with daisies.

Chocks away, a macho flying-suit worn with sensible sandals.
1943   Female pilot of the United States Women's Air Force Service.

Rush hour, tailored and tied in smart pinstripe suits, with crisp white shirts.
1967   Pop singer, Adam Faith, with his wife, Jackie Irving, in his and hers suits.

Naughty but nice, dancing in a see-through lace dress, with a long shawl.
1926   Dancer, Edmonde Guydens, at the Moulin Rouge nightclub in Paris.

Disco diva, twinkly underwear and a boa, perfect underpinnings for a night out.
1975   A model wearing a stretch triangular bra with matching sparkle tights.

Window dressing, little hats de rigueur and fashionable in the Fifties.
1955   Pamela Parks in the window of her millinery shop in Newark, New Jersey.

A feline too far, maxi, midi and mini in more animal skins than on the Serengeti.
1972   Models in coats made from various furs in a line-up on a London street.

Terrifically trendy, posing for pictures, a lovely leg clad in crocheted tights.
1967 British photographer, David Bailey, in a studio with model, Jean Shrimpton.

PHOTO CREDITS

gettyimages® gallery

Many of the images in this book are available for purchase please contact the gallery
+44 (0) 20 7291 5380. www.gettyimagesgallery.com

Getty Images have one of the largest and most varied photographic collections in the world with archives holding millions of original negatives, covering virtually every imaginable subject and style from the 1850's to the present day. The gallery uses this unique resource to offer beautiful affordable photographs hand printed in our darkrooms. Besides photography we also offer, interior design consultancy for businesses, exhibition and sponsorship opportunities